# BEGIN AGAIN

# BEGIN AGAIN

## James Baldwin's America and Its Urgent Lessons for Today

Eddie S. Glaude Jr.

Chatto & Windus
LONDON

1 3 5 7 9 10 8 6 4 2

Chatto & Windus, an imprint of Vintage

Chatto & Windus is part of the Penguin Random House group of companies
whose addresses can be found at global.penguinrandomhouse.com

Penguin
Random House
UK

First published in the United Kingdom by Chatto & Windus in 2021
First published in the United States by Crown in 2020

penguin.co.uk/vintage

Portions of this work first appeared, in different form, in *Time* magazine (time.
com) as 'A Mississippi Native Son's Notes on Civil War History' on 1 November
2017, and 'Don't Let the Loud Bigots Distract You. America's Real Problem
with Race Cuts Far Deeper' on 6 September 2018

A CIP catalogue record for this book is available from the British Library

HB ISBN 9781784744335
TPB ISBN 9781784744441

Printed and bound in Great Britain by Clays Ltd, Elcograf S.p.A.

The authorised representative in the EEA is Penguin Random House Ireland,
Morrison Chambers, 32 Nassau Street, Dublin D02 YH68.

Penguin Random House is committed to a sustainable future
for our business, our readers and our planet. This book is made
from Forest Stewardship Council® certified paper.

MIX
Paper from
responsible sources
FSC   FSC® C018179
www.fsc.org

*For his beautiful heart*

# CONTENTS

When I sat down to write *Begin Again* in 2018, two years after the disastrous election of Donald Trump, the world had not yet been seized by Covid-19. Families were enjoying the company of loved ones who soon would be gone, and the unimaginable grief that comes with the slaughter of innocents had not settled in. Most ordinary people went to work every day. They worried about paying bills and their children's future. White Americans continued to believe in their innocence even as white supremacy reared its ugly head. African Americans struggled as Trumpism flooded American politics. George Floyd and Breonna Taylor were still alive, but more dangerous storm clouds massed overhead.

In some ways, I wrote this book to deal with my despair and to make sense of what was happening in America. After the 2016 election I kept saying to myself, "They have done it *again*." Millions of white Americans had chosen Trump, and *we* would have to deal with the consequences of that choice. Trump exploited hatreds and fears. White resentment fueled his ascendance to the White House. But there was nothing unique about him except the explicitness of his lies and the wanton desire of some white folk (especially after eight years of a black president) that made him possible. In electing Trump, white America had reached for its latest fantasy to secure its belief that ours is, and always will be, a white nation. But in another sense, Trump is America's carnival mirror, a distorted reflection of ourselves and a consequence of our ongoing evasion to confront who we really are.

I found resources in James Baldwin's writing to help me understand this reality. Baldwin was clear about the lies that shaped the country as well as the self-understanding of those who believed in them. In "Nothing Personal," an essay he wrote to accompany the photographs of Richard Avedon, Baldwin put the point succinctly:

> We are afraid to reveal ourselves because we trust ourselves so little. . . . And in this labyrinth the person is desperately trying NOT to find out what he REALLY thinks. Therefore, the truth cannot be told, even about one's attitudes: we live by lies. And not only, for example, about race—whatever, by this time, in this country, or, indeed, in the world, this word may mean—but about our very natures. The lie has penetrated our most private moments and the most secret chambers of our heart.

Baldwin understood in 1964 that our problems in the United States went beyond who occupied the White House or the latest instance of American racism. We should understand in 2020 that Trump and the racism of his followers or the brutality of the police are not all that is wrong with us. These are just the outward manifestations of the rot at the heart of America. As I wrote *with* Baldwin about our current malaise, it became clear that the forces unleashed by this latest version of the American fantasy—and by the white people who cleaved to the very idea of being white and who menaced those who were not—threatened to destroy the very foundations of the country. Too many white Americans were willing to throw away this fragile experiment in democracy in order to hold on to the belief that they mattered more than others.

As the UK edition of this book goes to press, millions of Americans are going to the polls. It is, without any hint of exaggeration, the most important election of our lifetime. The stark divisions within the country—white/black, rural/urban, rich/poor, Republican/Democrat—are in plain view. And it feels as if the institutions and norms of our democracy are collapsing right in front of our bloodshot eyes. Covid-19 ravages the country. Americans die alone and those who love them must grieve with the regret of not being able to say goodbye properly. The economy is in tatters. Millions are unemployed and hunger grips the nation. But the top 1 percent continues to thrive; they are getting richer as death travels from door to door just a few blocks away. All the while the police keep killing black people, and we risk our lives protesting in the streets.

This election, then, comes at a time of moral reckoning. But I pray that we do not trade one fantasy for another: that a Trump defeat will somehow affirm America's inherent goodness and put a grateful Republic back to sleep. Presidential elections alone, no matter how momentous, do not settle the question of who we take ourselves to be. The answer to that question will emerge in what we do *after* November 2020.

In the end, America has to choose whether it will become a genuinely multiracial democracy, and this involves grappling with the past that continues to haunt our present. George Floyd, Breonna Taylor, Jacob Blake, and the countless others are the latest victims of what Baldwin described as the slave codes that have shaped the way black communities are policed in this country. We have to tell the truth about that. We have to tell the truth about a lot of things. As Baldwin wrote in 1962 in an essay for *The New York Times Book Review*, we have "to describe us to ourselves as we are now," without the crutch of our myths and illusions. For "the trouble is deeper than we wished to think: the trouble is in us. And we will never . . . conquer our cruel and unbearable human isolation—we will never establish human communities—until we stare our ghastly failure in the face."

The American fantasy, in all of its iterations, has disfigured our moral sense, because it requires that we lie to ourselves about what we have done and who we are. A lie that thrives on a kind of willful ignorance makes this place, and us, monstrous. When I sat down to write *Begin Again* I wanted to challenge the lie at its root and set the stage for what we must do after this all comes tumbling down.

3 November 2020

# Thinking with Jimmy

I arrived in Heidelberg, Germany, on a hot Saturday morning the day after leaving Newark, New Jersey. This was the beginning of my stay at Heidelberg University as the 2018 recipient of the James W.C. Pennington Award. Born on the eastern shore of Maryland in 1809, Pennington escaped slavery at the age of eighteen, learned to read and write, and was the first black man to attend classes at Yale University. He went on to become a minister, and in 1849, the Heidelberg Faculty of Theology awarded him an honorary doctorate. It was the first time, I believe, that a European university bestowed such an academic honor on an African American. And here I was, a country boy from Moss Point, Mississippi, who wrote about religion and race in the United States, flying across the world to accept an honor named after Pennington at a university founded in 1386.

I met James, an American graduate student from a small town in Michigan who was studying at Heidelberg, as I checked into my apartment, House 2, no. 64. He was charged with getting me settled on my first day at the university. The elevator wasn't working, so we walked up three flights of stairs with three weeks' worth of clothes in my suitcase. The apartment was small. I opened the door and immediately found myself in a kitchenette with the bathroom and shower right next to it. The stove had two burners. The oven was a microwave. Five steps in, I stood in my bedroom/living room/dining room. The bed doubled as a couch. Then I spotted my desk. Nothing else mattered after that.

The apartment, with its high ceilings that kept the room from closing in on you, had a dated feel, and comfort was not its primary concern. In fact, this part of the Heidelberg campus (and it is a stretch to describe it as a campus in any American sense) wasn't very appealing at all. All the buildings felt like they were constructed in the 1960s and '70s. Square monstrosities with little character. Strictly functional. James waited for me outside. We were going to buy my train pass, check out the grocery store, and travel to the *alte Stadt* (the old city).

As we entered the station, I heard screaming. People in front of us stood still and stared at some kind of commotion. I followed their eyes. Four policemen (*polizei*) were piled on a black man. One officer had his knee in the man's back; the others twisted his arms. His pants were halfway down his legs. His bare ass was exposed. The police pressed his head down into the concrete as if they were trying to leave the imprint of a leaf there.

With each attempt to cuff him, the man let out a bloodcurdling scream. All eyes were on him as the crowd stood by and watched intently, like spectators at a soccer game without any real attachment to the teams playing. I watched them as they watched the police and the black man. Their faces revealed nothing. They were inscrutable, at least to me. I had not been in Heidelberg for two hours, and police had a black man's face pressed down on the concrete with a knee in his back. He screamed again. I didn't understand his pained words. I didn't know what he had done, if anything. I only knew the screaming was all too familiar.

James turned beet red and, for some reason, felt the need to apologize *to me*.


There is a kind of isolation being in a place where you do not know the language. Words do not interrupt your vision. Silence allows you to see differently. During my short time in Heidelberg, I took in the landscape: the wildflowers, the cobblestone roads, the old buildings bleeding into new construction. One noticed a sadness. Perhaps it was the feeling of a place that had experienced the devastation of war or the effect of having a U.S. military base shut down and the struggle of figuring out what would happen next. I saw the whiteness of the place (a smattering of color here and there; a soul food restaurant that played Al Green and served only Ethiopian food) and heard the beauty and harshness of a language I could not understand. Whatever I was experiencing, even in that initial traumatic moment, I was not in the United States, and to my mind that was a good thing. I did not have to go on television and explain what happened at the train station. I did not have to explain it to James either.

I wondered, at the time, if this was what James Baldwin initially felt when he lived abroad: an escape from the constant demand to deal with what was happening in the States and what was happening *in him* because of it. Paris became a refuge of sorts in his early days. Whatever Baldwin faced there, at least he didn't have to deal with the barrage of racist nonsense here, and in the silence that his lack of French afforded him, he could reimagine himself. It is exhausting to find oneself, over and over again, navigating a world rife with deadly assumptions about you and those who look like you, to see and read about insult and harm, death and anguish, for no other reason than because you're black or black and poor or black and trans or . . . For me, the daily grind consumes. I cannot escape the news. I am drowning in it, and in all the nastiness of a country that seems, or feels, like it is going underwater.

Heidelberg afforded some critical distance, a brief refuge from it all. A small apartment in a place where I did not know the language offered *me* an opportunity to be still, to quiet my head, and to think about my country and the moment we currently find ourselves in.

I started this book outside of the United States. That seemed appropriate. It would give me a distinct vantage point to write about Donald Trump, race, and the current state of our politics. Plus, Baldwin insisted that it was outside of the United States that he came to understand the country more fully. My hope was to begin the writing in St. Thomas in a nice flat overlooking the Caribbean Sea, but Hurricane Maria took care of that dream. So I found myself in Europe, lecturing and teaching at a university where Hegel taught his *Phenomenology of Spirit* in the nineteenth century, and thinking about James Baldwin's America and what lessons it might offer our own.

At the end of the second week in Heidelberg, I decided to catch a quick flight from Frankfurt to Nice. I wanted to see Baldwin's home in Saint Paul de Vence, or what was left of it. I knew that his sprawling ten-acre property—the place with its "welcome table" that he finally called home for seventeen years—was being destroyed to make way for luxury apartments. I found it a fitting image for his later life and a somewhat ironic fulfillment of his own prophetic witness: capital and luxury running roughshod over everything. Even his sanctuary failed to escape.

I had never traveled within Europe before. They didn't give us papers to fill out. No one checked my passport. I simply walked off the plane that morning and into France. My taxi driver, Christophe (I imagined him as the white French counterpart of Black Christopher in Baldwin's novel *Tell Me How Long the Train's Been Gone*), a rather muscular white fellow who looked like he could be from South Jersey, drove toward my hotel. He seemed excited to practice his English. I mentioned the purpose of my visit: "I am going to Saint Paul de Vence to see the remains of the house of a famous African American writer." *The remains.* It was as if I were visiting a grave site.

Christophe interjected, "No. No. You should visit the place immediately." Nice would be cut off from traffic later in the day, he told me. France was preparing for a *national* dance party that evening (I found the idea of a "national dance party" odd). Plus, France's second game of the World Cup was scheduled at 4:00 P.M. He made an abrupt U-turn, and we headed toward Baldwin's home.

When we arrived in Saint Paul de Vence, Christophe walked with me down the Route de la Colle toward Baldwin's home. I saw the tips of moving cranes. We were close. Soon the beginnings of the new apartments came into view, concrete foundations with red wooden side rails for protection. Men were busily moving about. Below us was an absolutely stunning view of the countryside. I imagined Baldwin waking up, probably at midday, after a night of heavy drinking and intensive writing with coffee and cigarette in hand, stretching and looking out at the expanse. Readying himself for another day. Sounds of an active construction site interrupted the scene, especially that damn sledgehammer. Finally we arrived at what was left of Baldwin's house. Huge cranes lumbered. Bulldozers cleared land. And a sign on the wall said it all: LE JARDIN DES ARTS: 19 APPARTEMENTS DE GRAND LUXE AVEC VUE MER PANORAMIQUE. RÉSERVEZ MAINTENANT, SOTHEBY'S INTERNATIONAL REALTY.

From outside the fence, I saw portions of the main house still standing. Christophe said, "We should see if anyone is here. Maybe they will let us in." I thought that was rather brazen, but he walked up the stairs and knocked on the door. I must have looked unnerved. "What do we have to lose?" he asked, looking back at me with a slight smile. Two white women greeted us with decidedly British accents. They thought we were potential buyers: an African American man dressed in a blue linen shirt and cream-colored jeans with a muscular French guide. Made sense, I guess. I explained that I was working on a book with James Baldwin at its heart, and that I wanted to see the remains of his home. They seemed a bit defensive, declaring that the main portion of the home was being restored and would be a part of the new complex. The other part had been crumbling from neglect and had to be torn down. I asked if I could see the house. Nervously they agreed and walked out to the balcony, but immediately noted all of the construction work going on below. "It's too dangerous," they said. I could only view the house from there.

It looked like an excavation of an ancient ruin. The ground had been carefully cleared, and only the writing room of the historic house, once a beautiful villa with a lush garden and palm and orange trees, remained, exposed for the sun to beat down on its side. Contrasted with the new construction jutting out of the mountain, what was left of Baldwin's home looked old, scarred, and resigned to its fate. I imagined the owners of the new apartments, or at least some of them who cared to mention it, boasting that they lived at the home of a famous African American writer, only then to point out the panoramic view. Just above our heads, you could see the village of Saint Paul de Vence. The view was stunning. My heart broke.

The ruins were a fitting description for what Baldwin saw in the latter part of his life in the United States. He saw decay and wreckage alongside greed and selfishness. He saw, and felt deeply, the effects of America's betrayal of the black freedom struggle of the mid-twentieth century: The country had refused, once again, to turn its back on racism and to reach for its better angels, and our children were paying the cost. As I looked out onto the ruins and thought of the election of Donald Trump and the ugliness that consumed *my* country, I asked myself: *What do you do when you have lost faith in the place you call home?* That wasn't quite the right way to put it: I never really had faith in the United States in the strongest sense of the word. I hoped that one day white people here would finally leave behind the belief that they mattered more. But what do you do when this glimmer of hope fades, and you are left with the belief that white people will never change—that the country, no matter what we do, will remain basically the same?

Amid the rubble of the construction site and the signs promising luxurious living, I thought of Baldwin's witness in his later years as an answer to my questions and part of the reason why I needed to write this book. He grappled with profound disillusionment after the murder of Dr. King and yet held on to his faith in the possibility of a moment when we could all be fully ourselves, what he referred to as a New Jerusalem. I had to understand how he did that, and what resources, as he confronted his dark America, he might offer me as I confront the darkness of my own.

In the documentary *James Baldwin: The Price of the Ticket*, Baldwin's brother David powerfully recounted Jimmy's summation of his life; in that, I heard what I needed to do:

> I pray I've done my work . . . when I've gone from here, and all the turmoil, through the wreckage and rubble, and through whatever, when someone finds themselves digging through the ruins . . . I pray that somewhere in that wreckage they'll find me, somewhere in that wreckage that they use something I've left behind.

I started digging, and *Begin Again* is what I found.

I must admit this is a strange book. It isn't biography, although there are moments when it feels biographical; it is not literary criticism, although I read Baldwin's nonfiction writings closely; and it is not straightforward history, even though the book, like Baldwin, is obsessed with history. Instead, *Begin Again* is some combination of all three in an effort to say something meaningful about our current times. The book moves backward and forward, vacillating between the past and present as I think *with* Baldwin about this troubled period in American history.

To be sure, the idea of America is in deep trouble. Though many will find consolation in the principles of the founders or in the resilience of the American story, the fact remains that we stand on a knife's edge. Donald Trump's presidency unleashed forces howling beneath our politics since the tumult of the 1960s. For decades, politicians stoked and exploited white resentment. Corporations consolidated their hold on government and cut American workers off at the knees. Ideas of the public good were reduced to an unrelenting pursuit of self-interest. Communities fractured. Demographics shifted. Resentments deepened. The national fabric frayed, and we are all at one another's throats. Those restless ghosts underneath our politics now haunt openly, and a presidential election alone will not satisfy their hunger. A moral reckoning is upon us, and we have to decide, once and for all, whether or not we will truly be a multiracial democracy.

We have faced two such moments before in our history: (1) the Civil War and Reconstruction, and (2) the black freedom struggle of the mid-twentieth century. One has been described by historians as our second founding; the other as a second Reconstruction. Both grappled with the central contradiction at the heart of the Union. Abraham Lincoln's second inaugural address in March 1865 spoke directly to the cause of the war's carnage.

> Fondly do we hope, fervently do we pray, that the mighty scourge of war may speedily pass. Yet, if God wills that it continue until all the wealth piled by the bondman's two hundred and fifty years of unrequited toil shall be sunk, and until every drop of blood drawn with the lash shall be paid by another drawn with the sword, as was said three thousand years ago, so still it must be said, "the judgments of the Lord are true and righteous altogether."

Almost one hundred years later, Dr. Martin Luther King, Jr., gave voice to the aspirations of the second Reconstruction in his soaring "I Have a Dream" speech on the steps of the Lincoln Memorial in 1963.

> I say to you today, my friends, though, even though we face the difficulties of today and tomorrow, I still have a dream.

It is a dream deeply rooted in the American dream. I have a dream that one day this nation will rise up and live out the true meaning of its creed: "We hold these truths to be self-evident that all men are created equal."

Both moments were betrayed. One was undone by the advent of Jim Crow; the other by calls for law and order and the tax revolt by the so-called silent majority. The cumulative effect of our failure, in both instances, to uproot a pernicious understanding of race weighs heavy on our current crisis. Think of it this way: We already have two strikes.

Some may want to take issue with my reduction of our current malaise to the problem of race. What we face goes much deeper, they might argue. But I would beg to differ. At the core of this ugly period in our history is the idea that who "we" are as a country is changing for the worse—that "we" are becoming unrecognizable to ourselves. The slogans "Make America Great Again" and "Keep America Great" amount to nostalgic longings for a time under siege by present events, and the cascading crises we face grow out of, in part, the desperate attempts to step back into a past that can never be retrieved. The willingness of so many of our fellows to toss aside any semblance of commitment to democracy—to embrace cruel and hateful policies—exposes the idea of America as an outright lie.

In the archive at the Schomburg Center for Research in Black Culture in New York, I came across an undated handwritten note to Robert Kennedy from James Baldwin. The infamous meeting after the protests and violence in the streets of Birmingham, Alabama, between Kennedy, Baldwin, and a group of Baldwin's colleagues that included Lorraine Hansberry and Jerome Smith had ended horribly. Kennedy left the meeting suspicious of Baldwin, his motives, and his politics. The FBI file on Baldwin suggested as much. But on the occasion of the assassination of John F. Kennedy, on behalf of that same group, Baldwin wrote to Bobby Kennedy and expressed his sincerest condolences. He wanted Kennedy to see that the horrific murder of his brother should not be understood apart from the struggle they argued so fiercely about on May 24, 1963. "Whatever may have blocked your understanding of what we have tried to tell you of our suffering," he wrote, "is dissolved by suffering, and we beg you to allow us to share your grief. As we know that in these trying days to come, you share our struggle, for our struggle is the same." Baldwin wanted Kennedy to see what was at the root of all of our troubles: that, for the most part, human beings refused to live honestly with themselves and were all too willing to hide behind the idols of race and ready to kill in order to defend them. His insight remains relevant today because the moral reckoning we face bears the markings of the original sin of the nation.

But there is another, more specific concern that digging in the wreckage revealed. Baldwin had witnessed the promise and peril of the early days of the civil rights movement, rose to fame as a literary figure willing to risk everything on behalf of the movement, supported it financially, and even put his frail body on the line along with others in pursuit of a more just America. In an October 9, 1963, interview with Fern Marja Eckman, just two days after his participation in SNCC's Freedom Day demonstration in Selma, Alabama, Baldwin described what he saw there. He talked about the courage of everyday people as they stood in line, hungry and terrorized by Sheriff Jim Clarke and his men, to register to vote. He talked about his rage at the injustice of it all.

"The helmets were, you know, like a garden. So many colors," he recalled of the police who bullied the men and women waiting patiently in line to register to vote. "And with their guns and their clubs and their cattle prodders." Eckman asked him if he was afraid in the moment when the tensions rose between them and the Selma police. Baldwin said that he was furious. "The thing is you get—you're so scared—I was scared in the morning. Before it all began. And I was scared the first time I walked around there. But, later on, I wasn't scared at all. . . . Your fear is swallowed up by, you know . . . fury," he told her. "What you really want to do is kill all those people."

Baldwin saw the brutality of Jim Crow up close and witnessed its effects on those who struggled against the brutality, as well as on those who defended it. He also felt its effect on himself. He saw friends murdered in cold blood. The deaths of Medgar Evers, Malcolm X, and Martin Luther King, Jr., became symbolic of a broader and more systematic betrayal by the country. In Selma, Baldwin had described Sheriff Clarke and his deputies as manifestations of broader forces. These men "were deliberately created by the American Republic," he said. That same republic had now turned its back on everything black people and their allies fought for. Disillusionment and deep-seated pessimism set in among many of those, including Baldwin, who survived it all. Baldwin told Quincy Troupe in his last interview, in November 1987 (he died December 1, 1987):

I was right. I was right about what was happening in the country. What was about to happen to all of us really, one way or the other. And the choices people would have to make. . . . I was trying to tell the truth and it takes a long time to realize that you can't—that there's no point in going to the mat, so to speak, no point going to Texas

again. It's been said, and it's been said, and it's been said.
It's been heard and not heard. You are a broken motor.

One can read these words and conclude that Baldwin had given
up—that the cancer which ravaged his body had metastasized and
seized his spirit. But I think that's wrong. In the full view of the
wreckage of the movement, Baldwin realized he could not save
white Americans. No matter how hard he tried, no matter how
often he prophesied doom, the country refused to change. America simply doubled down on its ugliness, in *different* ways. White
Americans, he concluded, had to save themselves. This shift in the
later work of Baldwin—what the writer Michael Thelwell described to me as "the shift in Baldwin's *we*"—disturbed and unsettled those who had previously celebrated his genius. For the
white liberals who embraced him, Baldwin had succumbed to pessimism and turned his back on his artistic vision. He had, in effect,
given up on them and embraced the prattle of Black Power.

What many of his critics, then and today, fail to realize is that
Baldwin never gave up on the possibility that *all of us* could be
better. I found that insight in the rubble. Baldwin never relinquished the idea of the New or Heavenly Jerusalem found in the
book of Ezekiel and the book of Revelation, where, for him, the
idols of race and the shackles of obsolete categories that bound us
to the ground were no more. We still needed to fight for that. But
*we* would do so without the burden of having to save white people
first.

In writing this book, I wanted to understand more fully how
Baldwin navigated his disappointments, how he lived his refusal
to chase windmills any longer, and how he maintained his faith
that all of us, even those who saw themselves as white, could still

be better. I needed to understand how he harnessed his rage and lived his faith.

The problem, for me, was particularly acute, because of the country's *latest* betrayal: The promise of the election of the first black president had been met with white fear and rage and with the election of Donald Trump. The courage of young people in the Black Lives Matter movement as they protested police violence confronted the cynicism of large swaths of the nation. Dashed hopes and broken lives characterize our moment too. Ours, like the moments after the Civil War and Reconstruction and after the civil rights movement, requires a different kind of thinking, a different kind of resiliency, or else we succumb to madness or resignation. Baldwin, I believe, offers resources to respond to such dark times and to imagine an answer to the moral reckoning that confronts us all.

Although it has been many years now, I did not read James Baldwin seriously until graduate school, and even in my early days at Princeton, I was more interested in Ralph Ellison. Ellison, the author of *Invisible Man*, offered a sophisticated treatment of the race problem in the United States that left the ground fertile. His nonfiction essays brimmed with philosophical and literary rigor, and I could read them with my white classmates without having to manage their discomfort. Baldwin seemed, at least to me back then, to leave the ground scorched. He told the truth, but anger dripped from the page. When I read *The Fire Next Time*, I could not reconcile his rage with his talk of love. It was like Dr. King meets Henry James meets Malcolm X meets Freud. Baldwin was *too* personal. In contrast, Ellison remained hidden behind his elegant words and powerful insights. His mask fit perfectly. Baldwin's essays forced you to turn inward and confront whatever pain was there, and I did not want to do that. I damn sure didn't know what to do with *my* pain philosophically. Moreover, and this mattered most, I could not read him with my white colleagues without having to manage whatever *he* made *them* feel.

So I evaded Baldwin. My classmates wrote dissertations on him, one of which eventually became an important scholarly book. I hesitated because I knew that, if I let him get inside of my head—inside of me—he would force me to look at myself honestly as the precondition for saying anything about the world. I was right. I finally found the courage to read him seriously, and in his work I found a way of thinking and a language to express what was happening inside of me and what I was seeing in my country.

My engagement with Jimmy over these many years has been, in part, an arduous journey of self-discovery. Reading and teaching his words forced me back onto myself, and I had to return to *my* wounds: to understand the overbearing and vexed presence of my father in my head. As a child, the man scared me to death. A stare could freeze me. A tone could bring me to tears. I had to understand, as best as I could, how my father's rage lodged itself inside of me, why I really left home (ran away, actually) at sixteen to go to college, and how I closed myself off emotionally in order to protect the vulnerable child who simply wanted to hear the words "I love you" from him. Jimmy's essays demanded a kind of honesty with yourself, without sentimentality, before you could pass judgment on the world as it is. Lies, he maintained, gave birth to more lies. He insisted that we see the connection between the disaster of our interior lives and the mess of a country that believed, for some odd reason, that if you were white you mattered more than others. What we made of ourselves in our most private moments, we made of the country. The two were inextricably related, because the country itself reflected those intimate terrors that moved us about.

In this sense, I was wrong, in those early days, to think of Baldwin as simply a personal essayist. To be sure, autobiography was a central part of his nonfiction writing. But, at its core, Baldwin set out to understand the American riddle.

> *a place, at once, so free,*
> *yet so bound,*
> *always present, but never found*

He sought to wrap his mind around the complex bundle of evasions, denials, loves, and hatreds that made up the American project, and point a pathway forward to becoming new, different human beings.

Reading Jimmy, then, requires much more than an encounter with one's pain. It is a demanding practice: tracing his references (understanding his invocation of Henry James, Ralph Waldo Emerson, Marcel Proust, the blues, etc.), feeling his language (how he sits with the King James Bible, finds resources in Shakespeare, and revels in Black English), and tracking his insights across a wide array of work. Close to seven thousand pages of work. Since that fateful day in graduate school when I finally decided to "sit with him," I have been an ardent reader of James Baldwin. What I have learned over these three decades is that Baldwin's way of translating what he saw and making it real for others still has something to say to us. His understanding of America and his particular insights about its contradictions and failures endure and offer ways of seeing the country afresh.

But we cannot grab hold of what Baldwin is saying, I believe, if we fall into the trap of reading him in a straight line. There is so much more about him and about what he witnessed than the stale characterizations of a career in full bloom in 1963 and a writer in decline by 1972. Baldwin's work constantly folds back on itself. Earlier formulations are taken up in his later years, and the accents move because of what he has seen and experienced. Rarely does he cast aside old ideas for new ones. Instead, new experiences cast old ideas in a different light.

Reading *The Fire Next Time* alongside *No Name in the Street,* for example, reminds me of listening to John Coltrane's "Pursuance," the third part of his classic album *A Love Supreme.* Taking the same notes, rotating them, and using a different tonal framework, Coltrane frantically pursues enlightenment, and one gets the feeling as one listens that he is playing the same thing over and over again even when the solo is at its most dissonant. For me, reading Baldwin throughout his career feels like this: a manic pursuit of a radically different way of being in the world, where "niggers" and the white people who need them no longer exist.

*Begin Again* takes up this pursuance in our times. The book aims to think with Baldwin and to interrogate how an insidious view of race, in the form of Trumpism, continues to frustrate any effort to "achieve our country." To be clear, to think with Baldwin is not to imitate or replicate his thoughts but to grapple with the ghosts of history that shadowed his time and continue to haunt our own, to make explicit the ravages of memory as he bore witness, to sit with the traumas of betrayal then and now, and to acknowledge the overwhelming challenge of mustering the faith to continue to fight. Thus, the book moves about: gesturing to the past, abruptly turning to the present, drawing on Baldwin's biography and close readings of his essays, and ending with my thoughts about our current morass. Patience. Patience. Such a book requires a different kind of writing. Not simply straightforward political commentary or philosophical argument, but a kind of writing where my rage and vulnerability (in other words, my passions) are in full view, because the book itself is a desperate plea in the after times.

In the end, it makes sense to me that so many people today reach for Baldwin to help them understand this latest iteration of the American nightmare, but to my mind, they are only grasping a part of his gift. We cannot cordon off his rage and leave behind the later works. Jimmy saw something in those years leading up to the election of Ronald Reagan. He desperately sought to prepare us to endure what was to come if the country failed to make different choices. I guess he saw something like Donald Trump on the distant horizon, and, however bitter he seemed, he still wrote to us with love. He still played the same notes no matter how dissonant they sounded.

The American idea is indeed in trouble. It should be. We have told ourselves a story that secures our virtue and protects us from our vices. But today we confront the ugliness of who we are—our darker angels reign. That ugliness isn't just Donald Trump or murderous police officers or loud racists screaming horrible things. It is the image of children in cages with mucus-smeared shirts and soiled pants glaring back at us. Fourteen-year-old girls forced to take care of two-year-old children they do not even know. It is sleep-deprived babies in rooms where the lights never go off, crying for loved ones who risked everything to come here only because they believed the idea. It is Oscar Alberto Martinez Ramirez and his twenty-three-month-old daughter facedown, washed up on the banks of our border. Reality can be hard and heartless.

Revealing the lie at the heart of the American idea, however, occasions an opportunity to tell a different and better story. It affords us a chance to excavate the past and to examine the ruins to find, or at least glimpse, what made us who we are. Baldwin insisted, until he died, that we reach for a different story. We should tell the truth about ourselves, he maintained, and that would release us into a new possibility. In some ways, as I scoured the rubble and ruins of his life and works, this call for a different story was the answer I found to my own shaken faith. In his last novel, *Just Above My Head*, Baldwin provided the key to surviving and mustering the strength to keep fighting amid the after times:

> When the dream was slaughtered and all that love and labor seemed to have come to nothing, we scattered. . . . We knew where we had been, what we had tried to do, who had cracked, gone mad, died, or been murdered around us.
>
> Not everything is lost. Responsibility cannot be lost, it can only be abdicated. If one refuses abdication, one begins again.

# BEGIN AGAIN

# CHAPTER ONE

# The Lie

JAMES BALDWIN AND STOKELY CARMICHAEL FIRST MET DUR-
ing the heady days of the movement to desegregate the South.
Carmichael was a young activist and a member of a student group
at Howard University called the Nonviolent Action Group
(NAG), which sought to combat racism and segregation in Washington, D.C., and in the surrounding areas of Virginia and Maryland. NAG offered a snapshot of the civil rights movement's
future: Carmichael's fellow students in the group included Court-
land Cox, Michael Thelwell, Muriel Tillinghast, and Ruth Brown,
all of whom would go on to be influential leaders in the Student
Nonviolent Coordinating Committee (SNCC). On Howard's
campus, NAG sponsored a series of programs called Project
Awareness, which was designed to explore the full complexity and
richness of black life and to engage the controversies surrounding
the black freedom movement. It was through these programs that
James Baldwin was invited to campus.

During the spring semester of 1963, after the violent response directed at the movement in Birmingham, the group organized a symposium about the role and responsibility of the black writer in the civil rights struggle. They invited Baldwin, playwright Lorraine Hansberry, novelists John O. Killens and Ralph Ellison, and actor and playwright Ossie Davis. Ellison sent his regrets, and Hansberry was too ill to attend, but students packed the auditorium. Baldwin had just finished a speaking tour on behalf of the Congress for Racial Equality (CORE), and this audience was hungry to hear him speak. Malcolm X, in town by happenstance, dropped in to hear Jimmy hold forth. "Whenever I hear that this little brother is going to speak in any town where I am," he said, "I always make a point of going to listen, because I learn something."

Baldwin didn't disappoint. He was a captivating speaker, with a powerful, almost hypnotic cadence; if the desire to be a preacher had long ago left him, his ability to hold a crowd in his hand had not. "It is the responsibility of the Negro writer to excavate the real history of this country . . . to tell us what really happened to get us where we are now," he boldly declared from the stage at Howard. "We must tell the truth till we can no longer bear it."

After the symposium ended, Baldwin, Killens, and Davis joined a group of students in the small, cramped apartment of a few NAG members. The hour was late. Jimmy needed a glass of Johnnie Walker Black, but the liquor stores were closed. Someone knew a bootlegger. The impromptu rap session went on until sunrise. "Our older brothers reasoned with us like family," Carmichael, who would become known as Kwame Ture, later recalled, even though he confused the date of the panel and the subsequent events. "We had three years of struggle behind us," he said. "So was the March on Washington and Dr. King's Dream. John F.

Kennedy had recently been gunned down. The national mood was sore, tense, and uncertain, as was our mood." Everyone understood the burden the students carried on their shoulders. Despite their relative youth, they had already confronted the brutality of the South in an effort to desegregate lunch counters and to register black people to vote. Many had been beaten and chased down dusty roads in Mississippi and Alabama by the Klan and by white sheriffs. These students were the shock troops of the civil rights movement, and many suffered from the trauma induced by a region and a country reluctant to change. Pessimism and rage threatened to overwhelm them.

Baldwin worried about the young men and women like an older brother who did not know exactly how to protect them from the dangers he already glimpsed ahead. For him, the brutality of "Bull" Connor's dogs and firehoses in Birmingham had already foreshadowed what was to come, revealing a depth to the country's depravity that no single piece of legislation could cure.

As the meeting wound down, Baldwin was left to say the final words, and he brought the conversation full circle to the reason why the students had invited him to campus. "Well, here we are, my young brothers and sisters. Here's how matters stand. I, Jimmy Baldwin, as a black writer, must in some way represent you. Now, you didn't elect me and I didn't ask for it, but here we are." All eyes were fixed on him. "Everything I write will in some way reflect on you. So . . . what do we do? I'll make you a pledge. If you will promise your elder brother that you will never, ever accept any of the many derogatory, degrading, and reductive definitions that this society has ready for you, then I, Jimmy Baldwin, promise you I shall never betray you."

It was an avowal of love, and a declaration of his responsibility as a writer dedicated to speaking the truth.

"It is, alas, the truth that to be an American writer today means mounting an unending attack on all that Americans believe themselves to hold sacred," Baldwin wrote in 1962. "It means fighting an astute and agile guerrilla warfare with that American complacency which so inadequately masks the American panic." In this sense, Baldwin's view of the writer was a decidedly moral one. The writer puts aside America's myths and legends and forces a kind of confrontation with the society as it is, becoming a disturber of the peace in doing so.

By the time Baldwin sat down with the Howard students in 1963, he was at the height of his powers, if not yet the full-on disturber of the peace he would soon become. In a relatively short period of time since the publication of his first novel, *Go Tell It on the Mountain,* in 1953, his play *Amen Corner* in 1954, and his first book of essays, *Notes of a Native Son,* in 1955, he had become one of the most prominent African American writers and critics in the United States. With his view of the moral role of the writer; his faith in the redemptive possibilities of human beings, no matter their color; and his initial faith in the possibility that the country could change, Baldwin was catapulted to literary fame and emerged as one of the most incisive and honest critics of America and its race problem. His admirers stretched across racial and political spectrums. Malcolm X referred to him as "the poet of the revolution." Edmund Wilson described him as one of the great creative artists of the country.

Since the publication of *Notes of a Native Son,* Baldwin had insisted that the country grapple with the contradiction at the heart of its self-understanding: the fact that in this so-called democracy, people believed that the color of one's skin determined the relative value of an individual's life and justified the way American society was organized. That belief and justification had dehumanized entire groups of people. White Americans were not excluded from its effects. "In this debasement and definition of black people," Baldwin argued, white people "debased and defined themselves."

Baldwin's understanding of the American condition cohered around a set of practices that, taken together, constitute something I will refer to throughout this book as *the lie*. The idea of facing the lie was always at the heart of Jimmy's witness, because he thought that it, as opposed to our claim to the shining city on a hill, was what made America truly exceptional. The lie is more properly several sets of lies with a single purpose. If what I have called the "value gap" is the idea that in America white lives have always mattered more than the lives of others, then the lie is a broad and powerful architecture of false assumptions by which the value gap is maintained. These are the narrative assumptions that support the everyday order of American life, which means we breathe them like air. We count them as truths. We absorb them into our character.

One set of lies debases black people; examples stretch from the writings of the Founding Fathers to *The Bell Curve*. According to these lies, black people are essentially inferior, less human than white people, and therefore deserving of their particular station in American life. We see these lies every day in the stereotypes that black people are lazy, dishonest, sexually promiscuous, prone to criminal behavior, and only seeking a handout from big government. Baldwin made the Howard students promise him that they would never believe the lies the country told about them, because he knew that the lie would do irreparable harm to their souls, as it had done to the country.

Another constituent part of the lie involves lies about American history and about the trauma that America has visited throughout that history on people of color both at home and abroad. According to these lies, America is fundamentally good and innocent, its bad deeds dismissed as mistakes corrected on the way to "a more perfect union." The United States has always been shadowed by practices that contradict our most cherished principles. The genocide of native peoples, slavery, racial apartheid, Japanese internment camps, and the subordination of women reveal that our basic creed that "all men are created equal" was a lie, at least in practice. These weren't minor events in the grand history of the "redeemer nation," nor were they simply the outcomes of a time when such views were widely held. Each moment represented a profound revelation about who we were as a country—just as the moments of resistance against them said something about who we aspired to be.

But the lie's most pernicious effect when it comes to our history is to malform events to fit the story whenever America's innocence is threatened by reality. When measured against our actions, the story we have told ourselves about America being a divinely sanctioned nation called to be a beacon of light and a moral force in the world is a lie. The idea of the "Lost Cause" as just an honest assessment of what happened after the Civil War is a lie. The stories we often tell ourselves of the civil rights movement and racial progress in this country, with Rosa Parks's courage, Dr. King's moral vision, and the unreasonable venom of Black Power, culminating in the election of Barack Obama, are all too often lies.

Taken as a whole, then, the lie is the mechanism that allows, and has always allowed, America to avoid facing the truth about its unjust treatment of black people and how it deforms the soul of the country. The lie cuts deep into the American psyche. It secures our national innocence in the face of the ugliness and evil we have done.

In his 1964 essay "The White Problem," published in Robert A. Goodwin's edited volume *100 Years of Emancipation*, Baldwin placed the lie at the heart of the country's founding.

> The people who settled the country had a fatal flaw. They could recognize a man when they saw one. They knew he wasn't . . . anything *else* but a man; but since they were Christian, and since they had already decided that they came here to establish a free country, the only way to justify the role this chattel was playing in one's life was to say that he *was not* a man. For if he wasn't, then no crime had been committed. That lie is the basis of our present trouble.

American history would be contorted in the service of it: where efforts to resist the likes of slavery or to break the back of Jim Crow segregation would be conscripted into the grand story of America's greatness and its ongoing perfection. Slavery would be banished from view or seen as a mistake instead of a defining institution of systemic cruelty in pursuit of profit. That history would fortify our national identity, and any attempt to confront the lie itself would be sabotaged by the fear that we may not be who we say we are. For white people in this country, "America" is an identity worth protecting at any cost.

The symposium at Howard took place a few months after the publication of *The Fire Next Time,* and though the students may not have known it, like them, Baldwin stood at a crossroads. Behind him was the poverty of his Harlem childhood and the anguish of years in Paris. He had finally made himself into a writer. But from his perch in France, he had also seen the dawning of a mass movement in the United States and returned to bear witness to the courage and sacrifice of those he called "improbable aristocrats," like the Little Rock Nine, Dr. King, and the young people who sat in at lunch counters across the South. Behind him was the senseless murder of Medgar Evers and the carnage of Birmingham. In front of him was the promise of the March on Washington, and the death of those four little girls in the bombing of the Sixteenth Street Baptist Church, which broke that promise. Behind him was the sweetness and power of everyday people fighting for their freedom. In front of him was the bitterness and disappointment in a country that fought them at every turn.

What Baldwin saw in the eyes of the young people in that cramped little apartment in 1963, he felt in his bones. He knew the country was poised to betray them on behalf of the lie. Medgar's body offered ample evidence of that. In the face of such evil, the federal government continued to slow-walk substantive reform, and white people continued to be white people. Baldwin viscerally felt the students' rage and could easily understand how, in just two years, Carmichael would stand atop a bus in Greenwood, Mississippi, and shout "Black Power" and scare the hell out of the nation. Chickens must, after all, come home to roost.

Baldwin knew then that he would have to tell as much of the truth as possible about the betrayal and the rage, no matter the costs for him personally, and then tell a little more about what we would have to do to achieve our country. Such was the responsibility of the writer as he understood it, and especially in light of his promise to the Howard students that late night in a small apartment in Washington, D.C. In 1963, Baldwin could still hold out some hope that his work, and indeed, the work of Carmichael, King, and all of those unknown men and women who engaged in the movement, might have the effect of forcing white America to confront its belief in the lie. But that hope would soon fade.

Four years after the symposium at Howard, on December 11, 1967, Stokely Carmichael stepped off an Air France Boeing 707 at John F. Kennedy International Airport in New York City to find United States marshals from New York's Eastern District waiting to confiscate his passport. Carmichael had been on a blistering worldwide tour since his decision to step down in May of that year as the leader of SNCC. While in Paris, he boldly declared to four thousand people at the Palais de la Mutualité, "Our aim is to disrupt the United States of America, and we think our blood is not too high a price to pay. We don't want peace in Vietnam! We want the Vietnamese to defeat the United States of America!"

In the years since that all-night conversation with Baldwin, Carmichael, the optimistic kid from Trinidad, Bronx Science High School, and Howard University had become a fiery revolutionary. Repeated betrayals can create unexpected enemies. Carmichael had seen up close the horrors of the South and no longer believed that King's moral vision and his philosophy of nonviolence could save the country. Malcolm X was dead. So was Carmichael's comrade in SNCC, Jimmy Lee Jackson, who was beaten and murdered by an Alabama state trooper. Even with the passage of the Civil Rights Act of 1964 and the Voting Rights Act of 1965, the country seemed no closer to becoming a genuinely multiracial democracy. White people would not let that happen. They held firmly on to the lie.

Carmichael's rhetoric overseas set off a firestorm back home. His calls for revolution and his statements of solidarity with anti-colonial struggles in places like Cuba and Tanzania led many politicians to call for his arrest upon his return to the United States. A November 1967 editorial in the *Los Angeles Sentinel* declared, "It is time for the people here at home to recognize him for what he is—a traitor—and cut the puppet strings." A few months earlier, United Press International (UPI) reported that Senator Barry Goldwater of Arizona had said that if the attorney general was "worth his salt he would arrest Stokely Carmichael when he returns . . . and would try him under the laws of treason, and if found guilty, the penalty should be what the court would apply." In a *Los Angeles Times* report, Goldwater was even more strident: "If found guilty, put [him] to death."

As Carmichael stepped off the plane at Kennedy International Airport and into this tempest, Baldwin was in London spending time with his siblings Paula and David and David's partner, Carole Weinstein. David and Carole had found a quaint house on 36 Tedworth Square, just a few blocks off of King's Road in the middle of Chelsea, for Baldwin to finish his latest novel, *Tell Me How Long the Train's Been Gone.* The house had quickly become a gathering spot for an eclectic group of artists, activists, and friends; the writer Rudolph Kizerman described it as "a home, a hangout, a roof for the night, a love nest, a center of discussion, a restaurant, a place where everything happened, from the avant garde to the strictly eccentric to the situations without an answer." Amid the turmoil of the times and the disaster of his personal life—one relationship ended as another began—Baldwin had finally found a moment to rest. He did not have to tend to the volatility of another young lover or dwell on the latest disappointment dealt by Lucien Happersberger, the man who once held his heart. He simply enjoyed his siblings and friends, and the relative peace afforded in Chelsea from his hectic schedule.

But the incident at Kennedy International Airport disturbed him: That Stokely Carmichael was now widely viewed as a traitor by the press and politicians spoke volumes about the state of the country and of the movement itself. *Look where we have so quickly fallen,* Baldwin must have thought, *and look what has happened to those young men and women who dared to risk everything to save the country.*

Baldwin sat down to write a defense of Carmichael and to pen a powerful indictment of the nation's latest failure to live up to its promise. In doing so, he reached for the history of the movement, but here he tried to tell a more troubling story about what happened to many of the young people in the movement and about the stunning hypocrisy of the nation. He had in mind the brutal beatings the students endured in the South just to register to vote, the bitter disappointments they confronted when they engaged in electoral politics in Atlantic City at the Democratic National Convention, and the ongoing harassment and surveillance by the FBI. He guided the reader's attention to the "terror tactics" of American society, which says to "black boys and girls that . . . their lives are worth less than other lives, and that they can live only on terms dictated to them by other people." From Baldwin's point of view, Black Power was perhaps the only possible, or at least reasonable, response to the country's unwillingness to give up the lie.

"I first met Stokely Carmichael in the Deep South when he was just another nonviolent kid," Baldwin wrote, "marching and talking and getting his head whipped. . . ."

This time now seems as far behind us as the Flood, and if those suffering, gallant, betrayed boys and girls who were then using their bodies in an attempt to save a heedless nation have since concluded that the nation is not worth saving, no American alive has the right to be surprised.

As white America chose itself over a truly just and multiracial society, Baldwin set out to chart the nature of that betrayal and to offer an account of the devastation left in its wake. "What happened to those boys and girls, and what happened to the civil rights movement, is an indictment of America and Americans," he wrote. It remained "an enduring monument, which we will not outlive, to the breathtaking cowardice of this sovereign people." The young firebrands of Black Power were America's children, all grown up in the shadows of broken promises.

The rage that simmered just beneath the surface of *The Fire Next Time* finally came into full view. Jimmy's friends had always known he was angry. He knew it himself. His rage about the constraints of race in the United States was one of the reasons why he left for France in the winter of 1948, and that rage had always put him on edge. Baldwin responded to the smallest slights and had very little tolerance for the daily cuts and insults of racist America. I tell my students at Princeton that it was just down the street, at a restaurant on Route 1, that Baldwin hurled a glass at a waitress and shattered a mirror after he was refused service and ended up having to run for his life.

But something was different now, something best measured by his words in defense of Stokely. By 1967, Baldwin had grown even more disillusioned with the country, including the white liberals who had once celebrated him. His rage was no longer tempered by his faith in the possibility that America could change. In his early years, he had invested so much energy, in his writings and in his speeches, to warning white America of the costs to themselves and to the country of their commitment to the myths and legends of America. As Colin MacInnes, the British novelist and journalist, said in the literary magazine *Encounter* in 1965, "Why Baldwin speaks to us of another race is that he still believes us worthy of warning: he has not yet despaired of making us feel the dilemma we all chat about so glibly . . . and of trying to save us from the agonies that we too will suffer if the Negro people are driven beyond the ultimate point of desperation." As Baldwin sat down to write his defense of Carmichael, he questioned whether white America was worthy of warning at all.

Baldwin finished his essay defending Carmichael just after the New Year, 1968, but both the London *Times* and *The New York Times* refused to publish it. Black Power and Carmichael were simply anathema in a country at war in Vietnam and with itself. The Manchester *Guardian* ran the piece, but it would not be picked up by an American outlet until *The Los Angeles Free Press* ran it in February.

Beyond a mere defense of Carmichael, Baldwin offered a sober assessment of the fits and starts of the quest for black freedom in this country—what he would later call *the view from here*. Much of his nonfiction writing after 1963 involved warning the nation of the costs of ignoring the demands of the black freedom struggle. He urged Americans, as he always did, to plunge beneath the surface of the race problem and examine our interior agreement with ways of thinking that trapped us in the lie.

But Baldwin also wrote about what he viewed as the shattering of Dr. King's dream. He sought to understand what happened after the collapse of the civil rights movement (especially after Dr. King's murder in 1968), the emergence of Black Power, the significance of the rise of the black middle class and the so-called black underclass, and the scope of white America's commitment to resist fundamental change. He was no longer writing from the standpoint of someone energized by the movement who took it upon himself to bear witness to it, but rather as a witness to the reassertion of the American lie in the face of that movement.

In this light, and most important for our current moment, I think of Baldwin as a critic of the after times. I take that phrase, "after times," from Walt Whitman's 1871 treatise *Democratic Vistas*. For Whitman, out of the ashes of the Civil War emerged a nation bustling with the energy of commerce, "endowed with a vast and more and more appointed body" but "with little or no soul." In this context, national rage and fury served as warning signals that were "invaluable for after times." The phrase refers, at once, to the disruption and the splintering of old ways of living and the making of a new community after the fall. The after times characterize what was before and what is coming into view. On one level, it is the interregnum surrounded by the ghosts of the dying moment, and on another, the moment that is desperately trying to be born with a lie wrapped around its neck.

Baldwin wrote in another after times—that of the collapse of the civil rights movement, bearing witness to a time when many thought the nation was poised to change, only to have darkness descend and change arrested. Grief and trauma joined with disappointment as Baldwin watched white Americans turn away from the difficulties of genuine change, often embracing a nostalgic appeal for simpler days, when black people knew their place and weren't in the streets protesting, in order to justify their refusal to give up the lie.

Seeing this turn in real time, Baldwin understood the anger of Black Power and its harsh judgment of the country. He witnessed what was happening in ghettos, where the workings of the lie impoverished millions. He saw the beginnings of mass incarceration and its effects on black communities. He also felt the emotional trauma of dashed hopes and expectations, and the costs of the fight. Baldwin set himself the task to make sense of this vicious cycle in the country's history by naming the betrayal and exposing the lie that gave it such bite.

As a critic of the after times, Baldwin is like a blues singer who sings about the crossroads. He stands at the railroad junction, where he can go in multiple directions. He is betwixt and between possibilities. The crossroads or the railroad junction is a way station of the blues: a place where anguish and pain are faced, where everything seems to have gone wrong, and yet a kind of resilience is found in the painful phrasing of new possibility. In the after times, hope is not yet lost, even if the call to reimagine the country has been answered with violence. So the after times also represent an opportunity for a new America—a chance to grasp a new way of being in the world—amid the darkness of the hour. But as Jimmy understood, that opportunity rests on what we do in the moment.

To bear witness in the after times is hard on the soul. For Baldwin, time fractured at a dizzying pace as the possibilities of the movement gave way to the realization that white America would not give up what was required to finally end the racial nightmare. The moment was one of confusion. Everything seemed to collapse in on itself, and the path forward wasn't clear. With a gesture to Whitman, Baldwin cried out in *No Name in the Street*, "There are no clear vistas: the road that seems to pull one forward into the future is also pulling one backward into the past." The crossroads. The blues. In this sense, as Baldwin wrote in the "Black Power" essay, Carmichael did not invent anything new when he shouted "Black Power" atop a bus in Greenwood, Mississippi, in 1966. That young man from Howard, now a wizened veteran of

America's lie, "simply dug it up again from where it's been lying since the first slaves hit the gang plank."

If there is a reason that the arc of what I've described above seems so familiar—that the country finds itself on the precipice of significant change, only to turn its back on it all and double down on its historic ugliness—it's because I believe we, once again, find ourselves living in after times. Nearly half a century on, we are suffering through yet another terrible cycle in the tragic history of America.

Perhaps the most instructive example of the way the lie distorts our recent history can be found in how Barack Obama's election to the presidency was largely framed as an ending: a triumphant climax to the civil rights movement begun decades earlier. The elevation of a black man to the presidency, such a story suggested, represented the notion that all constraints had fallen away, that if a black man could hold the highest office in the land, then surely we as a country had finally and definitively overcome our racist past. In this story, what King began in Montgomery in 1955, Obama finished in triumph at Grant Park on election night 2008. To be fair, Obama himself did not discourage this reading of his own ascendance, even though a simple look at the American landscape at the moment of his election could not have made more plain the hollowness of this story. Still, the lie had a nice ring to it.

I would propose a different story, one in which Obama's presidency sounded not an ending but a beginning, the opening of a new moment when the lie and its dreadful consequences might once again be interrogated as it was during the civil rights movement, when the energy of activists and common citizens might be marshaled to bring forth a new country. We saw this in the tremendous response to the murder of Trayvon Martin, in the formation of Black Lives Matter, in the return of the phrase "white supremacy" to the lips of people of all colors to describe the arrangements of American life. Decades of pent-up energy were released into the streets, massed into protests. Civil disobedience found renewed appeal, as protesters tried to make plain to the nation the truth of the value gap.

No wonder, then, that in the last years of Obama's presidency we saw a resurgence of interest in Baldwin's life and work. Before Election Day 2016, Baldwin was everywhere in the Black Lives Matter movement. When residents erupted in Baltimore, Maryland, after the murder of Freddie Gray, one activist was seen outside the Western District police station with a sign quoting Baldwin: "Ignorance allied with power is the most ferocious enemy of justice." Activists throughout the Obama years appealed to Baldwin's critical insights on social media and reveled in his sexuality as a way of disrupting older forms of black politics (this black queer man represented a different kind of radicalism than the masculinist politics of black male preachers, they maintained). They sought out his works as a way of making sense of a country on the cusp of change, because they were protesting in the streets and walking the corridors of power demanding that change. With a black man in the White House, many believed that, even as the Tea Party shouted, as white nationalists panicked, and as Republicans obstructed, there was a genuine opportunity to fundamentally change the country. Nothing in our past would suggest this was possible, but nothing in our past suggested we would elect a black man president either.

Yet just as it did in response to the civil rights movement, the lie moved quickly to reassert itself. We soon heard cries of "All

Lives Matter." Cops were found not guilty in the killing of unarmed black men. Republican legislatures began to consider bills that would sanction protests. They also passed draconian voter ID laws that would affect the next election in places like Wisconsin. The anger of the Tea Party saturated the country's politics as many pundits described their economic angst and downplayed their cultural anxiety about the demographic changes in the country.

All of this was prelude to 2016, when chants of "Make America Great Again" took center stage. Trump barely won the election, but his victory felt like he had split the land in two, and whatever was released from below sucked up most of the oxygen. For many, the far right had taken hold of the reins of government. Trump refused to condemn white supremacists and neo-Nazis in Charlottesville. Tried to ban Muslims from entering the country. Turned on "enemies" within and without. He embraced draconian immigration policies—separating children from their parents and building tent cities to hold them—and declared the so-called caravan of refugees at the southern border a carrier of contagion (leprosy) and a threat to the security of the nation. Contrary to what he declared during his inaugural address, Trump did not stop the "American carnage." He unleashed it.

As the country lurched to the far right and reasserted the lie, Black Lives Matter went relatively silent, or it was no longer heard. Activists scattered. Many had suffered the trauma of their efforts. The disasters kept coming like waves, and many lives were shattered. Activists needed to step back and gather up the pieces. Some, like DeRay McKesson, ran for political office. Others, like Patrisse Cullors, Alicia Garza, and Opal Tometi, joined different organizing efforts or went back to college, like Kayla Reed, one of the leaders in the Ferguson uprising, who got her degree through a pilot program for activists at Washington University in St. Louis.

Some reached for more radical politics as networks disbanded. But, in Ferguson, Missouri, where Michael Brown was shot and killed and where a working-class black community captured the attention of the nation, seven activists died over the next few years after the cameras had been put away and reporters left town. The authorities reported that these activists had committed suicide, but some believed they were killed. Many others who risked everything in protest to change the country continue to work hard every day to get their lives back and to find some modicum of peace.

All that labor, the risk and death, seemed to have come to nothing, as activists and Americans in general hit Trump's wall face-first. The nation had turned its back on whatever vision of the country Black Lives Matter put forward. Police were still an ominous presence in many black communities as consent decrees, under the leadership of then attorney general Jeff Sessions, fell to the side like fallen dominoes stacked in a figure-eight pattern. Barack Obama was off vacationing on some island. He grew a nice beard, and Michelle Obama wrote her autobiography. Their symbolic significance quickly became the stuff of nostalgia. The Republican Party morphed into some monstrosity and became the Party of Trump, as if a recessive gene had been activated. All the while, 40 percent of America delighted in Trump's presidency. They had told themselves the lie that black and brown people threatened their way of life, and now they were poised to make America white again.

Trump is the dominant manifestation of *our* after times. His presidency is the response to the political and social possibilities of Barack Obama's election and the radical demands of the Black Lives Matter movement. Both Obama and Black Lives Matter indicated a significant shift in the political climate of the country.

And millions of white Americans did not like what they saw. Political scientists had already seen a pattern developing in our national politics, where racial attitudes were closely aligned with partisan identification: How one felt about black people or Muslims or immigration mapped onto how one voted. In many ways, party identification, particularly for white Americans, was becoming a proxy for racial identity. Obama's eight years in the White House worked like a massive release of fossil carbon in the political atmosphere and accelerated the linkage. For many, his ascendance signaled the end of entitlement for whites, and the protests in the streets over police violence solidified a deepening sense of racial anxiety.

Baldwin's words spoke to us powerfully in Obama's moment, as Black Lives Matter gained energy and the country opened up space to rethink race and confront the lie. But he also speaks to us just as powerfully, if not more so, in this moment of disillusionment, of promise deferred—especially to those young people of Black Lives Matter who risked so much to change this nation. I like to think of Jimmy as a moral compass. His writings and witness during his own after times offer direction and particular insight into how we might imagine beginning again in the face of yet another failure of America to give up the value gap. What might an honest reckoning with the country look like now? How do we muster the courage to keep fighting in the face of abject moral failure? To not abdicate our responsibility to fight for our children and for democracy itself? Baldwin's later writings are saturated with these questions. He sought to answer them while grappling with his own trauma, grief, and profound disillusionment with the moral state of the country and in the people who repeatedly choose the safety of being white over a more just society.

Throughout this country's history, from the Revolutionary period to Reconstruction to the black freedom movement of the mid-twentieth century, the United States has faced moments of crisis in which the country might emerge otherwise, moments when the *idea* of white America itself could finally be put aside. In each instance the country chose to remain exactly what it was: a racist nation that claimed to be democratic. These were and are moments of national betrayal, in which the commitments of democracy are shunted off to the side to make way for, and to safely secure, a more fundamental commitment to race.

We often reach for the language of "backlash" to describe these moments when the prospect of genuine change around racial matters hits a wall of resistance. It's a word we hear often today, one that registers that, for some people, the pace and substance of change have gone too far and, in doing so, threaten the very way of life that makes the reform possible in the first place. It is a genteel way of saying white people have had enough. Or it is another way of asking the old question, "What else does the Negro want?"

We should resist the language of backlash, not merely because it is inaccurate, but because it wrongly concedes the frame of the question. The term describes a political response to a problem that cuts much deeper than politics, suggesting that white people believe they have gone far enough in addressing black people's demands; it mistakes the substance of those demands for the underlying fears that have produced the politics and laws to begin with. As I wrote in my book *Democracy in Black,* even good laws are distorted by the persistence of the value gap, meaning that changes in laws, no matter how necessary, will never be sufficient to produce a healthier society. Only addressing the deeper fears can accomplish that. "Backlash" mistakenly views demands for fundamental dignity as demands for privileges, and, worse, suggests that creeping incrementalism is a legitimate pace of change when it comes to remedying the devastation of black lives.

"Backlash" fails to capture the response to the collapse of old hierarchies as people who were once relegated to the bottom rungs of society seek to move out of their designated spots. In critical moments of transition, when it seems as if old ways of living and established norms are fading, deep-seated fears emerge over loss of standing and privilege. Baldwin put it this way in the essay on Carmichael: "When a black man, whose destiny and identity have always been controlled by others, decides and states that he will control his own destiny and rejects the identity given to him by others, he is talking revolution." That threat to the social order releases fears that further contaminate our politics.

The word *backlash* covers in a cloak of innocence white fears and the politics that exploits them. Those fears throw us back into the pit and make tar babies of us all. During a speech at Kalamazoo College in 1960, later adapted and published in *Nobody Knows My Name,* Baldwin tried to show how those fears moved us about, how they dictated policies, and how they revealed what's at the heart of white identity in this country:

> They do not really know what it is they are afraid of, but they know they are afraid of something, and they are so frightened that they are nearly out of their minds. And this same fear obtains on one level or another, to varying degrees, throughout the entire country. We would never, never allow Negroes to starve, to grow bitter, and to die in

ghettos all over the country if we were not driven by some nameless fear that has nothing to do with Negroes. . . . It is only too clear that even with the most malevolent will in the world, Negroes can never manage to achieve one-tenth of the harm which we fear. No, it has everything to do with ourselves and this is one of the reasons that for all these generations we have disguised this problem in the most incredible jargon.

Talk of backlash is just one of the many disguises. In these moments, the country reaches the edge of fundamental transformation and pulls back out of a fear that genuine democracy will mean white people will have to lose something—that they will have to give up their particular material and symbolic standing in the country. That *fear*, Baldwin understood, is at the heart of the moral psychology of the nation and of the white people who have it by the throat. That fear, not the demand for freedom, arrests significant change and organizes American life. We see it in the eyes of Trump supporters. One hears it in the reticence of the Democratic Party to challenge them directly.

It is not enough to merely acknowledge these dark moments when the politics of fear threaten to overwhelm, as Jon Meacham does in his brilliant book *The Soul of America*, but then to move quickly to examples of hope that affirm the country's sense of its own exceptionalism. We fail to linger in the dark moments at our peril. To be sure, we have a vibrant democratic tradition and numerous examples of courageous voices who risked everything to defend its basic ideals. But these after times reveal the deep cellar of American life (that two-storied sense of the country), where the fears that move us about reside. They work like the recurring nightmare that frightens the child, because their power derives from a deep wound that overruns everything. One has to linger here. Move too quickly, and you set yourself up for another nightmare.

The path to a different America, Baldwin maintained, encompassed an acceptance of the reality of our country's racist past and present and how that has distorted our overall sense of who we take ourselves to be. But, as he wrote in *The Fire Next Time:*

> To accept one's past—one's history—is not the same thing as drowning in it; it is learning how to use it. An invented past can never be used; it cracks and crumbles under the pressures of life like clay in a season of drought. How can the American Negro's past be used? The unprecedented price demanded—and at this embattled hour of the world's history—is the transcendence of the realities of color, of nations, and of altars.

Close to ten years later in *No Name in the Street,* as he reflected on Black Power, Baldwin would state the point a bit differently, but with the same arc of intention. The point wasn't to declare ourselves color blind. We would have to fight it out in order to finally rid ourselves of the assumptions about who was valued more than others. That may have to involve black people celebrating their blackness, because it shatters their interior agreement with the lie. In this sense, one can only transcend color by passing through it, and uprooting the lie along the way:

> As the black glories in his newfound color, which is his at last, and asserts, not always with the very greatest polite-

ness, the unanswerable validity and power of his being—
even in the shadow of death—the white is very often
affronted and very often made afraid. . . . And one may
indeed be wary, but the point is that it was inevitable that
black and white should arrive at this dizzying height of
tension. Only when we have passed this moment will we
know what our history has made of us.

Trump and his supporters have shattered any illusion that we
might have passed through the moment. Some thirty years after
Baldwin's death we are still wrestling with the fact that so many
Americans continue to hold the view that ours is a white nation.

What can we learn from how Baldwin made his way through
the after times? How did he see his task as a writer in that moment, and what lessons can we draw from it about what we must
do in our own? We have to tell a different story about who we are
(by way of an honest encounter with our past) that challenges the
repetition of myths and legends in the guise of nostalgia for simpler times. And like Baldwin, we must never lose sight, as we finger the pain and disillusionment of our after times, of the
possibility of a New Jerusalem. We have to do this for all those
young people who risked everything to change the country—for
those who have gone mad, who gave us their last breath, and for
those who now face the temptation of accepting the world as it is
as opposed to what it can be. It is, after all, a declaration of responsibility and love.

Baldwin saw clearly what he was up against; he fully understood the power of the American lie. It is the engine that moves
this place. It transforms facts and events that do not quite fit our

self-understanding into the details of American greatness or features of our never-ending journey to perfection. The lie is the story that warps reality in this country, which means that resisting it involves telling in each moment a truer story, one that casts the lie into relief, showing it for what it is. And so Baldwin saw his role as that of bearing witness; that witness becomes a resource for what's possible. I think that's why Stokely Carmichael said Baldwin never betrayed us. Carmichael knew that no matter what happened, even when Baldwin disagreed with Black Power, Jimmy never conceded an inch to the lie. His witness remained true. And now, as then, someone must bear witness to the truth in the dark.

# CHAPTER TWO

# Witness

ON SEPTEMBER 4, 1957, HERMAN COUNTS, A PROFESSOR OF theology at North Carolina's Johnson C. Smith University, planned to drop off his daughter in the circle in front of Harding High School, which she was attending for the first time. Located off of West Fifth Street at the edge of downtown Charlotte, Harding was built in 1935 and stood as an important part of the city's landscape. It had been segregated since its founding, but in 1957 Harding finally faced the difficult challenge laid down by the 1954 Supreme Court decision in *Brown v. Board of Education*. Like most schools in the South, Harding resisted desegregation, and its students were prepared to resist the arrival of its first black student, Dorothy "Dot" Counts.

In anticipation of unrest, Charlotte police barricaded the main road to the school, so Dot had to get out and walk. Herman's friend Edwin Thompkins rode in the car with them and offered to join Dot while her dad parked. Herman looked at his daughter as she opened the door and reminded her of what he always told his family: "Hold your head high." He knew what she would face on the way into the building. Daily threats had set the stage for what was about to happen.

With Thompkins walking slightly behind her, Dorothy Counts, wearing a new red-and-yellow dress made by her grandmother, with a long bow that flowed beyond her waist, waded into a sea of white rage. She was only fifteen years old, one of four black students chosen to integrate the schools in Charlotte. The other three didn't face much resistance, because the White Citizens' Council had chosen Harding as the place to make their stand. And stand they did. Dot Counts confronted a wave of hatred that morning, all captured by the camera of Don Sturkey, a photographer for *The Charlotte Observer*. As she walked toward the school, white students, their faces contorted with hatred and unmistakable glee, screamed, "Nigger go back home" and "Go back to Africa, burrhead!" They threw sticks and chunks of ice. They spat on her new dress. The police refused to protect her, staying at the other end of the street and watching the spectacle from a distance. No school officials or teachers were present to calm the crowd or escort Dorothy to class. Instead, with her head held high on her lanky near six-foot frame, her brow furrowed with an intense stare that perhaps hid her fear, and her mouth twisted in a manner that revealed her horror and utter disgust, Dot walked a racist gauntlet to enter Harding High School.

She made the walk for just three more days before deciding never to return.

Don Sturkey's photos of Dot's harrowing experience soon traveled around the world, to great effect. In *No Name in the Street*, James Baldwin claimed that seeing newsstand images of Dorothy Counts while at the Sorbonne in Paris during the first Interna-

tional Conference of Black Writers and Artists led him to return
to the United States after years of being away from home. He was
covering the conference for the literary magazines *Preuves* and
*Encounter*, and he recalled the photos confronting him as he
walked from the meeting hall:

> Facing us, on every newspaper kiosk on that wide, tree-
> shaded boulevard, were photographs of fifteen-year-old
> Dorothy Counts being reviled and spat upon by the mob as
> she was making her way to school in Charlotte, North
> Carolina. There was unutterable pride, tension, and an-
> guish in that girl's face. . . . It made me furious, it filled me
> with both hatred and pity, and it made me ashamed. Some
> one of us should have been there with her! I dawdled in
> Europe for nearly yet another year, held by my private life
> and my attempt to finish a novel, but it was on that bright
> afternoon that I knew I was leaving France. I could, simply,
> no longer sit around in Paris discussing the Algerian and
> the black American problem. Everybody else was paying
> their dues, and it was time I went home and paid mine.

It makes for a galvanizing moment, with Baldwin moved to
leave Paris by the cruelty visited on a child. But this was not quite
the case. It could not have been the image of Dorothy Counts that
spurred Baldwin to give up France. The ordeal at Harding High
School happened in the fall of 1957, a year *after* the 1956 conference in Paris. In fact, the article Baldwin wrote at the time for
*Encounter*, later published in *Nobody Knows My Name* in 1961,
doesn't mention the Counts photograph at all. In that essay, his
memories reach for a different kind of sensory experience: "As
night was falling we poured into the Paris streets. Boys and girls,

old men and women, bicycles, terraces, all were there, and the people were queueing up before the bakeries for bread." No mention of a photograph. No momentous decision.

Baldwin's reflections on the photo of Dorothy Counts in *No Name in the Street* came some sixteen years after the events in Charlotte, and his memory failed him. In a sense, this was not a remarkable failure; throughout the beginning of that book, Baldwin warns the reader not to trust his memories. "Much, much, much has been blotted out," he writes, "coming back only lately in bewildering and untrustworthy flashes."

But it would be wrong to read this caution as mere reference to the fading memory of an aging mind. Instead, it is a consequence of trauma, not merely Baldwin's own, but the collective trauma experienced in the course of a decade and a half of the betrayal of the civil rights movement. Over the sixteen years since Dorothy Counts attempted to desegregate Harding High School, Baldwin witnessed up close the horrors of American racism. So many black children, in the South and in the North, had been subject to what she had experienced. Others had endured campaigns of violence against black people and the beatings and murder of protesters. Who knows how many black people line the bottom of the Mississippi River simply because they wanted to exercise their right to vote. Black leaders had been assassinated. Terror and disappointment had become defining features of the intervening years. And, through it all, America was still stuck in the morass of the lie.

Baldwin's mistake in recalling why he returned to the United States revealed how trauma colored his witness. Memories fragmented or were repressed. Painful moments were triggered by random encounters. Grief and loss often overwhelmed everything. In *No Name,* he tries to capture, at the level of form, the effect of this trauma: The book reads like the reflections of someone who has been traumatized, folding back on itself and twisting time as past and present collide and collapse into each other. Memories flood and recede. After recalling the assassination of Dr. Martin Luther King, Jr., and how King's death and funeral affected him, Baldwin wrote, "The mind is a strange and terrible vehicle . . . and my own mind, after I had left Atlanta, began to move backward in time, to places, people, and events I thought I had forgotten. Sorrow drove it there . . . and a certain kind of bewilderment." Here, in the after times, witness and trauma were inextricably linked.

So much of Baldwin's life was filled with traumatic experiences that left permanent scars. The difficulties of his childhood, the dangers of sexual predators, his experiences with white police in Harlem, and his own feeling of being trapped by it all weighed heavily on how he navigated the world. Those wounds shaped his artistic vision. The trauma guided his eyes (and his pen) to the pain that lurked in the shadows of human experience and the various ways we all try to avoid it.

By the year of Dorothy Counts's first day at Harding in 1957, nearly a decade had passed since Baldwin had fled Harlem for the City of Lights in fear of what might come to pass if he remained. In December of 1946, his close friend Eugene Worth had committed suicide by jumping off the George Washington Bridge. Whatever had driven Worth to that fatal choice—something about his life, perhaps, and about this country—Baldwin understood it. He felt that if he didn't leave the States, he too would end up at the bottom of the Hudson River, alongside the wedding rings he had tossed into it two years earlier when he rejected the life everyone expected of him. "My luck was running out," he said in a 1984 interview for *The Paris Review*. "I was going to jail, I was going to kill somebody or be killed."

Paris gave Baldwin the freedom to find—or better to create—a different self. Released from the stifling assumptions about black people in the United States, and the dangerous contradictions of the streets of Greenwich Village, Baldwin found breathing room in Paris to imagine himself anew. "I didn't have to walk around with one half of my brain trying to please Mr. Charlie and the other half trying to kill him," he recalled. "Fuck Mr. Charlie! It's his problem. It's not my problem. I felt that I was left alone in Paris to become whatever I wanted to become."

These early days in Paris, as his biographers note, marked Baldwin's manic attempt to become a writer. He was not so much overburdened with the racial politics of the United States—the tumult of the civil rights movement had not quite begun—as he was shadowed by the existential consequences of growing up black and poor in a society that despised you because you were black. In Paris, he embarked on a high-stakes quest for individuality, heightened by the pressing need to stay alive in a foreign country with little to no money.

During these years, Baldwin worked relentlessly to vomit up what he called "the profound, almost ineradicable self-hatred" America had lodged in his guts, a sickness that had started in his childhood home. So much of Baldwin's early life is bound up with his stormy relationship with his stepfather, David Baldwin, an itinerant preacher who came to New York from New Orleans in the early 1920s, one among the millions of black migrants who left the South and transformed America's northern cities. Baldwin famously wrote of his effort to escape the tyranny of his stepfather in a 1955 essay, "Me and My House," which would be reprinted as

"Notes of a Native Son." David Baldwin, the only father Baldwin ever knew, was consumed by his hatred of white people and his inability to provide for his ever-growing family. That hatred often spilled over into violence. He terrorized his children; eventually, along with tuberculosis, the hatred drove him mad. As the oldest child, Jimmy caught much of the hell and spent much of his life coming to terms with its effects on him. Imagine as a child grappling with the hurtful words that say you're ugly, he intimates to Fern Marja Eckman, his first biographer. "You take your estimate of yourself from what the world says about you. I was always told that I was ugly. My *father* told me that. And everybody else. But mostly my father. So I believed it. Naturally. Until *today* I believed it." The wound never fully healed. "I was to hurt a great many people by being unable to imagine that anyone could possibly be in love with an ugly boy like me," he wrote in the introduction to *The Price of the Ticket* in 1985.

As a boy caught in the throes of abuse, Baldwin struggled to find the space to be otherwise amid the challenges of being poor, black, and partly responsible for eight siblings. The mindless jobs he took and the scripted future he was expected to fulfill—a wife, kids, and a job at the post office—ate at his spirit. Friends like the artist Beauford Delaney offered him a glimpse of how to be different and to see the world differently, but Baldwin continued to struggle with his sexuality and his desire to become a writer. The hatred that consumed his stepfather threatened to consume him, and though he often directed that hatred and anger back toward David Baldwin, he was already beginning to understand the pointlessness in these feelings. No matter how much David Baldwin frightened his stepson, he was the victim of America's lie. He died believing, tragically, what white America said about him. Jimmy understood that. He also knew that hating his stepfather only imprisoned him. He had to leave that hate behind and confront his pain and trauma, if he was to ever truly be free. "I had told my mother that I did not want to see him because I hated him," he wrote of his stepfather in "Notes of a Native Son." "But this was not true. It was only that I *had* hated him, and I wanted to hold on to this hatred. I did not want to look on him as a ruin: It was not a ruin I had hated. I imagine that one of the reasons people cling to their hates so stubbornly is because they sense, once hate is gone, that they will be forced to deal with pain."

David Baldwin, Sr., died in 1943, when Baldwin was eighteen. By then, Jimmy had already concluded that writing was a matter of life and death. But he needed the freedom to confront and examine honestly the experiences—one might even say the terrors—that shaped how he understood himself, how he saw the world, and how he imagined the histories that shaped it all. For him, all three—the senses of self, society, and history—"simultaneously conspire[d] against and corroborate[d] one's fate." One had to work hard at self-creation—especially as a black person in America. The country had consigned black people to the bottom rung of the society, and the challenge was to avoid succumbing, as his stepfather did, to the fate that awaited one there. Jimmy concluded that the confrontation between who he was and who he was becoming could not happen on American shores. America would not allow him to be otherwise.

Still, once he got to France, Baldwin came to understand that leaving America behind would not be so simple. "It turned out that the question of who I was was not solved because I had removed myself from the social forces which menaced me—anyway, these forces had become interior, and I had dragged them across the ocean with me. The question of who I was had at last become a personal question, and the answer was to be found in me." America, and its racist assumptions, had indelibly shaped who Baldwin was. But, he insisted, we are not the mere product of social forces. Each of us has a say in who we take ourselves to be. No matter what America said about him as a black person, Baldwin argued, he had the last word about who he was as a human being and as a black man.

This conclusion was the result of what Socrates called the examined life, and it served as the foundation for Baldwin's broader witness. Just as we must examine our individual experiences and the terrors that shape how we come to see ourselves, together as a country we must do the same. The two are bound together. Such a realization set the stage for Baldwin to become the kind of poet he imagined himself to be—someone who could transform the daily experiences of being black in the world into the stuff of art; someone who could mold his individual suffering—even the vexed relationship with his stepfather—into a universal statement about what it means to be a fragile and fallen human being.

From France, Baldwin *had* to look toward America because, no matter his desire to leave the life that consumed his stepfather, he remained decidedly *of* this place. Any honest confrontation with his own experience demanded a reckoning of sorts with the quarrel he had with the country that made him. France gave him the critical distance to do so apart from the daily thousand cuts of American racism. Baldwin said about his time in France, "I got over . . . the terms . . . in which Americans identified me. . . . And I realized I'd never be controlled by them again. I didn't have to worry about acting like a nigger. I didn't have to prove anything to anybody."

And yet, as he struggled with his first novel, *Go Tell It on the*

*Mountain,* Baldwin realized that although he was distancing himself from American racism, he had to confront his identity *as* a black American. He had to do so as a profoundly moral question about who he took himself to be, as a matter of individual identity and how he would choose to live his life. Typically, the whole of the discussion of black Americans always began—and begins—with a deficit, with the idea that there is something not present that needs remedying. Baldwin doesn't begin with deficit. There was nothing to be ashamed of here. No need to approach the beauty of black life as somehow a tangle of pathology or simply a response to the doings of white folk. Instead, their extraordinary effort to live amid the ways of white folk constituted the raw stuff of art. Baldwin identified with those who survived the barbarism of slavery, withstood the horrors of white supremacy, and still had the creative power to make life swing. That exploration of the beauty of black life, with the help of Bessie Smith's blues, gave him access to the language and culture he heard in his head.

In the dank corners of Paris, a young Baldwin worked relentlessly to make himself into the kind of poet Ralph Waldo Emerson imagined in 1844, one who "shall draw us with love and terror," who sees through our comforting illusions, "chaunt[s] our own times and social circumstance," and speaks of the unique genius that is America. For Emerson, "America is a poem in our eyes" and what was needed, required even, was a poet to bring that vision to the page. Baldwin's vision of America was bound up with the lie that resided at the country's core. Its images could be nightmarish. Lynched bodies, with their private parts gone, swayed from poplar trees. Men and women nodded in piss-stained alleys. Children played in trash heaps. Boys were cuffed and beaten by police, for no reason other than because they were black. But more horrific than these crimes was the country's steadfast refusal to confront the truth that made them inevitable. "I am not talking about the crime: I am talking about denying what one does. This is a much more sinister matter," he wrote in "The White Problem." America was more than its "ample geography" that dazzled the imagination. It was a place that denied the contradiction between its commitments to freedom and democracy and its practice of slavery and white supremacy. Baldwin bore the scars and wounds of that idea and relentlessly questioned the contradictions that threatened, like "two warring souls," to tear him, and so many others, completely apart. It is from that deeply personal standpoint that he answered Emerson's call.

Going to France ultimately freed Baldwin to become the poet who could "describe us to ourselves as we are now" without the debilitating crutch of the lie, which Baldwin thought doomed every American's attempt to establish an identity free from the category of race that imprisoned us in the first place. As he wrote in his poignant 1953 essay, "Stranger in the Village,"

> At the root of the American Negro problem is the necessity of the American white man to find a way of living with the Negro in order to live with himself. And the history of this problem can be reduced to the means used by Americans—lynch law and law, segregation and legal acceptance, terrorization and concession—either to come to terms with this necessity, or to find a way around it, or (most usually) to find a way of doing both these things at once. The resulting spectacle, at once foolish and dreadful, led someone to make the quite accurate observation that "the Negro-in-America" is a form of insanity which over-

takes white men. In this long battle . . . the white man's
motive was the protection of his identity; the black man
was motivated by the need to establish an identity.

The political and social reality that results from what's at the
root of the "American Negro problem" overruns our moral sense
and distorts any substantive idea of who we are as individuals. This
is the real American dilemma: acknowledging the moral effects of
a way of life emptied of genuine meaning because of a lie that
denies the things we have done. We are trapped like flies on sticky
paper, and the spectacle of our struggles has led some to lose their
minds and others to hate themselves for being stuck on the fly-
paper in the first place.

These, then, are the twined purposes at the heart of Baldwin's
poetic vision. He is not only motivated to transform the stuff of
experience into the beauty of art; as a poet he also *bears witness* to
what he sees and what we have forgotten, calling our attention to
the enduring legacies of slavery in our lives; to the impact of systemic discrimination throughout the country that has denied generations of black people access to the so-called American dream;
to the willful blindness of so many white Americans to the violence that sustains it all. He laments the suffering that results from
our evasions and refusals and passes judgment on what we have
done and not done in order to release ourselves into the possibility
of becoming different and better people. He bears witness for
those who cannot because they did not survive, and he bears witness for those who survived it all, wounded and broken.

As Emerson said, "the poets are liberating gods." They "unlock
our chains, and admit us to a new scene." Or, as Baldwin put it in
his essay "Why I Stopped Hating Shakespeare," the poet is called
"to defeat all labels and complicate all battles . . . to bear witness,

as long as breath is in him, to that mighty, unnameable, transfigur-
ing force which lives in the soul of man, and to aspire to do his
work so well that when the breath has left him, the people—all
people!—who search in the rubble for a sign or witness will be
able to find him there."

In Paris, Baldwin sought the critical distance necessary to reimagine himself apart from the assumptions and stereotypes of race
that saturated American life. He needed the space to see himself
and the country differently. However, this wasn't an abstract or
academic exercise for him. His very life depended on it. Jimmy
knew he could not survive accommodating to the way black people were forced to live in this country. Only madness or murder
awaited him there.

So his return to the United States wasn't simply a political
choice, as he seems to suggest in *No Name*. He needed the family
he loved so dearly but had left behind. He wanted the comfort of
black American culture—the sounds of the language, the taste of
the food, its joys and pains. He wanted to experience again the
elements of black life that danced around in his imagination and
made its way into his writing. He first returned to New York for a
period of nine months in 1954, bringing his play *Amen Corner* and
the essay that would become "Notes of a Native Son." He felt out
of place. His years in Paris had created what felt like an unbreach-
able distance between him and the life he had left behind when he
first moved to France. Old friends felt like strangers. And, of
course, they didn't know him any longer; he had been gone for six
years. But he returned to Paris only to find that it was no longer
the same either. "Until I came back to America, I didn't realize
how many props I'd knocked out from beneath me. And, among

them, as it turned out, was the prop of Paris," he said to Fern Eckman. "I was almost as lonely in Paris when I went back as I had been here." France had not become home.

For this reason, Baldwin's return to Paris in the fall of 1955 was riddled with a mixture of excitement about his modest literary success in the States and deepening depression. An intense love affair had finally ended, and Baldwin could only see ahead of himself a life of "fantastically unreal alternatives to my pain," where even if he achieved fame he would not have love. Alone and desperate, he took an overdose of sleeping pills only to call his friend Mary Painter to tell her what he had done. She rushed to his side with a friend and helped save his life. Even in despair, Baldwin realized as he looked back on that time that something profound had changed in him. "I guess I was making up my mind, in some interior, strange, private way, about what I would do with the rest of my life," he said. "And I think I was suspecting—though I don't think I could have put it that way then—that I couldn't really hope to spend the rest of my life in France. The attempt would kill me."

It was in late September of 1956, after his attempted suicide, that he found himself at the Sorbonne covering the International Conference of Black Writers and Artists. It would have been a year after that, if indeed he saw it at the time, when Baldwin noticed Don Sturkey's photo of Dorothy Counts with her slightly twisted mouth, her unshakeable pride, on the covers of newspapers.

Her photo was not the reason he decided to leave Paris. But when Baldwin finally went to the South in 1957 at the suggestion of *Partisan Review*'s Philip Rahv, he found Dot's story. He arrived in Charlotte in the fall, after she had withdrawn from Harding High School. A woman, he reported, told him of the mob and of the spit that dripped from the hem of Dorothy's dress. Several white students, he was told, begged Dot to stay. "Harry Golden, editor of *The Carolina Israelite*, suggested that the 'hoodlum element' might not have so shamed the town and the nation if several of the town's leading businessmen had personally escorted Miss Counts to school."

But even when Baldwin wrote about his trip south two years later, in a 1959 article for *Partisan Review*, he did not mention the particular image of Dorothy he later claimed made such an impression on him. He offered instead a description of *the end* of Dorothy's ordeal, her decision to leave the school and the regrets and trauma that accompanied it. Years later, in *No Name in the Street*, he would start at *the beginning*, with the image of her amid the hatred on her first day, and use the famous photo of Dorothy to justify his own decision to join the fray. Trauma did not come at the end, rather, it framed the story.

Looking back, after the deaths of Medgar Evers, Malcolm X, and Martin Luther King, Jr., the photo with all of its pathos, anguish, and pride represented for Baldwin in 1972 the demand to bear witness to what was happening in 1957 and to what had transpired since, which led to his recollection of it in *No Name in the Street*. Dot's eyes captured the trauma of that journey. Baldwin sought to narrate what happened on the eve of a social movement that would attempt to transform the country, and to testify to that odd combination of trauma and grit, which he now knew so well, seen in a fifteen-year-old black girl's courage that spurred *him*, so he believed, to leap into the fire.

Narrating trauma fragments how we remember. We recall what we can and what we desperately need to keep ourselves together. Wounds, historical and painfully present, threaten to rend the soul, and if that happens, nothing else matters. Telling the story of trauma in fits and starts isn't history in any formal sense. It is the way traumatic memory works: recollections caught in "the pitched battle between remembering and forgetting." Facts bungled on behalf of much-needed truths. We try to keep our heads above water and tell ourselves a story that keeps our legs and arms moving below the surface.

By 1972, Baldwin can be forgiven for forgetting some things. He was trying to hold himself—hold us—together, after all. Four years into Nixon and the reassertion of the lie in the name of the "silent majority," the previous decade's struggle for equality was already receding into history, having changed laws but done little to address the value gap. In *No Name*, Baldwin moved from the image of Dorothy Counts to the events of the civil rights movement and, in the shadow of the dead and broken, sought to tell a story about the past that would, at least, give us some sense of direction in an uncertain moment. His misremembering sought to orient us to the after times of the civil rights movement and to call attention to the trauma and terror that threatened everything. "What one does not remember," he reminds the reader, "is the serpent in the garden of one's dreams."

Baldwin's view of traumatic memory is pretty consistent. In "Many Thousands Gone," written in 1951, he makes the point about the relationship between memory, trauma, and the past.

> Wherever the Negro face appears a tension is created, the tension is a silence filled with things unutterable. It is a sentimental error, therefore, to believe that the past is dead; it means nothing to say that it is all forgotten, that the Negro himself has forgotten it. It is not a question of memory. Oedipus did not remember the thongs that bound

his feet; nevertheless the marks they left testified to that doom toward which his feet were leading him. The man does not remember the hand that struck him, the darkness that frightened him as a child; nevertheless the hand and the darkness remain with him, indivisible from himself forever, part of the passion that drives him wherever he thinks to take flight.

Some thirty years later, in his last book, *The Evidence of Things Not Seen,* about the Atlanta child murders, Baldwin begins with a meditation on the difficulty of remembering the patterns of the past and separating that from what he imagines himself to be able to remember. "Terror cannot be remembered," he writes. "One blots it out. The organism—the human being—blots it out. One invents or creates, a personality or a persona. Beneath this accumulation (rock of ages!) sleeps or hopes to sleep, that terror which the memory repudiates."

The cruel irony, of course, is that the terrors move us about. We dig trenches to redirect the memories and to get them to flow away from us. But, like the waters of the Mississippi River, the memories always return, flooding everything no matter how high we build the stilts.

Although he was writing about the murdered and missing children of Atlanta, Baldwin revealed the deep fears that shaped his own memories.

It has something to do with the fact that no one wishes to be plunged, head down, into the torrent of what he does not remember and does not wish to remember. It has something to do with the fact that we all came here as candidates for the slaughter of the innocents. It has something to do with the fact that all survivors, however they accommodate or fail to remember it, bear the inexorable guilt of the survivor.

He had survived the storms of the modern black freedom movement and lived, no matter the burden of guilt, to tell the story— especially on behalf of those who could not. "My memory stammers," he wrote. "But my soul is a witness."

In the end, we cannot escape our beginnings: The scars on our backs and the white-knuckled grip of the lash that put them there remain in dim outline across generations and in the way we cautiously or not so cautiously move around one another. This legacy of trauma is an inheritance of sorts, an inheritance of sin that undergirds much of what we do in this country.

It has never been America's way to confront the trauma directly, largely because the lie does not allow for it. At nearly every turn, the country minimizes the trauma, either by shifting blame for it onto fringe actors of the present ("These acts don't represent who we are"), relative values of the times ("Everyone back then believed in slavery"), or, worst, back onto the traumatized ("They are responsible for themselves"). There has never been a mechanism, through something like a truth and reconciliation commission, for telling ourselves the truth about what we have done in a way that would broadly legitimate government policies to repair systemic discrimination across generations. Instead, we pine for national rituals of expiation that wash away our guilt without the need for an admission of guilt, celebrating Martin Luther King Jr. Day or pointing to the election of Barack Obama, and in the process doing further damage to the traumatized through a kind of historical gaslighting.

This is the sinister work of denying the crime Baldwin wrote about. We lie and cover up our sins and mute the traumas they cause. We dissociate the trauma from our national self-understanding and locate it, if at all, in the ungrateful cries of grievance and victimization among those who experienced the pain and loss. "The biggest bigots are the people that call other people bigots," George Wallace declared in 1968. By this logic, we identify scapegoats to bear the burden of our sins. Undocumented workers and Muslims become the "niggers" to fortify our sense of whiteness. We find security and safety in fantasies of how we are always, no matter what we do and what carnage we leave behind, on the road to a more perfect union.

The lie works like a barrier and keeps the nastiness of our living from becoming a part of the American story, while those who truly know what happened remember differently. "What is most terrible is that American white men are not prepared to believe my version of the story, to believe that it happened," Baldwin declared. "In order to avoid believing that, they have set up in themselves a fantastic system of evasions, denials, and justifications, [a system that] is about to destroy their grasp of reality, which is another way of saying their moral sense." The marks of Oedipus's thongs remain, and some, like a Greek chorus, can see exactly where all of this is leading us.

When Baldwin returned to the United States in 1957, he knew he couldn't readjust to the country's racism.

The whole system. The whole set-up. I knew I had to be in opposition to it. I couldn't adjust to it. . . . That was why I went south. I thought—the thing to do, you know, if you're sitting around in a hotel room for a month or two months, wondering what you're going to do next and drinking too much and really terribly occupied with yourself, that the thing to do is to, at any price whatever, is get in touch with something which is more than you. Throw yourself into a situation where you won't have time to weep. So I went south. Because I was afraid to go South.

Baldwin, forever the blues man, ran toward the trouble. But later, from the vantage point of 1972 and all that had happened since, he could not help but say, in the words of the old gospel song, "my soul looks back and I wonder how I got over."

Baldwin found Dorothy Counts in the South, as well as Dr. King and many others. In *No Name*, he bore witness to their trauma, and to that of many other black people throughout the region as he told the true story about the civil rights movement. But Baldwin did not only bear witness to the trauma visited on black people; he also revealed the damage at the heart of white people who embraced the hate and caused the terror.

In *No Name*, when Baldwin recalls his first visit to the South, he says that he "felt as though [he] had wandered into hell." He wasn't talking about the hellish lives led by black southerners, but rather how the racial dynamics of the region had hollowed out white southerners. The lies and violence had so distorted and over-taken the private lives of white people in the region that their lived lives felt empty. Baldwin's travels through the South took him from Charlotte to Little Rock, then on to Atlanta, Birmingham, Montgomery, and Tuskegee. When he first wrote about the trip in 1959 for *Partisan Review*, he kept a certain distance from the material, "more or less impersonal," he recalled. But in *No Name*, Baldwin conveyed the trauma of the experience. He could not re-call how long he had been on the road, but upon his return Baldwin wrote that he felt overwhelmed and was paralyzed by what he called "a kind of retrospective terror." The terror was not rooted in a fear for his safety or a fear of dying at the hands of racist bigots. Instead, what shook Baldwin at his core was a "realization of the nature of the heathen." The white southerner had to lie *continuously* to himself in order to justify his world. Lie that the black people around him were inferior. Lie about what he was doing under the cover of night. Lie that he was Christian. For Baldwin, the accumulation of lies suffocated the white southerner. So much so that Baldwin reached for Dante's *Inferno* to express his feelings about it all: "I would not have believed that death had undone so many."

Baldwin recounts an experience of sexual assault at the hands of a powerful white man considered a friend of the "Negro." The man was drunk and he reached for Baldwin's cock.

> It was frightening—not the gesture itself, but the abjectness of it, and the assumption of a swift and grim complicity: as my identity was defined by his power, so was my humanity to be placed at the service of his fantasies. If the lives of those children [black children who were attempting to integrate schools in Little Rock, Arkansas] were in those wet, despairing hands, if their future was to be read in those wet, blind eyes, there was reason to tremble.

For Baldwin, the assault revealed the consequence of the refusal to confront the untruths that undergird the South in particular and the country in general. These people, he insisted, could not be trusted to transform the nation. They couldn't even trust themselves. The powerful white man, who with a phone call "could prevent or provoke a lynching," lived a desperate lie, not only about race, but about his desire, and the result of it was that he could not genuinely love because he was blind to the actual human being right in front of him.

"I watched his eyes, thinking, with great sorrow, *The unexamined life is not worth living*," Baldwin wrote. "The despair among the loveless is that they must narcoticize themselves before they can touch any human being at all. They, then, fatally, touch the wrong person, not merely because they have gone blind, or have lost the sense of touch, but because they no longer have any way of knowing that any loveless touch is a violation, whether one is touching a woman or a man."

The complex web of race and sex immobilized the South. One needed only to look carefully at the people to see that what happened after the sun went down betrayed the lie of hard-core segregationists. Under the cover of night, the very people they despised as less than themselves became the object of their carnal desire. Monstrous intimacies defined the region and gave life to a host of fantasies that regularly debased men and women—especially white men and women—and fueled the lies that sought to hide it all in plain sight.

Black people had to navigate this reality. Their lives depended on it. Baldwin recalled landing at Montgomery's airport and feeling the intense hatred in the eyes of three white men who watched him struggle with his typewriter as he walked to the car of a member of the Montgomery Improvement Association who finally arrived to pick him up. "I had never in all my life seen such a concentrated, malevolent poverty of spirit."

In *No Name in the Street*, this "poverty of spirit" constituted the backdrop of Baldwin's recollection of the heroic effort of the civil rights revolution. In a beautiful passage, he wove together the memory of his own experience with the early stirrings of the movement, and then set them against the hatred of the airport men:

> What had begun in Montgomery was beginning to happen all over the South. The student sit-in movement has yet to begin. No one has yet heard of James Foreman or James Bevel. We have only begun to hear of Martin Luther King, Jr. Malcolm X has yet to be taken seriously. No one, except their parents, has ever heard of Huey Newton or Bobby Seale or Angela Davis. Emmett Till had been dead two years. Bobby Hutton and Jonathan Jackson have just mastered their first words, and with someone holding them by the hand, are discovering how much fun it is to climb up and down the stairs. Oh, pioneers!—I got into the car and we drove into town: the cradle of the Confederacy, the whitest town this side of Casablanca, and one of the most wretched on the face of the earth. And wretched because no one in authority in the town, the state, or the nation, had the force or the courage or the love to attempt to correct the manners or redeem the souls of those three desperate men, standing before that dismal airport, imagining that they were holding back a flood.

Baldwin tries to convey the pace of time in this passage. He leaves pregnant and unspoken the deadly costs that followed. These were the early and heady days of the movement, but he was writing about it from the vantage point of its denouement. By 1972, Angela Davis had already been on the FBI's most wanted list and jailed. Bobby Hutton and Jonathan Jackson were dead.

Malcolm dead. Martin dead. Baldwin's recollection of this moment in the past sets in stark relief what has tragically happened since and what has not changed in a country full of innocents.

In this context, his memory of Dorothy Counts comes more fully into view. For Baldwin, the photograph captured the tortured energy and promise of earlier days. It marked, like the passage about the encounter at the Montgomery airport, the brutal passage of time—from the heady days of the bus boycott to the darkness of the after times. Some thirteen years after that fateful trip to the South, after Martin King's assassination and Carmichael's cry of "Black Power," the photograph of Angela Davis on the cover of *Newsweek* magazine—handcuffed, her jaws clenched, a wig covering her gorgeous Afro, wearing glasses, a blue satin shirt, and a black skirt—revealed the truth of what had happened in the interim.

Ever since that first journey to the American South, Baldwin understood exactly what his calling required, even when the times became dark and sullen. "I think I really understood and probably for the first time that what you are doing, as a writer, or any kind of artist, was not designed to, you know, to make you special or to even isolate you. . . . What your role was, it seemed to me, was to bear witness. To what life is—does—and to speak for people who cannot speak. That you are simply a kind of conduit." This isn't the work of a spokesman, he would later clarify in a *New York Times Book Review* interview with Julius Lester in 1984. He wasn't a partisan of any particular ideology or a leader of some civil rights organization. Baldwin had to capture what moved in the guts and what was desperately desired among the people, what happened in the country, and in the moment; he had to write about all of that and about what and who was lost.

Baldwin put it this way to Fern Marja Eckman: "You're at the mercy of something, which has nothing to do with you, nothing to do with your career, nothing to do with your ambitions, nothing to do with your loneliness, nothing to do with your despair. It had to do simply with the division of labor in the world—and this was your job. This is what you were here to do. Y'know, to translate somehow, if you could, by whatever means you could find, the way I see it—in any case, you know, I found myself in the deep South, looking at the eyes of a black boy or girl of 10. Y'know? To make it real. To force it on the world's attention."

In so many ways, these last two sentences best illustrate what Baldwin means by being a witness. Tell the story. Make it real for those who refuse to believe that such a thing can happen/has happened/is happening here. Bring the suffering to the attention of those who wallow in willful ignorance. In short, shatter the illusion of innocence at every turn and attack all the shibboleths the country holds sacred.

Don Sturkey's images of Dorothy Counts find their inheritors in pictures and videos we see today of the suffering of black people at the hands of police forces. We have become a world of people using their cellphone cameras to bear witness, filming the brutality of police or recording the callousness of white people who feel threatened by black people who they believe don't belong in their space. A brief search of the Internet could easily pull up footage of racist encounters in parks and grocery stores, incidents that unfold while black and brown people are simply walking down the street or trying to move into an apartment or attempting to check into a hotel. The footage reveals the insults and cuts—the danger and the death—that happen daily in this country that many white Americans don't want to know about. We saw police in Arizona accost a family at gunpoint because a four-year-old allegedly stole a doll from the dollar store. We saw Eric Garner say, over and over again, "I can't breathe." We witnessed in real time on Facebook Live the shooting and death of Philando Castile. And we heard the babies in cages on the borders crying for their parents.

The footage shatters the innocence, but just as in Dot Counts's time, it does not guarantee anything like justice. In fact, we're inundated with the horror and the risk, becoming numb to it all. Most people seem to just click to the next thing. But we cannot become numb.

We are told every day not to believe what we see happening all around us or what we feel in the marrow of our bones. We are told, for example, that Trumpism is exceptional, a unique threat to our democracy. This view that Trump, and Trump alone, stresses the fabric of the country lets us off the hook. It feeds into the lie that Baldwin spent the majority of his life trying to convince us to confront. It attempts to explain away as isolated events what today's cellphone footage exposes as part of our everyday experience. Exceptionalizing Trump deforms our attention (it becomes difficult to see what is happening right in front of us) and secures our self-understanding from anything he might actually represent. If anything, Trump represents a reassertion of the belief that America is, and will always be, a white nation.

Today, our task remains the same, no matter its difficulty or the magnitude of the challenge. Some of us must become poets, but we all must bear witness. Make the suffering real and force the world to pay attention to *it,* and not place that suffering all at the feet of Donald Trump, but understand it as the inevitable outcome in a country that continues to lie to itself.

I look back, and from this vantage point, with my eyes wide open, I see the illusion for what it was and is. I am overcome with a kind of "retrospective terror" when I think about the police killings of black people and the fact that most were never prosecuted, and reflect on the death and madness of those young people—our babies—who risked everything with Black Lives Matter, and the compromises of so many, including some of my friends, who hoped to finally walk the corridors of power. All of it comes into full view. Illusions of substantive change stand alongside the reality of what really happened during the Obama years. And each time I see and hear Donald Trump, I try to beat back the rage and hold myself together.

What we are living through, even with our cellphone cameras, is not unlike what Baldwin and so many others dealt with as the black freedom movement collapsed with the ascent of the Reagan revolution. This latest betrayal by the country joins with the underlying trauma caused by all the previous betrayals. That trauma carried over, and it shapes implicitly how we imagine and respond to our current days. This is the undertow of black politics: traumatic memories that cling to our choices like ghosts who can't find peace as white America refuses to change again.

Like Baldwin, we have to bear witness to it all and tell the story of how we got here—and then, just maybe, we can muster the resolve and will to push this damn rock up the hill again.

# CHAPTER THREE

# The Dangerous Road

ON MARCH 16, 1968, JAMES BALDWIN WALKED TO THE PODIUM at a fundraiser at the Anaheim Disneyland Hotel to introduce Dr. Martin Luther King, Jr. Baldwin had returned to Los Angeles from New York in February after Columbia Pictures bought the rights to Alex Haley's *Autobiography of Malcolm X* and asked him to write the script. He ended up in Los Angeles navigating the "sharks" of Hollywood as he tried desperately to bring *his* story of Malcolm to the screen. The road ahead was long. Baldwin wanted Billy Dee Williams to play the lead, but the studio had other actors in mind—there were rumors someone had even suggested a darkened Charlton Heston.

While Baldwin was in California, though, he found himself responding to a request to say a few words in Anaheim before King's speech. The fundraiser was meant to replenish the coffers of the Southern Christian Leadership Conference (SCLC) and to help fund King's upcoming Poor People's Campaign. Money had become direly necessary. Dr. King wanted to make the case for massive direct action in Washington, D.C., on behalf of America's poor, but he would need to marshal greater financial resources than ever before. Desegregating lunch counters didn't cost much, but ending poverty would cost the nation billions of dollars. Sentimentality alone could not pay the bill.

But King found that many who once supported his desegregation efforts in the South were less than enthusiastic about his agenda around jobs and poverty. The *Los Angeles Times* reported that King "had found that some of the white groups he was counting on for support have held back for fear his campaign would turn to chaos." The idea of occupying the nation's capital with poor people scared the hell out of some activists—even some on the board of SCLC. For others like Bayard Rustin, a trusted adviser of Dr. King since the days of the Montgomery bus boycott, such an act of civil disobedience courted violence and threatened to turn even more white Americans against the civil rights agenda. Rustin wanted the membership of SCLC to focus on electing Democrats to political office, not on building a tent city or blocking bridges or staging sit-ins at congressional offices. Nevertheless, Dr. King persisted, and William Rutherford, the executive director of SCLC, wrote to the actor Marlon Brando to enlist his help. Brando, in turn, had organized the Anaheim fundraiser.

How Baldwin ended up as part of the program is unclear, though Brando may have invited him, since the two were close. In any case, Baldwin had not been expecting to give an introduction for King, and he hesitated as he approached the podium. When he reached the microphone he announced, in a somewhat halting manner, his surprise. His subsequent introduction of King said little about King himself, only that "Martin" had spent most of his time, in the early years of the civil rights movement, "in and out of jail . . . trying to redeem what we claim we live by." Instead, Baldwin told a brief story about the promise of those early days and how that promise was betrayed by the country. He recounted a history of how they had arrived at this moment in 1968. It was not a triumphant story, rather one shot through with disappointment and frustration.

"What Rosa Parks was saying in 1956 in Montgomery and what the Negroes were saying in their march for 381 days," he intoned, "the country did not want to hear or did not hear." Once again he invoked the quick passage of time between the beginning of the movement and the volatility of 1968, and the ugliness and sorrow experienced in between. "As time rolled on and kids, including people like Stokely Carmichael, were being beaten with chains, going to jail, marching up and down those dusty highways, trying to change the conscience of this country, still nobody heard and nobody cared." Baldwin's introduction of Dr. King was all about America's betrayal, not a story about America's progress on racial matters. He spoke about the wall of white supremacy that clearly stood in the way of fundamental transformation in the country, and about the urgency they all faced at what was fast becoming the crossroads. His was an effort to jog the memory and, by extension, the moral conscience of the audience by telling a different story about what happened to a movement on the brink of failure.

When King reached the podium, he did not acknowledge Baldwin specifically, instead offering generic thanks to all of those who spoke before him. At some point that evening, the two men spoke privately. "We sat down in a relatively secluded corner and tried to bring each other up to date. Alas, it would never be possible," Baldwin recalled in *No Name in the Street*. "We had first met during the last days of the Montgomery bus boycott—and how long ago was that? It was senseless to say, eight years, ten years ago—it was longer ago than time can reckon."

Baldwin's general sense of the encounter was that King was a bit skeptical of him. Although Baldwin had known King since his first trip to the South in 1957 and had worked beside him and on behalf of the movement over the years, he felt that King and those around him were discomfited by his presence. "Martin and I had never got to know each other well, circumstances, if not temperament, made that impossible," he wrote. On King's side, at least, a certain suspicion never dissipated. In 1963, King had been caught on tape by the FBI expressing his concern about Baldwin: He didn't want to appear on television with him because Baldwin "was generally uninformed regarding his movement" and might be mistaken as a civil rights leader. The press may have given Baldwin that label, but King did not see him that way. To King, Baldwin was just one celebrity among many willing to lend his star power to help the movement. I can't help but think, although King never said it explicitly, that Baldwin's queerness unsettled him.

By the time of the fundraiser, the distance between them was widened by Baldwin's sympathies with the militancy of the younger generation. He was in Hollywood, after all, writing a screenplay on Malcolm X. Just a month before the King event, he had hosted a joint birthday party and fundraiser for Huey P. Newton, the jailed leader of the Black Panther Party, published his "Black Power" essay vigorously defending Stokely Carmichael, and appeared with Carmichael recently in Los Angeles. In 1968, King felt the intense pressure of these radical groups and personalities as he wrestled with the shifts in the political and social climate of the times. Once lauded as one of the most respected men in the world, he now found himself persona non grata as the nation turned its back on his moral vision. His position on the Vietnam War led some to call him a traitor and some so-called black leaders to denounce him. *The New York Review of Books* declared that he had been "outstripped by the times." One young black woman who supported Carmichael had even gone so far as to accuse King of selling out the Selma movement as he and other members of the SCLC board arrived for a meeting in Washington, D.C.

Baldwin had long seen this turn against King on the horizon. Some seven years before the fundraiser in Los Angeles, in 1961, he had penned an article for *Harper's Magazine* entitled "The Dangerous Road Before Martin Luther King." In it, he noted the difference in King's voice from the heady days of the bus boycott and detailed the challenges King was destined to face as a black leader in a revolutionary time. "He was more beleaguered than he had ever been before, and not only by his enemies in the white South," Baldwin wrote. "Three years earlier, I had not encountered very many people—I am speaking now of Negroes—who were really critical of him. But many more people seemed critical of him now, were bitter, disappointed, skeptical. None of this had anything to do . . . with his personal character or integrity. It had to do with his effectiveness as a leader. King has had an extraordinary effect in the Negro world and therefore the nation, and is now in the center of an extremely complex cross fire."

King had to confront, Baldwin argued, the meaning and significance of the radical shift in the movement caused by the student sit-ins. The black freedom movement had upended traditional custodial models of black leadership that were codependent with the white world. These leaders, and Baldwin distinguished them from "genuine leadership," had come to power not so much because of their efforts "to make the Negro a first class citizen but to keep him content as a second class one." Now leaders like Roy

Wilkins of the NAACP and Whitney Young of the National Urban League were being confronted by their children, who rejected the underlying premise of the world that made "the traditional black leader" necessary in the first place. It was in this crossfire, Baldwin maintained, that King found himself:

> It is the sons and daughters of the beleaguered bourgeoisie—supported, in the most extraordinary fashion, by those old, work-worn men and women who were known, only yesterday, as the "country niggers"—who have begun a revolution in the consciousness of this country which will inexorably destroy nearly all that we now think of as concrete and indisputable. These young people have never believed in the American image of the Negro and have never bargained with the Republic, and now they never will. . . . There is no longer any basis on which to bargain.

Moving forward, Baldwin believed, King's leadership would be judged according to this standard. In 1961, many had already begun to question his methods as no longer consonant with what was necessary to challenge the lie. By 1968, as Baldwin watched King speak in Anaheim, the clarity and force of the country's refusal to address the lie had left King in a near impossible position, unable to deliver the change black America so desperately sought and yet seemingly unwilling to take the more radical measures that some believed necessary for its deliverance.

To be sure, Baldwin had been aware back in 1961 of the distinct possibility that the country would be unwilling to change. He understood that the road ahead was full of potholes and golden apples that could distract our attention from the goal of genuine transformation of the country. Quoting the philosopher William

James, Baldwin knew that "our futures are rough," particularly in a place so obsessed with the future. By 1968, he also knew how the passage of the civil rights and voting rights acts a few years earlier offered white America the sense of self-congratulation that Black Power was now denying it. Seen in this way, the civil rights movement could easily be conscripted into a story of how Americans perfected the Union, where all of their sacrifices would become, with vicious irony, proof of America's inherent goodness. The history they were making, in real time, could be bent in the service of the lie. For Baldwin, the movement had to challenge that lie at its root or it would consume us all, which is why, perhaps, he had dedicated his own introduction of King to telling a true story of the movement.

Though the two men would never manage to bridge the vast gulf their circumstances had opened between them, King shared Baldwin's understanding of what the movement's history meant. After Baldwin had finished speaking and the applause had died down, King gave a speech that echoed Baldwin's account. He too sought to tell a true story of the movement. And again, it wasn't a narrative of American triumphalism, where he recalled his "I Have a Dream" speech or lauded the passage of the civil rights laws as important steps toward a more perfect union. On this night, both King and Baldwin resisted any effort to draft the civil rights movement into that story. Instead, as King conveyed the gravity of the moment in 1968 and the necessity for the Poor People's Campaign, he conjured, without a hint of nostalgia, a history of the heroism of everyday people acting against all odds, a history no less full of disappointment and trauma. He expressed a sense that the movement was losing the battle for the soul of the nation. King didn't mince words: America was a decidedly racist country. "The problem can only be solved when there is a kind of coalition of conscience," he said. "Now I am not sure if we have that many consciences left. Too many have gone to sleep. But there are some left. And we gotta be that . . . creative minority, ready to do battle for the sacred . . . issues of life. Ready to do battle for the principles of justice, goodwill, and brotherhood."

But, like Baldwin, King struggled with America's commitment to the belief that white people mattered more and to the lie that made it palatable:

> I must honestly confess that I go through moments of disappointment when I have to recognize that there aren't enough white persons in our country who are willing to cherish democratic principles over privilege. But I am grateful to God that some are left.

As King brought his speech to a close, he tried to reach for the promise of America. "I believe we are going to get there [freedom] because, however much she strays away from it, the goal of America is freedom." His somber tone and the sadness in his eyes betrayed the hopeful words.

The importance of history had been in full view for both Baldwin and King just a few weeks earlier at a Carnegie Hall event in New York City, celebrating what would have been the one hundredth birthday of W.E.B. Du Bois, the great African American intellectual and co-founder of the NAACP. Du Bois, after seven decades of fighting for racial justice in the United States, had given up on America and died in exile in Accra, Ghana, on the eve of the March on Washington in 1963. On this evening, February 23, 1968, an extraordinary gathering of scholars, entertainers, and activists celebrated his life. Although Baldwin had been working on an essay about Du Bois, he chose instead to read his recent piece, "Black Power." Here, at this celebration of Du Bois, who dedicated his life to exposing America's lies, Baldwin sought to shift the balance of concern around Black Power from criticism of the misguided turn to militancy among young black people to an honest assessment of the conditions in the country that made such a turn necessary in the first place. As he would do just a few weeks later in Los Angeles, he set out to tell a different history.

King disagreed with the rhetoric and symbolism of Black Power. He found no use for what he called "a mystique of blackness" or "the angry militant who failed to organize." But he, too, was a student of Du Bois's work and understood what Du Bois taught regarding "our tasks of emancipation." "One idea he insistently taught," King told the audience that night, "was that black people have been kept in oppression and deprivation by a poisonous fog of lies that depicted them as inferior, born deficient, and deservedly doomed to servitude to the grave." He went on to say that "so long as the lie was believed the brutality and criminality of conduct toward the Negro was easy for the conscience to bear."

Du Bois's life offered both men a blueprint for the longevity of struggle. He never gave up on his search for truth—even though he gave up on the idea of America—and he fought until his last breath for freedom and justice. King's remarks that evening were shadowed by a note of despair even as he reached for hope. It was 1968. The country was in turmoil, and he would be dead in less than two months. "Negroes have heavy tasks today," he told the assembled. "We were partially liberated and then re-enslaved. We have to fight again on old battlefields" and although black people have been fighting for freedom "for more than a hundred years and even if the date of full emancipation is uncertain, what is explicitly certain is that the struggle for it will endure."

Before he was killed at the Lorraine Motel on April 4, 1968,

Baldwin and King would be together one last time for a fundraiser in New York City. Baldwin didn't have a dark suit for the occasion. So he ran out to purchase one and had it fitted. "Two weeks later," as Baldwin famously recalled in *No Name in the Street*, "I wore this same suit to Martin's funeral."

Baldwin had returned to California to work on the Malcolm X film. Instead of staying in the Beverly Hills Hotel, he rented a house in Palm Springs. He was still in a pitched battle with the executives at Columbia about the direction of the film. In April, he was sitting by the swimming pool with Billy Dee Williams at his house in Palm Springs listening to Aretha Franklin when the phone rang. Baldwin picked it up to hear the voice of his friend David Moses: "Jimmy—? Martin's just been shot. He's not dead yet, but it's a head wound—so—."

Baldwin dropped the phone and wept.


Baldwin and King, no matter the temperamental distance between them, moved together as they struggled to make real the promise of American democracy. King was the preacher, Baldwin the poet—and, of course, the two are interchangeable. Billy Dee Williams said that "Martin's death was with Jimmy for a long time. I doubt if he ever got over it. Much of his hope died with King."

Baldwin was not naïve about the human capacity for evil, especially among white folk. He knew intimately what it meant to be vulnerable to the whims of others who held a certain kind of power over you. "If you're a Negro, you're in the center of that *peculiar* affliction," he said, "because *anybody* can touch *you*—when the sun goes down. You know, you're the target of everybody's fantasies." Instead, what shocked him was the fact that white America killed someone who espoused love, an apostle of nonviolence. King's death revealed the depths of their debasement and the scope of our peril.

Baldwin wrote of King's murder and the funeral:

> Perhaps even more than the death itself, the manner of his death has forced me into a judgment concerning human life and human beings which I have always been reluctant to make. . . . Incontestably, alas, most people are not, in action, worth very much; and yet, every human being is an unprecedented miracle. One tries to treat them as the miracles they are, while trying to protect oneself against the disasters they've become.

Baldwin struggled to come to terms with the meaning of King's death, what his murder said about the country, about white people, about human beings in general. How would he hold back despair, and how would he, if he could muster the strength, tell the story now that King was in the coffin?

Baldwin, the poet, sought to account for the confusion, the mourning of loss, and the trauma it caused. He had to gather up the pieces—not only of himself, but of black folk—buried beneath the disaster that was the country. That work kept his despair at arm's length. To be sure, King's death, just like Medgar Evers's, Malcolm X's, and all the others, did not stop time. White people didn't stop being white people. Two days after King's murder, eighteen-year-old Bobby Hutton of the Black Panther Party was killed by Oakland police officers. Robert Kennedy was murdered two months later. Cities burned throughout the country. The Tet Offensive revealed the brutal carnage and senselessness of the war. Police rioted in Chicago at the Democratic Convention. The country lurched to the right with the election of Richard Nixon, who exploited white America's fears and insisted "that minorities were undercutting America's greatness."

Baldwin and black America had to mourn and make sense of unimaginable loss with little time to grieve because the nastiness of the white world kept coming at them. With little time to mourn, we carried our dead forward in our resentments and unresolved questions. All of which gave black politics—and certainly gave Baldwin's voice—an edge. King's death had revealed the bitterness at the bottom of the cup.

What Baldwin saw on that dangerous road that led to King's death in Memphis was the difficult question of whether or not the country had the courage to confront its demons. Could America tell itself the truth about how we all arrived at this moment? Did America have the moral stamina to do the work required to surrender the comfort of its lies?

In July of 1968, just a few months after King's assassination and against the backdrop of American cities burning, Baldwin gave an interview to *Esquire* magazine. He set the tone of the interview with his answers to the magazine editors' first two questions.

Q. How can we get the black people to cool it?

A. It is not for us to cool it.

Q. But aren't you the ones who are getting hurt the most?

A. No, we are only the ones who are dying fastest.

The editors did not see how the moral burden of America's racial nightmare rested not with the black people rioting in the streets but with those white people who insisted on holding so tightly to the belief that they were somehow, because of the color of their skin, better than others who were not white. These people, Baldwin argued, had to see themselves otherwise. Passing new laws or declarations of unending sympathy or acts of racial charity would never be enough to change the course of this country. Something more radical had to be done; a different history had to be told.

Now Baldwin spoke directly to the editors—and, by extension, to white America. I imagine his brow furrowed, with a slight smile in the beginning, only later turning to an intense gaze:

> I'm not trying to accuse you, you know. That's not the point. But you have a lot to face. . . . All that can save you now is your confrontation with your own history . . . which is not your past, but your present. Nobody cares what happened in the past. One can't afford to care what happened in the past. But your history has led you to this moment, and you can only begin to change yourself and save yourself by looking at what you are doing in the name of your history.

On August 12, 2017, twenty-one-year-old James Fields, Jr., a self-proclaimed neo-Nazi from Maumee, Ohio, punched the gas of his 2010 gray Dodge Challenger and roared down a narrow street full of counterprotesters at the Unite the Right rally in Charlottesville, Virginia. Thirty-two-year-old Heather Heyer, who was born in Charlottesville but raised in nearby Ruckersville, was among the crowd. According to people who knew her, Heyer had dedicated much of her life "standing up against any type of discrimination." It made sense that, along with her close friends, she decided to join the protests downtown against white supremacist hate. As

Fields's speeding car sent shoes, cell phones, and bodies flying into the air, Ryan Kelly, a photographer for *The Daily Progress*, captured the carnage. Framed between the image of Marcus Martin falling behind the car's back bumper, one red-and-white Air Jordans-clad foot horribly twisted in the air and the tattooed torso of an unidentified white man in mid-somersault is the image of Heyer. She is leaning to the side in horror as the muscle car hits her and plows through the crowd.

Heyer died at the scene. Cornel West, who marched with other clergy to protest the rally, witnessed people frantically trying to resuscitate her. The Central District office of the chief medical examiner in Richmond declared the cause of death as blunt force injury to the chest. Thirty-five others were also injured, some seriously. Fields was eventually convicted of first-degree murder and eight counts of malicious wounding and sentenced to life in prison.

The occasion of this carnage was a bitter battle over American history and how we ought to publicly remember the past. In March 2016, Wes Bellamy, Charlottesville's vice mayor and a member of its city council, advocated for the removal of Confederate monuments to Robert E. Lee and Thomas "Stonewall" Jackson. Zyahna Bryant, a high school freshman, joined Bellamy's effort. She circulated a petition demanding the removal of the Robert E. Lee statue in Lee Park (now Emancipation Park) and submitted it to the council. During a February 6, 2017, meeting, the city council by a vote of three to two agreed to remove the statue, which is when all hell broke loose.

White nationalists saw an opportunity to exploit the removal of the statue for their own purposes. Since Donald Trump's election they had been emboldened by his overt appeals to white identity. In fact, social scientists found a direct correlation between

Trump's election and a surge in hate crimes across the country. But the violence was only one disturbing consequence of Trump's rhetoric; in Charlottesville, in the early days of the monuments controversy, these white nationalists reasserted themselves into the country's national politics. For them, the actions of the Charlottesville city council amounted to an all-out assault on white people: The so-called soldiers of political correctness had disfigured and distorted southern history in particular and American history in general. Their outrage prompted the Unite the Right rally, the largest gathering of white nationalists and neo-Nazis in recent memory. The day of the rally became a violent spectacle as gun-toting neo-Nazis clashed in the streets with members of antifa, an anti-fascist movement, and other counterprotesters. It ended with Fields's murderous drive on Fourth Street. Cornel West told me he had never seen such hate.

It is telling, to me, that such brutality broke out over a fight regarding the symbols and uses of American history. I have said that America is an identity that white people will protect at any cost, and our history—our founding documents, our national heroes, our actions that cast us as a moral force in the world—is the supporting argument that underpins that identity. This history is inseparable from the landscape and built environment of the country; in many ways both, from the monuments to the way communities are spatially organized, reinforce that story subtly and overtly. When Dr. King declared that the country's moral vision had been clouded by "a poisonous fog of lies" and Baldwin said in *Esquire* that we needed to look at what we are doing in the name of our history, both made clear that this history, the story we tell ourselves about what the country is and thus who we are, shapes the world we make going forward. That insight is no less true now. The Confederate monuments question makes plain that the history we tell ourselves is a key battleground for the country's future.

For white nationalists the answer is clear. Those who embrace the cruelty of America's history have every reason to celebrate Confederate heroes. The Confederacy represents a triumph of a certain understanding of the country where the superiority of white people is evident in the social, political, and cultural arrangements of the nation. From that perspective, open-air tributes to white supremacy make sense.

The more complex question is what we do with all of those who are willing to condemn neo-Nazis like Richard Spencer but who still claim the Confederate statues as part of their "heritage." These are the folks, as Mitch Landrieu, the mayor of New Orleans, writes in his book, *In the Shadows of Statues,* "whose ancestors fought in the Civil War, [who have a] popular interest in historical events." These are the people for whom Judge Richard E. Moore of the Charlottesville Circuit Court ruled in April 2019 that the Confederate statues must remain in Emancipation Park. "While some people obviously see Lee and Jackson as symbols of white supremacy others see them as brilliant military tacticians or complex leaders in a difficult time," Judge Moore wrote in his nine-page letter detailing his decision. "In either event the statues to them . . . still are monuments and memories to them, as veterans of the Civil War."

The controversy over the Confederate statues reflects this complex relationship between history and memory, between what actually happened and the kinds of stories we tell about what happened and for what purpose.

After Charlottesville, American historians weighed in on the debate. They showed that the statues were not erected as contemporaneous historical memorials of the Civil War. Most were built many years later, either between the 1890s and the first decades of the twentieth century (when most of the Confederate veterans began to die) or in the 1950s, with the demand for racial equality intensifying. They were monuments to an ideology—physical representations of the superiority of white people and a way of life that reflected that fact. This was the "Lost Cause" erected in public space: the claim that the Civil War wasn't about slavery but was a heroic and admirable defense of the southern way of life.

That such public education is even necessary is evidence of the power of the lie to protect America's innocence. Why? Because we have had this conversation before: Black people challenged these monuments on ideological and historical grounds even as they were being built. That challenge, for example, sits at the heart of W.E.B. Du Bois's classic 1935 book *Black Reconstruction*, the final chapter of which, "The Propaganda of History," is devoted to exposing the lies at the heart of the historiography around Reconstruction. Du Bois unmasked the racist assumptions shaping the influential works of political scientist John W. Burgess and historian William A. Dunning, both of Columbia University. The Dunning School, the first generation of trained historians to write about Reconstruction, told the story of the period as one of extensive overreach of federal power and the corruption of northern carpetbaggers, and viewed the granting of political rights to former slaves as "a monstrous mistake." In rejecting the historical scholarship of Dunning and his students, Du Bois put it this way: "We have too often a deliberate attempt so to change the facts of history that the story will make pleasant reading for Americans." Du Bois's devastating criticism notwithstanding, their lies held firm.

As if to underscore the point, King's speech at the centennial celebration of Du Bois was an extended meditation on Du Bois's chapter, "The Propaganda of History." King spoke about the lie of Reconstruction, and his words speak directly to us now:

> White historians had for a century crudely distorted the Negro's role in the Reconstruction years. It was a conscious and deliberate manipulation of history, and the stakes were high. The Reconstruction was a period in which black men had a small measure of freedom of action. If, as white historians tell, Negroes wallowed in corruption, opportunism, displayed spectacular stupidity, were wanton and evil, and ignorant, their case was made. They would have proved that freedom was dangerous in the hands of inferior beings. One generation after another of Americans were assiduously taught these falsehoods, and the collective mind of America became poisoned with racism and stunted with myths.

In so many ways, the people who promulgated the lie, those Frederick Douglass called the "apostles of forgetfulness," helped build monuments to their willful amnesia. They turned their backs on the promise of emancipation and rejected the idea that black people could be full-fledged citizens in the United States. Even America's bard, Walt Whitman, expressed such sentiments in 1874. "As if we had not strained the voting and digestive caliber of American Democracy to the utmost for the last fifty years with the millions of ignorant foreigners," he declared, "we have now infused a powerful percentage of blacks, with about as much intellect and caliber (in the mass) as so many baboons." The Confederate statues represented the triumph of this sensibility in public space. The history that justified their construction banished, once and for all, the horrors of slavery (or simply reduced them to a mistake) and fortified the assumptions that black people were not fit for freedom. In both cases, American identity was left safe and secure.

Three days after the murder of Heather Heyer and the violent display of white supremacy in Charlottesville, President Donald Trump held his infamous press conference in Trump Tower. He blamed "both sides" for the violence and flatly rejected the idea of removing the Confederate statues, employing a not-so-deft piece of moral relativism:

> George Washington was a slave owner. Was George Washington a slave owner? So will George Washington lose his status? Are we going to take down—excuse me—are we going to take down statues to George Washington? How about Thomas Jefferson? What do you think of Thomas Jefferson? You like him? . . . Are you going to take down the statue? He was a major slave owner.

In Trump's hands, the celebration of the Confederacy—of a region that committed treason and did so to defend the institution of slavery—*was* American history. Robert E. Lee was no different from the Founding Fathers. Trump wanted to use the moral failings of the Founding Fathers to give Lee cover. By playing on the assumption that Washington and Jefferson are essentially "uncancellable" in most Americans' eyes, he sought to suggest there were two sides of the argument for Lee as well, or that taking down statues of Lee was somehow a slippery slope that would lead to the unraveling of our basic moral assumptions about American history.

In an interview on Fox News's "The Ingraham Angle," Trump's then chief of staff, General John Kelly, weighed in on the debate as well. "Well, history's history," Kelly proclaimed. "You know . . . it's inconceivable to me that you would take what we think now and apply it back then. I think it's just very, very dangerous. It shows you . . . a lack of appreciation of history and what history is." For Kelly, we can't wash history clean of wrongdoing (as if that was the objective of the protests). We can't hold the past to moral standards that are our own (as if there weren't white and black abolitionists in the nineteenth century who also condemned slavery). Instead, he reached over a generation of historical scholarship to reclaim a debunked version of the Civil War and Reconstruction that allows us to remember without judgment and without sin. The Civil War simply becomes "history as our heritage," where, as Kelly said, "men and women of good faith on both sides made their stand," where "Robert E. Lee was an honorable man" and the war happened because of "the lack of an ability to compromise."

Obviously I disagree with Trump and Kelly here, but I think their understanding of history affords an opportunity to grapple with Baldwin's insistence that we look at what we are doing in the name of our history and how that might enable us, if we're honest, to tell the story of America differently. Trump, for all his bluster, actually asks a necessary question, even if he thinks the answer is obvious: What do we do with George Washington? For Trump it's a binary question framed around statues. Do they stay up or come down? But that's not how history works; it's more complicated than that. What does the story, for example, of slavery and Reconstruction, or of George Washington and Thomas Jefferson, look like when told in a way that neither glosses over the cruelty and failures of the country nor demonizes every aspect of the society, fully lionizes the men, or damns them to hell? To be sure, the shelves of libraries at universities and colleges across the country are full of books that treat these historical moments and figures in critically balanced ways. What I am referring to here, however, is the kind of story we tell that comes to us as a critical feature of our identity as Americans.

Something like this issue confronted the community at Princeton University, where I teach. In November 2015, the Black Justice League, a student activist organization on campus, staged a thirty-three-hour sit-in in the president's office. This was part of a nationwide student action on college campuses in support of the student protests at the University of Missouri. As one of the Black Justice League's many demands, the students requested that the administration "publicly acknowledge the racist legacy of Woodrow Wilson," rename the Wilson residential college and the Woodrow Wilson School of Public Policy, and remove the mural of Wilson in Wilcox dining hall. This demand cut to the heart of Princeton's self-understanding. In Princeton lore, Woodrow Wilson is the reason we are an elite modern university; much of who we are as a serious institution of higher learning has been attributed to him. But the students wanted the university to complicate the story it told itself about Wilson, to acknowledge what his racist legacy meant to its black students, and how that legacy represented in public space devalued them. Just think of walking in a building, the students argued, sleeping in a dorm, or eating your meals in a place named after someone who thought you were an inferior human being. The sit-ins drew national attention, and the university found itself struggling with its own story.

Spurred by the students' protest, Princeton's president, Christopher Eisgruber, and the school's board of trustees established a board-level committee to reexamine the ways the university commemorated Wilson. Scholars, biographers, and members of the university community were invited to contribute to the overall conversation. I thought emerita professor Nell Painter spoke to the heart of the matter. "It's all about the questions we ask," she said. "The questions have changed. I mean, the questions always change. That's why we keep writing history."

In the end, Princeton chose not to remove Wilson's name from the buildings, but the administration did agree to complicate its story of Woodrow Wilson and acknowledge his racism. Signage around campus and within the dormitories tells a fuller story about Wilson's segregationist past and Princeton's complicated racial history. One sign located near the easternmost arch in East Pyne Hall, for example, tells the story of Jimmy Johnson, a black janitor who worked on campus in the mid-nineteenth century. Another plaque stands outside of John MacClean House, the home of the president of the university from 1756 to 1878, and lists the sixteen enslaved men, women, and children who were owned by the Presbyterian ministers who served as presidents of the school. The university also agreed to diversify representation across the campus. One of the adminstration's most important decisions was to rename West College, a prominent building on campus that houses the dean of the college and the admissions office, after the Nobel Prize–winning writer Toni Morrison.

The issue is far from resolved. Black students at Princeton aren't interlopers. They aren't guests on campus or the beneficiaries of charity who should be grateful to be at the school. They are an intergral part of the Princeton community, unlike in Woodrow Wilson's day. And, like the other students on campus, they should feel a sense of possession of the university. Much more work needs to be done in this regard, but the student protest brilliantly forced the university to reassess its past in the full light of its current values. How, what, and who we celebrate reflects what and who we value, and how we celebrate our past reflects ultimately who we take ourselves to be today.

The ordeal at Princeton helped me think about Trump's question about what to do about Washington and Jefferson as slave owners and Kelly's view of "what history is." We have to *get the facts right* as best as we can. Otherwise, history becomes what Du Bois referred to as "lies agreed upon." We can't just casually leave out the facts that complicate how we might see a historical personality or view a historical event. Washington held slaves, and he didn't treat them very well. Jefferson wrote brilliantly about democracy and held slaves, exploited Sally Hemings, and wondered aloud in *Notes on the State of Virginia* if black people were biologically inferior. It's clear, for example, that the histories that represented slaves as "happy darkies" were lies, and D. W. Griffith's representation of Reconstruction in *The Birth of a Nation* was a lie. The facts showed them to be so. But this particular story of slavery and Reconstruction reveals that the facts alone aren't enough. *Interpretation matters:* What we do with the facts, the kinds of questions we ask about them, and for what ends, matter.

For some, the fact that Washington and Jefferson owned slaves disqualifies them as moral exemplars. For others, they may have been wrong in owning slaves, but that fact alone stands alongside other more admirable aspects of their lives. Most people aren't wholly saints or completely devils. William Dunning's and D. W. Griffith's interpretation of Reconstruction was different from Du Bois's. Each interpretation revealed something about what was valued (and the power dynamics that often reflected winners and losers), and how the past as told spoke to the present. One way to think about this is that our appeals to history often aim to help us clarify and justify our commitments in the present. And one way to think about the difference between competing accounts of a historical moment, like those of Dunning and Du Bois, is to ask ourselves how that past reflects our current commitments and what kind of world that past might commend to us now.

When we memorialize the Confederacy with monuments to Robert E. Lee and "Stonewall" Jackson, what exactly are we commending? It's never simply the military genius of a general, as Judge Moore suggested. The Confederate monuments are memorials to a way of life and a particular set of values associated with that way of life. To suggest they are not is just dishonest. The students at Princeton asked a similar question about Woodrow Wilson: What does the university's uncritical celebration of him commend *to us*? Again, who and what we celebrate reflects who and what we value. This is why in moments of revolution or profound cultural shifts one of the first things people remove are symbols of the old values. Lenin's and Stalin's statues, for example, had to fall, but it is telling that Robert E. Lee continues to stand tall in parks across the United States—even in Charlottesville, Virginia, where Heather Heyer died.

It should be said that even when we get the facts straight as best as we can and we offer interpretations of the past that acknowledge the evils and best approximate who we aspire to be, there is no guarantee that those who have borne the brunt of the previous histories will accept the story being told. *Reception matters too*. Given their views of black people, I don't have to accept George Washington, Thomas Jefferson, or Walt Whitman as *my* democratic heroes. They can't be stuffed down my throat. Declarations of their historical significance aren't enough. Baldwin put it this way in *No Name in the Street:* "One may see that the history, which is now indivisible from oneself, has been full of errors and excesses; but this is not the same thing as seeing that, for millions of people, this history . . . has been nothing but an intolerable yoke, a stinking prison, a shrieking grave." Because we have been forced to accept the lies, the histories themselves, Baldwin argued, have little value in the battle over the meaning of our history, because "we have never been free to reject [that history]." Being *free* to reject the stories, for Baldwin, is the precondition to becoming open to accepting them on one's own terms. That is unsettling for some, especially for white Americans who expect that black people should all be grateful patriots.

How we tell the story of Washington and Jefferson, how we grapple with the horror of slavery and the constant betrayals, is inextricably tied to the values animating the kind of persons and the kind of society we aspire to be. The protests and counterprotests over the monuments bring these issues to the fore, and they force a reckoning with the horrors and brutal practices that are a constitutive part of who we are as Americans. Therein lies the difficulty: any admission of such evils in our past is so thoroughly damning that some white people are loath to admit the reality in any form. For those who cling to the idea of America, so to speak, the fear is that such an admission about, for example, the evil of slavery would make us—and the idea—completely irredeemable. How can the shining city on the hill be capable of such evil? We would rather find comfort and safety in the lie than try to resolve this question. But, in the end, we have to allow this "innocent" idea of white America to die. It *is* irredeemable, *but that does not mean we are too.*

This is not an easy conclusion to accept. One of the unique features of American nationalism is how closely interwoven the idea of America is with the individual identity of white people in this country. American history corroborates a particular sense of the self rooted in liberty, self-reliance, and hard work. That history validates who white Americans take themselves to be, and the lives they lead, in turn, validate the specialness of America itself and its mission to the world. Emerson put the point baldly in his journals: "My estimate of America," like my "estimate of my mental means and resources, is all or nothing." To say then that the idea of white America is irredeemable is the equivalent of removing the stone that keeps our sense of ourselves in place. Without the idea, the whole house comes tumbling down. But if we don't rid ourselves of the idea of white America, we seal our fate.

If the condition of the love of country is a lie, the love itself, no matter how genuine, is a lie. It disfigures who we are because we engage in self-deceit. In the end, we have to free ourselves of the hold and allure of such a self-deceiving love because that is the only way we can imagine ourselves anew and love truly.

For Baldwin, if the country continued to believe the lie and to embrace a history that obscured its deadly consequences, then King's death would be in vain. And we—all of us—would remain on this godforsaken racial hamster wheel, running around and around, littering the landscape with dead bodies and destroyed souls. Charlottesville was just another tragic example of that history's stranglehold on the country.

In August 1965, Baldwin penned an essay for *Ebony* magazine titled "The White Man's Guilt," a relentless indictment of white America. Already it had been a difficult year. Malcolm X was assassinated in February. In March, the world witnessed the brutality of Selma. And on August 11, Watts exploded. The special issue of *Ebony*—black with a white face in profile and a cover line announcing "The White Problem in America"—hit the stands as people took to the streets. In his essay, Baldwin demanded a wholesale confrontation with a history that white America desperately avoided. Here he made clear the view of history he would later invoke in the 1968 *Esquire* interview:

> White man, hear me! History, as nearly no one seems to know, is not merely something to be read. And it does not refer merely, or even principally, to the past. On the contrary, the great force of history comes from the fact that we carry it within us. . . . And it is with great pain and terror that one begins to realize this. . . . In great pain and terror because . . . one enters into battle with that historical creation, Oneself, and attempts to recreate oneself according to a principle more humane and more liberating.

An honest confrontation with the past had everything to do with the kinds of persons we understood ourselves to be and the kinds of people we aspired to become. Baldwin's demand was a decidedly moral one: He wanted to free us from the shackles of a particular national story in order that we might create ourselves anew. For this to happen, white America needed to shatter the myths that secured its innocence. This required discarding the histories that trapped us in the categories of race. "People who imagine that history flatters them," he wrote in *Ebony*, "are impaled on their history like a butterfly on a pin and become incapable of seeing or changing themselves, or the world."

Trump and his legions invoke a history to justify their belief in the value gap. In doing so, they stand in the long lineage of white people in the United States who have used a certain understanding of the past to reinforce the injustices of the present day. Baldwin's moral vision requires a confrontation with history—with slavery and with the ongoing consequences of the after times—

shorn of the rosy tint of American innocence in order to overcome its hold on us. Not, in the end, to posit the greatness of America, but to establish the ground upon which to imagine the country anew and that greatness can be found there. Otherwise, we all remain impaled on an unseemly history, like a *dead* butterfly on a pin.

All of this is hard work, almost Sisyphean labor, in a country so wedded to its legends and so in need of its illusions. Black folk have sacrificed generations trying to fight it all, and here we are in the second decade of the twentieth-first century, with Charlottes-ville and so much more in our rearview mirror and in front of us, still fighting for an understanding of American history that will finally set white folk free.

Here we are today living in the shadows of the disaster that is Trumpism and grappling with our own temptation of despair. Ours is "a cold Civil War." We have those who are desperately holding on to a vision of the United States that has never really made sense, at least to me, and those who are fighting for the birth of a new America. But, even in the fight, the divisions in the country feel old and worn. Today feels like we are fighting old ghosts that have the country by the throat.

In his reflections on Dr. King, Baldwin wrote that we were witnessing the death of segregation as we knew it, and the question was how long and how expensive the funeral would be. If only he knew. We are still in that funeral procession. To be sure, a world is dying, but we have been slow-walking to put it in the grave, and the costs are mounting. How many of our children are languishing in failing schools? How many of our loved ones are rotting in prisons and jails? How many are breaking their backs trying to make ends meet only to fall deeper and deeper into holes full of economic quicksand? How many have we put in the ground? And how many souls have been darkened because of the corrosive effects of America's original sin?

Something has died. But the ghosts will not leave us alone. True freedom, for all Americans, requires that we confront them directly. Maybe tell a different, better story about how we arrived here. Tell the ghosts to go on and rest; we've got this now. All of which requires that we work even harder for a better world; that we put aside the old fears and the histories that justify them in order to finally bury that old Negro and the white people who so desperately needed him, and finally begin again.

# CHAPTER FOUR

# The Reckoning

RONALD REAGAN WAS INAUGURATED GOVERNOR OF CALIFOR-
nia in January 1967, and in May of that same year an armed delegation of Black Panthers entered the state capitol in Sacramento.
They were there to protest the Mulford Act, which restricted the
carrying of loaded firearms in public spaces. The legislation had
been drafted in response to the Panthers' armed community patrols of police in Oakland.

In black and brown communities, the Oakland Police Department had earned the reputation for "head-knocking brutality."
Many people feared them. The police weren't in black communities to protect the people, Huey P. Newton suggested in his memoir, *Revolutionary Suicide:* "Instead they act as the military arm of
our oppressors and continually brutalize us." Newton and Bobby
Seale founded the Black Panther Party for Self-Defense in October 1966, in part as a response to that brutal repression. Listed

among the party's demands was "an immediate end to POLICE BRUTALITY and MURDER of Black people."The Panthers' community patrols were aimed at inspiring black and brown communities to fight back and served as a warning to law enforcement of the party's willingness to defend its communities with violence, if necessary. The theater of armed black men monitoring police captured the imagination of Oakland and of the country. It certainly caught the attention of legislators in Sacramento. The Mulford Act was an attempt to shut it down.

More than two dozen Panthers, armed with open-carry handguns, rifles, and shotguns, descended upon the capitol as state legislators deliberated about the act. About ten of them made it all the way to the assembly chamber before the state police responded. Camera bulbs flashed. News organizations reported that the state capitol had been invaded. Regularly scheduled news and radio programs were interrupted to broadcast a statement by Bobby Seale. Standing on the steps of the statehouse in front of the press with an exasperated state police officer by his side, Seale read what the Panthers called "Executive Mandate Number 1." He insisted that black people "take careful note of the racist California Legislature, which was considering legislation aimed at keeping the black people disarmed and powerless." He urged black people to openly resist violent police departments.

This was not Dr. King's nonviolent movement. Black Power had arrived in full force.

By what would become known as the "long, hot summer" of 1967, urban rebellions exploded in 159 cities across the United States—in states from Florida to Nebraska; on college campuses in Jackson, Mississippi, and Houston, Texas; and in places like Boston's Roxbury neighborhood and Cincinnati, Ohio, where the National Guard was deployed. In Newark, New Jersey, where the riots were particularly intense, twenty-six people were killed. Hundreds more were injured. A week after the riots in Newark, Detroit exploded, leaving forty-three people dead, more than seven thousand arrested, and the city devastated. The Panthers had come to represent the rage and discontent being expressed in urban unrest across the country.

Their hard stance exemplified the new militancy that challenged King's vision of nonviolent resistance. The cover of the July 20, 1967, issue of *The Black Panther*, the party's official newspaper, featured a photo of three white-helmeted police officers, their guns drawn, handcuffing a black man in a Newark street. The caption read, "How can any Black man in his right mind look at this picture in Racist Dog America and not understand What is Happening?" The photo was framed by headlines: POLICE SLAUGHTER BLACK PEOPLE, GUNS BABY GUNS, and THE SIGNIFICANCE OF THE BLACK LIBERATION STRUGGLE IN NEWARK.

The Panthers' challenge to the status quo went beyond the specific vision of King to the very style of black leadership that characterized much of the civil rights movement. In that same issue of *Black Panther*, Eldridge Cleaver, the party's minister of information, penned a damning screed against the NAACP entitled "Old Toms Never Die Unless They are Blown Away." The once venerable organization, Cleaver argued, had become a shell of itself. Its leadership had finally succumbed to the reformist impulses present since its beginnings, and at a moment when reform seemed to many a fool's errand and revolution the only way forward. "The white liberals who helped found the organization exercised a restraining, moderating influence on policy," Cleaver wrote. The organization had become "a pernicious, subversive force in the black community."

A photograph of Dr. King and NAACP president Roy Wilkins

sat in the middle of the column, striking emblems of the so-called Uncle Tom. Both men were now seen, at least in the early days of the Panthers' newspaper, as "the white man's Negro leaders," as "niggers in the window" who were delighted to be there. Underneath Cleaver's condemnation and covering most of the page was an illustration drawn by Emory Douglas, the brilliant artist responsible for much of what would become the celebrated graphic art of the party. Douglas's "Bedfellows . . . NAACP and Others" illustrated the confluence of forces supporting the police who brutalized black communities: the John Birch Society, Minute Men, the White Citizens' Council, and President Lyndon Baines Johnson. Bootlickers needed to be blown away, the paper ominously declared. Indeed, a "Bootlickers gallery," a montage of photographs, was set above the rest of the article on a subsequent page. Surrounding a caricature of Lyndon Johnson's head in a cowboy boot being licked by a black man were images of Massachusetts senator Ed Brooke, Dr. Martin Luther King, Jr., Bayard Rustin, Floyd McKissick—*and* James Baldwin.

The animating idea behind Douglas's visual art and the ideology of the party as a whole was not to reform the system in order to include black people but, rather, to foster a revolution at the level of perception and experience—to fundamentally transform the entire society and assert a virile black manhood, in the form of the party itself, at its helm. At this early stage of the organization's development, the leadership embraced a form of black nationalism associated with Malcolm X. Like Malcolm after he left the Nation of Islam, the Panthers believed that black people should own and control the vital interests of their communities. We were a nation within a nation, an internal colony, caught up in global forces that put us in solidarity with other oppressed people in the country and around the world. Unlike many of the black nationalist organizations at the time, however, the Panthers believed in cross-racial coalitions as a necessary component of a truly revolutionary politics. But, for them, black people—specifically the black people at the very bottom of American life—were the true revolutionary class. In this light, black leaders committed to reform, like Dr. King and apparently James Baldwin, were ruthlessly condemned for standing in the way of revolution. It was the ultimate realization of Baldwin's fears about King and black leadership in "The Dangerous Road."

This exacting judgment of those seen as traditional black leaders was, in part, a desperate conclusion drawn from the experience of deepening poverty, chronic unemployment, and the many deaths among the black poor at the hands of the police. By 1966, the year of the party's founding, the record of monumental betrayal was clear. The lives of poor black people bore witness to that fact, especially in places like Oakland, where the original Panthers lived. The nation had clearly refused to concede to the demands of the civil rights movement. Moreover, the refusal itself, at least from the vantage point of those disaffected with Dr. King's philosophy of nonviolence, revealed that moral appeals did little to transform the circumstances of black people's lives, since white Americans did not seem to view the issue of race in moral terms. In fact, white people seemed to give less than a damn about the sinfulness of racism. Power was at the heart of the matter, the Panthers maintained, and power should be pursued, morality be damned. Who controlled government, who controlled the economy, who controlled and dictated the prospects of our futures—that was all that mattered. Moral appeals like Dr. King's only distracted from that fact and from the need for the wretched of the earth, with the Black Panther Party as the vanguard, to overthrow it all.

Baldwin's inclusion among "the bootlickers" indicated that he would not be spared the judgment of Black America's disaffected youth. By 1967, Baldwin was in a no-man's-land of his own—and the country's—making. Just a few years earlier he had been touted as the darling of white liberals; his novels had received their most enthusiastic approval and marked him as the most eloquent interpreter of the race question in the country. But now he had gained the ire of those same people; those who, as he noted, "reproached me for my ingratitude." His politics were changing, and his writing with it. He knew now that liberal reform was not enough to fundamentally change the country; Selma, Birmingham, and the murders of Medgar and Malcolm had made that clear.

And yet Baldwin knew as well that the ideological focus on blackness and separatism by some within the Black Power movement represented its own kind of trap. The Panthers may have escaped this particular problem with their commitment to cross-racial politics, but Baldwin worried that their rejection of the moral underpinnings of the fight set them up for failure as well. "I would like us to do something unprecedented," Baldwin wrote in 1967, "to create ourselves without finding it necessary to create an enemy." In interviews with leading magazines, on television shows and in speeches across the globe, he had relentlessly deconstructed America's race problem as, at its root, a fundamentally moral question with implications for who we take ourselves to be. Sure, policy mattered. Power mattered. But in the end, for Jimmy, what kind of human beings we aspired to be mattered more.

And I am convinced he was absolutely right, especially for *our* after times.

———

Baldwin's view of Black Power was marked, as is so much of his thinking, by nuance and complexity, two characteristics that felt increasingly out of fashion among too many black activists and the Manichaean world they inhabited as the 1960s unfolded. He grasped early on, as he wrote in "The Dangerous Road," that the sit-ins of young students represented a radicalization of the movement and a direct challenge to traditional models of black leadership. But even then he identified more with those students than with Dr. King and his fellow preachers in SCLC. In 1963, Baldwin lectured throughout the South to raise money for CORE, and he viewed SNCC as a more radical organization than any of the traditional civil rights organizations. According to David Leeming, Baldwin even became a member of both groups. Baldwin knew the student activists had experienced the brutal terror of the South, and that the experience had changed them. He remembered what he saw in the eyes of those Howard students in 1963 and what he saw in them in 1967. Faith in the capacity of the country to change by way of nonviolent appeal had been irreparably shaken. He understood that for those young people who languished in black ghettos in American cities in the North and in the West, "We Shall Overcome" had become a minstrel tune in the soft-shoe dance white folks demanded of black protesters. Nonviolent protests had become safe, the litmus test of whether one was a "good Negro" or the proverbial "bad nigger."

By 1967, then, Baldwin saw how the appeals to morality at the heart of Dr. King's philosophy and of the civil rights movement could seem entirely unacceptable for young people hardened by the country turning its back on the movement. That realization did not change the fact that a moral sickness lay at the heart of the country's malaise, but Baldwin understood that a more radical course of action was needed. The "disaster [was] upon us," he wrote. White America's choice to remain racist made Black Power necessary. In this sense Baldwin saw Black Power as a response, and a justifiable one at that, to the beginning of the after times.

And yet Baldwin by no means accepted Black Power uncritically. He worried about the turn to separatism among certain groups within the Black Power movement, which he thought was a philosophical and practical dead end. No matter what happened we were, and would always be, American. The future of black people in this country resided not in some fantastical elsewhere but here. Baldwin never changed his mind about that.

He also rejected appeals to solidarity based on some essential, fixed idea of blackness. The particular histories and experiences of black people mattered more than the idea of race. Baldwin insisted that black people should not get hung up on "some mystical black bull-shit. That's how the whole fucking nightmare started." Here he echoes the point he first made almost two decades earlier in his essay "Everybody's Protest Novel": "We find ourselves bound, first without, then within, by the nature of categorizations." Black identity politics, for Baldwin, was only a means to an end. They could never be an end in itself because a certain acceptance of blackness sprung the trap, imprisoning us in the very categories we needed to escape. "Perhaps the whole root of our trouble, the human trouble," Baldwin wrote in *The Fire Next Time*, "is that we will sacrifice all the beauty of our lives, will imprison ourselves in totems, taboos, crosses, blood sacrifices, steeples, mosques, races, armies, flags, nations, in order to deny the fact of death, which is the only fact we have."

Even as Baldwin framed his critique of Black Power, his willingness to take the movement seriously at all came with a cost. For some critics and at least one biographer, Baldwin's turn to Black

Power marked the beginning of the end of him as an artist. *Tell Me How Long the Train's Been Gone,* the novel he had been working on in Istanbul and finished at the house in London, was finally published in 1968 to some of the worst reviews of his career. "It is possible that Baldwin believes this is not tactically the time for art, that polemical fiction can help the Negro cause more, that art is too strong, too gamy a dish for a prophet to offer now," wrote Mario Puzo in *The New York Times Book Review.* "And so he gives us propagandistic fiction, a readable book with a positive social value. If this is what he wants, he has been successful. But perhaps it is now time for Baldwin to forget the black revolution and start worrying about himself as an artist, who is the ultimate revolutionary." Hilton Als, looking back from a vantage point of two decades, would go as far as to say that "by 1968, Baldwin found impersonating a black writer more seductive than being an artist." The power of Baldwin's pen had been corrupted, Als maintained, by the bitterness and venom of the young militants. Jimmy's desperate desire to remain relevant and be accepted by them, some opined, led him to become a sycophant to what they saw as the wild and bombastic claims of the young.

To my mind, implicit in some of this criticism was a rejection of Baldwin's politics as much as his art. We can see it in the ways his critics frame Black Power, almost always seeing it as a political step too far. Baldwin, in contrast, saw Black Power as a justifiable, even inevitable, response to white America's betrayal of the civil rights movement. But his political shift did not stop there. In the years after *The Fire Next Time,* Baldwin openly questioned capitalism—even commending, with Bobby Seale, a "Yankee Doodle"–type socialism. He relentlessly criticized white supremacy, railed against U.S. imperialism, and prophesied the end of the West. In his open letter to Angela Davis in 1970, he succinctly summarized that politics: "We know that we, the blacks, and not only we, the blacks, have been, and are, the victims of a system whose only fuel is greed, whose only god is profit. We know that the fruits of this system have been ignorance, despair, and death, and we know that the system is doomed because the world can no longer afford it—if, indeed, it ever could have. . . . The enormous revolution in black consciousness which has occurred in your generation . . . means the beginning or the end of America." The shift in Baldwin's politics included a full-throated, if vague, criticism of the *systems* of exploitation. Perhaps his flirtation in his younger years with the Young People's Socialist League and Trotskyism had not been completely cast aside. For most of his critics, his politics were a step too far.

Those same critics who rejected Baldwin's politics were also unsettled by the shift in the audience of concern in Baldwin's work. Through the 1960s, Baldwin turned his attention away from the gaze of white America and focused more directly on the well-being and future of black people. The nature of his "we" changed. We can begin to see the shift, at least in tone, after the killing of Addie Mae Collins, Cynthia Wesley, Carole Robertson, and Carol Denise McNair in the Sixteenth Street Baptist Church in Birmingham and in his 1964 play *Blues for Mister Charlie,* based on the murder of Emmett Till. But the substantive shift, in my view, happened after King's assassination. Something changed in him, something one can hear in his interviews and speeches, and read in his short editorials and letters. Formulations like "We cannot be free until they are free" in *The Fire Next Time* give way to "we'll share it or we'll perish, and I don't care" in "Black Power." In a way, the shift in Baldwin's work mirrors one of the central moves of the new black militancy: He turns inward and explores what *we* need to do to secure our freedom because no one is going to do it for us.

Baldwin was no longer concerned about saving the souls of white people or warning them of the consequences of their failure to change. "We cannot awaken this sleeper, and God knows we have tried," he declared. "We must do what we can do, and fortify and save each other."

That shift—the shift in his "we"—matters in how we read his engagement with Black Power and his later work. For decades, a standard view of Baldwin's post-1963 writing held that he had lost a step, that his rage and politics got the best of him, and that his fame kept him from giving his art the attention it needed. James Campbell, an early biographer, wrote that after 1963, Baldwin's "voice broke." Others, like Darryl Pinckney, offered a more nuanced, but similar, account: "The news in his later essays is in his mood of supposed candor. He is correcting, refusing to moderate his negativism about the US, and therefore neither betraying nor being betrayed anymore. It is as though he were settling accounts, criticizing, by being more damning, an earlier self for having mastered such a blameless voice." In other words, Baldwin had let white America off the hook in his early writings, and he was now committed, in order to redeem himself, to condemning them and the country to hell.

The writer Albert Murray hit Baldwin where he knew it would especially hurt. He claimed that Baldwin had turned his back on the lessons of Henry James, writing, "[James] did not oversimplify the virtues of heroes, the vice of his villains, the complexity of their situation or the ambiguity of their motives." Baldwin's literary gifts had become subordinate to politics. Another critic put the point this way: "Baldwin abdicat[es] . . . his responsibility as a serious writer . . . in the course of his decision, enthusiasm, and willingness to assume the role of racial spokesman and representative." Henry Louis Gates was even more direct. "By 1973 the times had changed; and they have stayed changed. . . . But Baldwin wanted to change with them. That was his problem. And so we lost his skepticism, his critical independence."

I think that much of this criticism fails to take seriously the continuity of themes running through Baldwin's body of work: that he continued to examine questions of American identity and history, railed against the traps of categories that narrowed our frames of reference, insisted that we reject the comfort and illusion of safety that the country's myths offered, and struggled mightily with the delicate balance between his advocacy and his art. Critics preferred to think of the old man going bad in the teeth; that, somehow, he had failed to account for the changing times or became a caricature of himself. But I contend that Baldwin's later work was a determined effort to account for the dramatic shift *in* the times, not a concession to them. He took seriously the politics and aesthetics of Black Power, and he gave expression to his disappointment and disillusionment with the forces that made the election of Ronald Reagan possible. Some critics simply disagreed with his politics and disliked his shift in moral concern.

For as much as these evolving views troubled Baldwin's white liberal friends and supporters, he in turn had become profoundly suspicious of some of them. He cited their behavior during the McCarthy era, cowed in the face of the witch hunts, and their failure to push back against the country's response to the civil rights movement. Despite their claims of commitment to racial justice, Baldwin saw them, in their actions, as co-conspirators in maintaining the belief that white people mattered more than others. White liberals weren't loud racists. They were simply racial philanthropists who, after a good deed, return to their suburban homes with their white picket fences or to their apartments in segregated cities with their consciences content. Baldwin was not shy about calling this out. "I am a little bit hard-bitten about white liberals," he said in New York City in 1969 as he sat alongside Betty Shabazz, the widow of Malcolm X, at a House select subcommittee hearing on a bill aimed at establishing a national commission on "Negro history and culture." "I don't trust people who think as liberals. . . . I don't want anybody working with me because they are doing something *for* me."

The nuance and complexity that estranged Baldwin from old friends and fellow travelers was similarly lost on the editors of the Black Panther newspaper in 1967. In their world the villains were clear and distinct, and its heroes looked a lot like themselves. Baldwin's inclusion among the image of "bootlickers" reflected, it seems to me, their refusal—or, more specifically, Eldridge Cleaver's refusal—to see the complexity of Baldwin's view of race and the true nature of his quarrel with America. For many proponents of Black Power, even among younger artists like Leroi Jones and Ishmael Reed (both of whom would later change their minds), Baldwin was just another black liberal talking about love while cities burned, a relic of a bygone era obsessed with the moral state of white people.

Baldwin would not formally meet the Black Panthers until October 1967. His friends Reggie and Helen Major and Kay Boyle helped arrange the meeting in the Bay Area at the apartment of Connie Williams, an old friend who cooked a big West Indian dinner for them. He hit it off with Huey P. Newton (and so did his sister, Gloria), and he met Cleaver, though reports of the meeting hardly suggest comity. According to Reggie Major, Cleaver spent most of the evening "cowering in the back room." I imagine Jimmy's eyes darting back and forth. He would later write, "I felt a certain constraint between us. I felt that he didn't like me—or not exactly that: that he considered me a rather doubtful quantity." As with Dr. King, and Cleaver was explicit about his discomfort, Baldwin's queerness unsettled him.

Even before that fateful meeting, Cleaver had already judged Jimmy and found his ideas and his masculinity wanting—and for Cleaver, these two elements were inseparable. He perceived Baldwin as a homosexual who projected his perverse love of white men onto the black freedom struggle. He seized upon Baldwin's nuance as a kind of failure of nerve in the revolutionary moment. Jimmy's desire "not to create enemies," his insistence on love, and ultimately, his version of a new kind of humanism shorn of constraining categories like race and sexuality rested upon, for Cleaver, a deep-seated self-hatred. To be sure, Cleaver's idea of himself as a virile black man was central to his politics. For him, white supremacy emasculated black men and denied them access to the benefits of patriarchy. Thus, politics became black men fighting for their place among white men. Baldwin's words, his life really, called all of that into question.

Cleaver was in prison for rape and assault and not yet a Panther when on June 1, 1966, *Ramparts*, a New Left, Catholic political magazine, published his essay "Notes on a Native Son," later included in his book *Soul on Ice*. In that essay, he infamously wrote, "There is in James Baldwin the most grueling, agonizing, total hatred of the blacks, particularly of himself, and the most shameful, fanatical, fawning, sycophantic love of the whites that one can find in any black American writer of note in our time."

I have always wondered why the editors at *Ramparts* published Cleaver's essay. Despite moments of insight, for the most part he moves about Baldwin's writings like a rabid animal in closed quarters. Were the journal's editors fascinated by the fact that Cleaver wrote quality prose from behind bars? Or was it a staging of sorts of the latest "battle royal," that moment in Ralph Ellison's *Invisible Man* where blindfolded black boys brutally fought over pennies on an electrified floor for the entertainment of rich southern white men—only, in this case, for radical white revolutionaries in a glossy magazine? Indeed, Baldwin had himself participated in 1949 in a similar battle with Richard Wright, the author of the novel *Native Son*. And just as Cleaver now called out Baldwin for "hatred of the blacks," nearly two decades earlier Baldwin had accused Wright of the same thing, connecting *Native Son* with Harriet Beecher Stowe's *Uncle Tom's Cabin* and accusing Wright of failing to represent fully the complexity of black life. Ironically, Cleaver would hold Baldwin to account for his criticism of Wright.

Cleaver's essay opens by acknowledging the importance of Baldwin's writings to his own sense of himself. But Cleaver finds Baldwin's essay "Princes and Powers," the same 1957 essay on the International Conference on Black Writers and Artists whose coverage by Baldwin set the stage for his misremembering the photograph of Dorothy Counts in *No Name*, to be deeply troubling. And to be fair, on some level the essay does leave much to be desired. Baldwin's understanding of the geopolitics surrounding decolonization appears limited. He comes off as someone decidedly committed, despite his criticisms, to the exceptionalism of the American project. What set the American delegation to the conference apart from all the other black people there, Baldwin maintained, was the fact that they were born in an open and free society. He also arrogantly insisted that "the American negro is possibly the only man who can speak of the West with real authority."

But the section of the essay that really raised Cleaver's hackles was Baldwin's rejection of negritude and his criticism of the idea that there was something that connected all African peoples no matter their particular histories and contexts—a unified African identity. Cleaver misread Baldwin's rejection of the idea of an African identity as a rejection of his connection with African peoples around the globe. And for Cleaver, this rejection becomes *the* clue: Baldwin "was defending his first love—the white man" and revealing himself as a "self-hating negro." Cleaver then turns to the "Autobiographical Notes" prefacing *Notes of a Native Son*, and there, in stark relief on the page, finds Baldwin revealing his ugly secret: "This did not mean that I loved black people; on the contrary, I despised them, possibly because they failed to produce Rembrandt." There it was: Baldwin hated *us* because we were not *them*.

Of course, Cleaver misapprehends the essential point. His was a world of hypermasculinist politics, full of virile black men slaying enemies and defending distressed damsels. Such romance, even dressed in revolutionary linens, had no place in Baldwin's imagination. His world, our world, was much too complicated for such sentimentality. The paragraph in the "Autobiographical Notes" that contains the so-called clue Cleaver quotes actually explores the effects of growing up in a world defined by the value gap. Baldwin's hatred and fear of white people led him to a devastating judgment about himself and about black people generally. The emotions are intimately intertwined and deeply felt. Hatred and fear of the world as it is overwhelm the young Baldwin. He is willing to express that vulnerability on the page and, in doing so, opens up the possibility of a different way of being in the world.

Baldwin's rejection of negritude grew out of his understanding that the answer to the value gap was not to retreat into the safety of an idealized black world—to "flip the script," so to speak, and make all that is black worthwhile. Ultimately, we would not find comfort in an easy identity secured from the vagaries of history that determines who we are, or an identity that denies how indelibly shaped we are by the places we sometimes reluctantly call home. Instead, the answer lay in fully accepting, in all of its complexity, who we are.

For Baldwin, even in his later work, the category of race all too often pulls us out of the places where the hard work of self-examination happens. It can easily become an illusion of safety, because so many questions are settled beforehand by the assumptions and stereotypes that come with our understanding of race. Baldwin rejected that illusion, without qualification. He did so even in the darkness of the after times and amid the despair he so desperately sought to hold off. Fixed identities and static categories that deny the complexity of who we are block the way to that new creation Baldwin so desired, and we end up stuck right where we are.

Baldwin returned to this insight from "Autobiographical Notes" in his introduction to *Nobody Knows My Name*.

> The question of color, especially in this country, operates to hide the graver questions of the self. That is precisely why what we like to call "the Negro problem" is so tenacious in American life, and so dangerous. . . . The questions which one asks oneself begin, at last, to illuminate the world, and become one's key to the experience of others. One can only face in others what one can face in oneself. On this confrontation depends the measure of our wisdom and compassion. This energy is all that one finds in the rubble of vanished civilizations, and the only hope for ours.

Even though Baldwin understood Black Power, its condemnation of white America, and its insistence on black self-determination as a reasonable and, in some ways, wholly justifiable response to the country's betrayal of the civil rights movement, he never rejected the idea, found in this formulation, that we are much more than the categories that bind our feet. We, too, must never forget this insight.

"Color," as he wrote in 1963, "is not a human or personal reality; it is a political reality." Color does not say, once and for all, who we are and who we will forever be, nor does it accord anyone a different moral standing because they happen to be one color as opposed to another. But, again, Baldwin is not naïve. He understands history's hold and the politics that make it so. As he wrote in *The Fire Next Time*, "as long as we in the West place on color the value that we do, we make it impossible for the great unwashed to consolidate themselves according to any other principle." It makes all the sense in the world, then, that black people would look to the fact of their blackness as a key source of solidarity and liberation. White people make black identity politics necessary. But if we are to survive, we cannot get trapped there.

No matter his rage and no matter his embrace of the basic impulses of Black Power, Baldwin never succumbed to the view that the fact of our blackness determines the substance of who we are. Nor did he accept the conclusion that white supremacy necessitated we hate white people. In an interview with Nazar Buyum in Istanbul in 1969, with Black Power blazing across the country and throughout the black diaspora, Jimmy's emphasis on love returns.

If only [people] could trust that "thing," they would be less afraid of being touched, less afraid of loving each other, less afraid of being changed by each other. Life would be different. Our children would not be the victims that they are now, we would not be either. But for some reason love is the most frightful thing; something that the human being is most in need of and dreads most.

This view of love remained consistent across the body of his work, woven together with his rejection of categorization and its threats to overwhelm the complexity of who we actually are. Baldwin made the point explicitly in that same interview:

Like all poets . . . I am full with the question of how the human being will be put to right. You know, it is for this reason that all this black, white, Armenian, Turkish, Greek, Jewish, etc., etc., etc., never carried any meaning for me. The question is how to fix ourselves. Give birth to ourselves. To make us live free of all these swaddling clothes, free of these habits.

Black Power could never overrun this robust idea of our individuality. Categories, especially racial categories, remain the bait in the trap. Instead, Baldwin insisted that we reach for a better self, and that involved leaving the "swaddling clothes" and certain "habits" behind. Swaddling clothes call forth the image of a baby, of innocence wrapped tight and secure. But in Baldwin's hands, the clothes refer to a refusal to grow up, and those habits indicate an unwillingness to leave behind childish things. The text of 1 Corinthians 13:11 comes to mind: "When I was a child, I spake as a child, I thought like a child, I reasoned like a child. When I became a man, I put aside childish things." America had to finally grow up.

Cleaver's damning judgment of Baldwin's alleged hatred of black people dovetailed with another long-standing criticism, one levied by Langston Hughes, among others, that Baldwin was unduly focused on white people in his early writings: that he was obsessed, in a way, with them and our role in securing their salvation. Baldwin even wrote to his nephew, "The really terrible thing, old buddy, is that *you* must accept them with love. For these innocent people have no other hope."

But again, these criticisms missed the nuance of Baldwin's thinking, especially what seems to me to be his ideas on the moral relationship between black people and white people. If Baldwin seemed "obsessed" with white people in his early writing, it was because he still believed that black people needed to play some role in the moral salvation of white people, a belief that flowed directly from his reframing of the traditional formulation of "the Negro problem."

Deployed as the title of an 1891 racist tract by a future Virginia senator, "the Negro problem" was meant to characterize the question of what was to be done with black people. Of course, the question goes all the way back to the founding of the nation, as the likes of Thomas Jefferson and James Madison worked to reconcile the reality of slavery with their ideas of democracy. Yet what is consistent across these periods is that in terms of "the Negro problem," the Negro *is* the problem—this approach is framed by how he should fit into society when freed from bondage, what will be his place among his obvious superiors, and how we might respond to his demand for equality. And the problem often takes the form of the pressing question "What more does the Negro want?"

By the publication of *The Fire Next Time*, Baldwin had turned this question on its head. The problem wasn't black people or simply reconciling our practices with our creed. The problem was white people. For Baldwin, there was no such thing as "the Negro problem."

Baldwin, like many black writers before and after him, understood the effects of growing up in a society like our own. The looming danger, as he said to those young students at Howard University in 1963, involved believing what the country said about them—that they would take the lies as truth and let them fester in their spirits. Baldwin put it this way in his essay "The Uses of the Blues":

> I'm talking about what happens to you if, having barely escaped suicide, or death, or madness, or yourself, you watch your children growing up and no matter what you do, no matter *what* you do, you are powerless, you are *really* powerless, against the force of the world that is out to tell your child that he has no right to be alive. And no amount of liberal jargon, and no amount of talk about how well and how far we have progressed, does anything to soften or to point out any solution to this dilemma. In every generation, ever since Negroes have been here, every Negro mother and father has had to face that child and try to create in that child some way of surviving this particular world, some way to make the child who will be despised not despise himself. I don't know what "the Negro Problem" means to white people, but this is what it means to Negroes.

The fact of growing up, of coming of age, in a place that holds all sorts of negative stereotypes about who you are and what you are capable of, along with the country's racist history of torture, rape, and murder and its supposed ideals of democracy—all of it inevitably distorts your sense of self.

Baldwin maintained that navigating this contradiction was the true "Negro problem"—not a problem *of* black people, but a problem *for* black people presented by the problem *with* white people. The fact that we have to work so hard to prevent this nonsense from taking root in our children has little to nothing to do with us, he argued. *It is a consequence of white America's problem.* We are simply trying to keep our heads above water and prevent our babies from drowning.

Contrary to what we are told, then, the race problem does not involve understanding the pathologies of black culture, the failures of black families, or the so-called dim intellect of a race. The problem does not entail the question of what black people want. For Baldwin, the problem rested at the feet of white America. All they had to do was look down.

> We have invented the nigger. I didn't invent him; white people invented him. I've always known, I had to know by the time I was 17 years old, that what you were describing was not me and what you were afraid of was not me. It had to be something else, you had invented it so it had to be something you were afraid of and you invested me with. . . . I've always known that I am not a nigger. But, if I am not the nigger, and if it's true that your invention reveals you, then who is the nigger? I am not the victim here. . . . So I give you your problem back. You're the nigger, baby, it isn't me.

This is Baldwin's revolutionary act: to shift or invert the "white man's burden." The problem is not us. Instead Americans must understand as best we can, because our lives depend on it, the consequences of this deadly projection. Through this lens, the "black man's burden" is the brutal behavior of white people in thrall to a lie. By way of the horrors of slavery, black people became the depository for many of the dangers and terrors white America refused to face. We are *made* the sexualized beasts, the violent criminals, the reckless and shiftless primitives ruled by passions with no regard for Christian restraint. We are *made* niggers continuously (an act that is transferable to others who aren't white). All of this, Baldwin maintained, revealed more about white Americans than black people.

In Baldwin's early formulation of the problem, the solution rested partially on the shoulders of black America. If black people were ever to break loose from the image projected onto us, we had to help white Americans put aside the false image of themselves. They had to see how they were, in fact, the niggers. In politics this would involve the redemptive power of suffering and love evidenced in Dr. King's philosophy and the civil rights movement. In our daily lives it would entail the difficult task of love: for black people to break free from the assumptions about who they were and, in doing so, lovingly open up space for white people to see themselves otherwise. It was the only way, Baldwin believed in those early days, we could *all* be free.

Baldwin's understanding of Black Power came, in part, with a rejection of this view. He rejected not so much the analysis that turned the so-called Negro problem on its head as he did the faith that we could convince those who were so deeply invested in being white that they should see themselves otherwise. He lamented that we cannot do what Thoreau called us to do: "awaken the sleeper." The costs of America's lies had become too much to bear. The dead kept piling up. By 1968, Baldwin admitted that he was not the man he used to be and, in a fit of rage, shouted that he could care less about what happened to the country. White people deserved whatever happened to them, he said. The problem is that *we* don't deserve any of it.

In Baldwin's *Esquire* interview in July 1968, one can see the rage dripping from the page. Barely a month removed from the murder of Dr. King, he spares no one in his criticism of the country. Baldwin offered an account of why black people were rioting in the streets and shifted the burden of responsibility for "cooling" down the tensions onto white America. "White people cooling it means a very simple thing," he told the interviewer.

> Black power frightens them. White power doesn't frighten them. Stokely [Carmichael] is not, you know, bombing a country out of existence. Nor menacing your children. White power is doing that. White people have to accept their history and their actual circumstances and they won't. Not without a miracle they won't.

One can see here in this answer that, in some ways, Baldwin had mastered the idiom of Black Power. Invective. Excess. A relentless truth telling, without concern for civility or comfort.

And yet Baldwin ends the interview in a way that brings the problem back to its moral underpinnings, the way he always saw it. When asked how he would talk to someone who was ready "to tear up the town," Baldwin revealed what truly mattered to him:

> All I can tell him, is that I'm with you, whatever that means. I'll tell you what I can't tell him. I can't tell him to submit and allow himself to be slaughtered. I can't tell him that he

should not arm, because the white people are armed. . . . what I try to tell him, too, is if you're ready to blow the cat's head off—because it could come to that—try not to hate him; for the sake of your soul's salvation and for no other reason. But let's try to be better, let's try—no matter what it costs us—to be better than they are. You haven't got to hate them, though we have to be free. It's a waste of time to hate them.

Baldwin never relinquished the belief that, at bottom, the problem we faced as individuals and as a nation was, and remains, fundamentally a moral one: It was and will always be a question about who we take ourselves to be. Hatred, in the end, corrodes the soul. And as Baldwin said, "I would rather die than see the black American become as hideously empty as the majority of white men have become." The shibboleth of an essential blackness or mindless rage could lead us there. Only love can fortify us against hatred's temptations.

With Black Power, something dramatic happened in America. One could see it in the defiance of those who shouted the words. Baldwin understood, or so he hoped, that the Panthers and those who took up the mantle of Black Power had finally broken loose from the stranglehold of a view of the world that killed his stepfather and so frightened him as a young man, that view which led him to "despise black people, because they didn't have Rembrandt." Black people no longer conceded to what this country said about them. "To be liberated from the stigma of blackness by embracing it is to cease, forever, one's interior agreement and collaboration with the authors of one's degradation," he wrote. What Baldwin said to Fern Marja Eckman in 1965—"Fuck Mr. Charlie"—had become, at least for a moment, a generalized sentiment.

At the end of *The Fire Next Time,* Baldwin prophesized that if the relatively conscious whites and blacks failed to do the work necessary to "achieve our country," we would all face the fire. He was right. The country doubled down on its idols. Cities burned and the embers remained for much of the decade. The end of *No Name in the Street,* however, is not a prophecy; it is a reckoning with the failure inherent in the after times. The country had not heeded his warning. Baldwin wrote, "It is terrible to watch people cling to their captivity and insist on their own destruction. I think black people have always felt this about America, and Americans, and have always seen, spinning above the thoughtless American head, the shape of the wrath to come." The time between the two books and the horrors of what happened in the interim led Baldwin to simply note the fact: It is up *to white people* to release themselves from their own captivity.

But I am not comfortable ending here, and it is *not* the lesson for *our* after times. Baldwin's shift in concern is real. In the face of white America's repeated refusal and betrayal, he insisted that we tend to ourselves (we have to raise our babies, he was fond of saying) and leave behind the old idea that it is our task to save white Americans. But this conclusion does not change the substance of his analysis of our moral malaise. Even in *No Name,* he understood that the embrace of color was only a means to a broader end; relinquishing the stigma of blackness was just as difficult as "surmounting the delusions of whiteness." For him, the country had to go through this phase around color in order, finally, to get beyond it. Baldwin still hoped, even in his angriest of moments, that we, and I am convinced he meant *all of us,* could be better. Here is that staunch commitment in *No Name,* the book dripping with so much grief and rage:

> To be an Afro-American, or an American Black, is to be in the situation, intolerably exaggerated, of all those who have ever found themselves part of a civilization which they could in no wise honorably defend—which they were compelled, indeed, endlessly to attack and condemn—and who yet spoke out of the most passionate love, hoping to make the kingdom new, to make it honorable and worthy of life.

But it is not our task to save white people: That old idea has provided comfort for far too many across generations who continued to hate and harm. It works like a ready-made absolution: White people will be forgiven for their sins, because that's what black people do. We forgive them. And they sin again. Baldwin was right to give up on this folly.

We have to give up this folly too. Much is made today of the necessity to reach out to the disaffected Trump voter. This is the latest description of the "silent majority," the "Reagan Democrat," or the "forgotten American." For the most part, we are told, these are the high-school-educated white people—working-class white people—who feel left out of an increasingly diverse America. These are the voters left behind by a Democratic Party catering to so-called identity politics—as if talking about a living wage and healthcare as a right, or affordable education, or equal pay for women, or equal rights for the LGBTQ community, or a fair criminal justice system, somehow excludes working-class white people. We are often told *they* are the heartbeat of the country, and we ignore them at our peril.

But to direct our attention to these voters, to give our energy over to convincing them to believe otherwise, often takes us away from the difficult task of building a better world. In some ways, they hold the country hostage, and we compromise to appease them. It reminds me of General Kelly's belief that the Civil War happened only because of an unwillingness to compromise—he wanted to compromise with the slaveholding South! But, all too often, that compromise arrests substantive change, and black people end up having to bear the burden of that compromise while white people get to go on with their lives. American history is replete with examples of attempts to convince those who reject substantive change in the country and what happens as a consequence. C. Vann Woodward's famous formulation in *The Strange Career of Jim Crow* poignantly characterizes one example that General Kelly would have done well to remember: "Just as the Negro gained his emancipation and new rights through a falling out between white men, he now stood to lose his rights through the reconciliation of white men." Tending to "the Trump voter," in that generalized sense, involves trafficking in a view of the country that we ought to leave behind. We can't compromise about that.

Baldwin came to understand that there were some white people in America who refused to give up their commitment to the value gap. For him, we could not predicate our politics on changing their minds and souls. They had to do that for themselves. In our after times, our task, then, is not to save Trump voters—it isn't to convince them to give up their views that white people ought to matter more than others. Our task is to build a world where such a view has no place or quarter to breathe. I am aware that this is a radical, some may even say, dangerous claim. It amounts to "throwing away" a large portion of the country, many of whom are willing to defend their positions with violence. But we cannot give in to these people. We know what the result will be, and I cannot watch another generation of black children bear the burden of that choice.

Our task is not to retreat into the illusions of an easy identity politics either. Talk of identity politics often runs aground because we find comfort and safety in the appeal to unique experiences that are essentially our own and bind us to others *like us*. Instead of seeing that politics as one way to make claims about unjust practices—"I am treated unjustly because I am seen this way"—and imagining solidarity and identity as growing out of the fight against those practices, we reach for something deeper, something that exists apart from history and prior to experience, that connects us to one another. What Baldwin called "mystical black bullshit!" I sometimes saw and heard, in various forms, in the Black Lives Matter movement. Appeals to identities often shut down conversation or resulted in arguments that led to deep divides that could not be bridged, or they took time to heal in a moment that didn't seem to offer much time.

I am not echoing here the stale criticisms of identity politics that we hear on the political left and right in this country. My concern isn't that appeals to identities like race or sexuality distract from more fundamental questions like class or that individuals, not groups, are what really matter. More often than not these sorts of criticisms come from the mouths of those who fail to see how *they* are engaged in identity politics. They take their whiteness, their straightness, their maleness for granted. What matters—and Baldwin suffered the label of bootlicker, in part, for making this point—is that categories can shut us off from the complexity of the world and the complexity within ourselves. For Jimmy, "complexity is our only safety." He understood that "identities are invented: an identity would seem to be arrived at by the way in which the person faces and uses his experience. It is a long drawn-out and somewhat bewildering process." There is nothing simple or obvious about it. Embracing one's identity does not settle the matter at hand; it is the result of a life lived fully, not one with our heads stuck in the sand searching for that essential grain.

This way of thinking is hard in a Republic that "has told itself nothing but lies" for its own safety. But, Baldwin insisted, even at the height of Black Power, that we think and see ourselves otherwise. Amid a controversy with the *Liberator*, a monthly New York–based black journal that ran from 1960 to 1971, Baldwin, who was also a member of its advisory board, wrote an open letter in 1967 denouncing the journal's anti-Semitism and proffered a vision of the goal of our struggles.

> If one accepts my basic assumption, which is that all men are brothers—simply because all men share the same condition, however different the details of their lives may be—then it is perfectly possible, it seems to me, that in re-creating ourselves, in saving ourselves, we can re-create and save many others: whosoever will. I certainly think that this possibility ought to be kept very vividly in the forefront of our consciousness. The value of a human being is never indicated by the color of his skin; the value of a human being is all that I hold sacred; and I know that I do not become better by making another worse. One need not read the New Testament to discover that. One need only read history and look at the world—one need only, in fact, look into one's own mirror.

Our task, then, is not to save Trump voters nor is it to demonize them. Our task is to work, with every ounce of passion and every drop of love we have, to make the kingdom new! The first step involves what I called in *Democracy in Black* a "revolution of value." This involves telling ourselves the truth about what we have done. It entails implementing policies that remedy generations of inequities based on the lie. It requires centering a set of values that holds every human being sacred. All of this will be made possible by grassroots movements that shift the center of gravity of our politics. And, in the end, we must resist Ibsen's ghosts, the "old ideas and beliefs" that cage us in categories and assumptions about who we are and what we are capable of and blind us to the beauty of others, never forgetting that categorization refers only to the different conditions under which we live; it doesn't capture the essence of who we are. Our task involves shaking loose the warm "swaddling clothes" that secure us in our prejudices and prevent us from confronting our fears. Our task means speaking truth to power and looking the darkness of our times squarely in the face without the security of legend or myth, and without the comforting idea that black people will save *you*.

In the end, facing the bleakness of his time almost destroyed Jimmy. It took everything in him to survive it and to bear witness on the other side. How he survived may very well help us as we risk everything for a new America.

# CHAPTER FIVE

# Elsewhere

On June 26, 1972, *The New York Times* published an article about Baldwin's return to the United States. *No Name in the Street* had recently arrived in bookstores, and Jimmy spoke of "a new determination to live." He was energized, with not only a new book on the shelves but another novel scheduled to be delivered before long. Still, the interview made clear that his new outlook was hard earned. He had survived a dark period in his life, the depths of which had almost cost him everything.

*No Name* was his first major book since his 1968 novel *Tell Me How Long the Train's Been Gone*. The intervening years had been difficult. Dr. King's death had thrown him into a deep depression. He had attempted suicide again in 1969 and been hospitalized. "For a time it went badly because I was on the edge of something I didn't want to admit," he told the *Times* reporter. He struggled mightily to come to terms with the murders of his friends. "The list is long," he said. Then there was the question of the movement itself. The civil rights struggle, Baldwin noted, had been "buried with Martin Luther King," and he wasn't sure what the country would do next.

For a period after 1968, he found it difficult to bring himself to write—he was flailing. His only books to appear at the turn of the decade were transcribed conversations with the renowned anthropologist Margaret Mead and the young poet Nikki Giovanni, along with a few scattered articles and interviews. The murders, the seeming death of the movement, and the election of Richard Nixon, signaling that the country had turned its back on real change, all conspired to seize his pen.

But then in 1970, in an interview with John Hall that appeared in the *Transatlantic Review*, Baldwin gave word of a new work. "For the past year I've been in Istanbul," he told Hall, "writing a long essay on the life and death of what we call the civil rights movement." He had finally found the will and space to reckon with his trauma, grief, and rage on the page—to reckon with the collective trauma and rage of the Black Power movement—and to bear witness for those who did not survive the betrayal and witness to what happened to those who did. But, Jimmy said, it was taking everything in him to give birth to this "Mighty Mother Fucker."

By 1972, after Baldwin's brother David had snatched the manuscript of *No Name* out of his hands and delivered it to his editor at Dial Press, the book was in the world. Baldwin declared to the *Times* reporter, "I'm beginning again." *No Name* represented that new start. It was his unvarnished assessment of what had happened to the movement and to him. The book was, in a certain way, an answer to *The Fire Next Time*. America had refused to heed his prophetic call in 1963, and too many had paid the price of that refusal. Now the country faced the fire, and something radically different was required of us, and of him as an artist. Tinkering around the edges would only seal our fate.

Baldwin took the title of *No Name in the Street* from Job 18:16–20, a declaration of the fate of the wicked.

> *His roots shall be dried up beneath, and above shall his branch be cut off.*
>
> *His remembrance shall perish from the earth, and he shall have no name in the street.*
>
> *He shall be driven from light into darkness, and chased out of the world.*
>
> *He shall neither have son nor nephew among his people, nor any remaining in his dwellings.*
>
> *They that come after him shall be astonished at his day, as they that went before were affrighted.*

This was the damning conclusion drawn from his own experience of the country's failures and evident in the fiery rhetoric of young black militants across the nation. *No Name* was prophecy drenched in the blood of Baldwin's wounds. It was the book that made sense of his journey from the heights of the civil rights movement to the lows of Dr. King's murder and the uncertainty of the after times.

Ever since *Notes of a Native Son* Baldwin had sought to understand, as best as he could, the contradictions of the country. He did so as an artist desperate to make sense of a place that rejected its own reality, *and* as a black man from Harlem who had to survive the consequences of those contradictions. This kind of work was extraordinarily personal for him. The ups and the downs, the refusals and the deaths, were felt in the marrow of his bones, and he worked hard to figure out how to get it all on the page. Bayard Rustin said of Baldwin, "People sometimes didn't understand Jimmy's intense identification with people in the Movement. He often came off a platform after speaking trembling with emotion. It's a wonder to me such intensity didn't wear out that frail body long ago." It almost did. *No Name* was the book that announced his survival.

Upon its appearance, *No Name* did little to reverse shifting opinions about Baldwin among critics. *The New York Times* was only slightly more complimentary of this effort than of *Tell Me How Long the Train's Been Gone,* saying that the new book "evades the crucial question" and that "for the most part, the ideological discourse is either too abstract and facile or too obvious to impress." Summing up its reception, *The New York Review of Books* noted that "Baldwin's newest essay seems to have been received with general disappointment."

The critics barely noticed the formal innovations of the book: that Jimmy tried to mirror the fragmenting of memory by trauma in the very way the book was structured. The first sentence of the second paragraph in *No Name* lets the reader know that something different is about to unfold: "Much, much, much has been blotted out, coming back only lately in bewildering and untrustworthy flashes." Time folds back on itself as he repeatedly shifts between the past and the present. A fragment of memory triggers an extended reflection in the book—readers of Toni Morrison's *Beloved* should notice an ancestor. Concern about a linear story is cast aside, because Baldwin found a form to capture and reflect his experience of the after times. That insight would then shape his subsequent writing of *If Beale Street Could Talk* and *Just Above My Head.*

But, more important, critics failed to note how *No Name* sought to make sense of the after times. The book had not succumbed to the ideological pressures of the times, but rather sought to explain how we had arrived there. At the heart of *No Name* is the reality of loss: The country's betrayal of the civil rights movement had left in its wake a trail of the dead, and we needed to come to terms with the bodies. Baldwin continued to do what his vision of the artist required: He sought to bear witness to what happened, to offer a language to describe the betrayal, and, in doing so, offer us a chance to outlive it. In this sense and because of the difficulty of the times, *No Name* is one of his best books and, perhaps, his most important work of social criticism.

In Baldwin's effort to capture his grief and pain, and as he sought to imagine a way forward for black people and for America, the distinction between autobiography and history collapsed. In this sense, he was like the Old Testament prophet Jeremiah, who, with great personal pain, sought to rebuke the Jews who had surrendered to idolatry and depravity. Jeremiah's prophecies could not be separated from his individual suffering and grief, his sense of isolation, and the costs for him to speak God's truth in a world committed to its sins.

Like Jeremiah's, Jimmy's social vision was deeply connected with his own psychic anguish. In fact, from the beginning, he arrived at his broader conclusions about the country and about human beings, generally, through a relentless exploration of his own pain, fragility, and vulnerability. The mental and psychic collapses over the course of his life figured centrally in what and how he wrote. The wounds caused by his stepfather, the pain of growing up poor and black, and the feeling of isolation as a queer black man (he would say that he had to create himself as if he had no antecedents) along with his deep sense of loneliness shaped how he saw and experienced the world.

In *No Name*, Baldwin struggled with his collapse in the face of the death of people he loved and the tragic end of the movement to which he had given so much of his life. His effort to gather up the pieces of his own life became, in a way, an account of America itself, one indistinguishable from the other, both indelibly marked by trauma and by the lies told to conceal that trauma. In doing so, critics would declare that Baldwin had given up on a space apart from politics from which to write as an artist. Everything had become politics, even his personal anguish. But *No Name* stands in a literary tradition of American writing that goes back, again, to Ralph Waldo Emerson. In the middle of the political and economic crisis of the Jacksonian era in the 1830s, for example, Emerson set out to confront what he called "the emphatic and universal calamity" of the times. This required looking back and rereading "the whole of the past . . . in its infinite scope." Emerson even declared, "Let me begin anew!" He did so in order to reclaim the American idea *in himself*, for Emerson stood as the representative American, no matter the ugliness and political failures of Jacksonian democracy. Here individual American identity became illustrative of the greatness of the country: The two, like a double helix, were inextricably connected, so much so that the biography of an individual life like Emerson's could stand as an account of America itself.

But Baldwin didn't have the luxury of Emerson's detachment from the ugliness of the day or the belief that his own identity was bound up with the idea of America itself—because that idea, in part, relied on a lie *about him*. Looking back and rereading the whole of the American past involved, for Baldwin, not so much claiming the inheritance of the Puritan fathers as his own, but confronting the scope of what felt like infinite betrayals and consequent traumas. Looking back meant confronting history in his own broken, wounded identity and accepting what that identity revealed about our national character and the lies that shaped it.

Ironically, in light of Emerson's claims, it turned out that *we* were the representative Americans, because our experiences exposed the lie at the heart of the nation. As the novelist Ralph Ellison wrote in *Invisible Man,* "Who knows but that, on the lower frequencies, I speak for you." The turn to autobiography in *No Name* does not secure the American idea against the revelation of the country's ugliness and failures. For Baldwin, that idea cracks and crumbles under the weight of his, *our,* story.

*No Name* was a book shadowed in grief, and that grief made it terribly difficult to finish. Baldwin would even say, later, that "it was grief I had been avoiding." In the 1970 interview with Hall, as he struggled with writing, Baldwin mentioned that he still believed what he had written in *The Fire Next Time:* We could, if we allowed ourselves to be vulnerable like lovers, end the racial nightmare and achieve our country. "But the price will be high, higher than I might have thought when I wrote that," he said. "Nothing has altered in America, except that white people have simply raised the price, and raised it so high that fewer and fewer black people will be willing to pay it." All of this demanded a general reassessment of the state of the country and of potential next steps. As he put the point to an Associated Press reporter in 1969,

It began to be very clear to black people in the United States that what *Time* magazine calls "the troubled American" is not going to listen, does not want to know, does not want to hear the truth about the situation of the American black. And one of the results of that is that everybody involved in it has to rethink his situation, to rethink his strategy.

When Baldwin sat down with the *Times* reporter in 1972, finishing *No Name* had reenergized him to step into the next phase of his witness, which involved, among other things, telling the story about the necessity and perils of Black Power. He had just completed a fundraising tour for Angela Davis, who had been placed on the FBI's Most Wanted list in October 1970 because the weapons used by seventeen-year-old Jonathan Jackson as he stormed the Marin County courthouse to free his brother, George, were traced back to her. She fled and was eventually captured, only to have her handcuffed image on the cover of *Newsweek* magazine. In one of the few pieces written during the period before *No Name* was published, Baldwin penned a powerful open letter to Angela Davis, later published in *The New York Review of Books*. He famously wrote: "We must fight for your life as though it were our own—which it is—and render impassable with our bodies the corridor to the gas chamber. For, if they take you in the morning, they will be coming for us that night." Baldwin's letter, Davis told me as we sat in the Yankee Doodle Tap Room in Princeton, New Jersey, helped build an international movement to free her. "I don't know where I would be today if that letter hadn't circulated," she said. They could have locked her up and thrown away the key or put her to death. "His letter was so impactful at the time," she told me, "they decided to title the edited collection of prison letters *If They Come in the Morning*, after the last line of the essay."

Baldwin brought all of that history to the interview with the *Times*. None of it had been easy to live. Along with the heavy grief over the movement and the country, he had suffered in other ways as well, including a severe bout of hepatitis that hampered his ability to write. His vision of Malcolm X would not make it to the screen as the debacle of his dalliance with Hollywood finally came to a disastrous end. Another personal relationship had fallen apart, leaving him alone, once again, amid all the public adoration. He would come to learn firsthand that he too was in the crosshairs of the new militancy as he traveled back and forth to the United States and found himself, at once, defending Black Power and fending off criticism that he had, in fact, sold out to "the man"—even as he raised money for the Black Panthers and, later, for Angela Davis and the Soledad Brothers. All of this made *No Name* especially difficult to write; it also gave the book sharp edges that made it a powerful and knotty read.

Baldwin understood that what kept him from writing cut much deeper than physical sickness or ideological confusion. "I thought it was psychological," he said. Jimmy felt useless in the face of everything that was happening in the country and in his life. He also believed he kept getting sick, citing the effects of the panic and fear of sitting down and writing onto the page what was going on in his head. His illness, real in its effects on his frail body, amounted to a cunning evasion. Baldwin found himself desperate; only after an extended stay in the American hospital in Paris did he find the will to keep fighting, to live. As he put it, "I simply discovered you can [live], you see. . . . I decided I have no right nor reason to be despairing. But I do not believe in the promise of America in the same ways. There will be no moral appeals on my part to this country's moral conscience. It has none."

King's death buckled Baldwin's knees. Jimmy struggled to come to terms with what was happening in the country, around the world, and in him. He was only able to bounce back from the trauma of it all in the comfort of friends and loved ones, who provided him momentary respite from the center of the political storm and who loved him unconditionally. They offered him a place to gather together himself and his thoughts. A reinvigorated

Baldwin told the *Times* reporter, "The tangible thing that happened to me—and to blacks in America—during that whole terrible time was the realization that our destinies are in our hands, black hands, and no one else's."

Baldwin did not come to this realization in America. He came to it, mostly, during an extended stay in Istanbul, Turkey, where he lived on and off for roughly a decade. Unlike in Paris, he was not yet famous in Istanbul. The city had long offered him solace, and the quiet space to get his work done. It was here that he either started or completed some of his more important work, including *Another Country, The Fire Next Time, Blues for Mister Charlie, Tell Me How Long the Train's Been Gone,* and *No Name in the Street.* But between 1968 and 1972, Istanbul helped Baldwin make sense of the collapse of the civil rights movement. From this ancient, complex landscape that balanced Islam and Christianity, he conceived of how he would move forward not only in his creative work but in his work as a witness. This place at the intersection of Europe and Asia, a city among the ruins of a long-lost empire, in a country that struggled to imagine itself as modern in a world overrun by U.S. power, offered Baldwin the distance necessary to look back and the love of his friends to staunch his wounds and tend to his scars.

Charting Baldwin's time in Istanbul maps onto the major transitions in his life. When he showed up unexpectedly at Engin Cezzar's door in 1961 in the middle of a wedding, almost penniless and in dire need of space to finish *Another Country,* Baldwin had not yet become an internationally famous American writer. Standing in the doorway of this simple home in Taksim Square, eyes exhausted with a tattered suitcase in hand, he was simply a forlorn artist desperately trying to finish a novel that threatened, as he said, to drive him to suicide.

Baldwin had met Engin, a Turkish theater actor and graduate of the Yale School of Drama, in New York through the Actors Studio workshop production of *Giovanni's Room* in 1958. Not much came of the play, but Baldwin and Engin developed a close friendship that would last for more than thirty years. When Engin returned to Turkey, he offered Baldwin a place to stay if he was ever in Istanbul. Baldwin had traveled to the South and confronted the terror of American racism head on. He saw up close the burgeoning black freedom movement that had called him home from France in the first place. Three years later, he stood at Engin's door unannounced. "Baby, I'm broke, I'm sick. I need your help." Cezzar recalled him saying,

> Let's face it—I saved Jimmy in a very, very bad period in his life. He was losing his health, losing his objectives, his motivations . . . broke as hell. The man had to be taken care of. It so happened that I was insisting, that I knew the situation—I said, "you come here"—to save himself. I don't want to sound like he came to Istanbul and that was a renaissance or whatever. I was a friend who was offering him my friendship, my house, my family, my food, my bed. In a situation where he could rest, he could write, not worry about food, drink, or where he was going to sleep that night. He had a room in my house. . . . We were not hungry, not dirty, but it was not luxurious.

By the end of 1961, Istanbul and the community Baldwin found there, which included Engin, the journalist Zeynep Oral, film and theater actor Ali Poyrazoğlu, and the African American singer Bertice Reading, just to name a few, enabled him to finish *Another Country*. Less than two years later, with the publication of *The Fire Next Time*, Baldwin would become that famous American writer, known throughout the world. He was a long way from the letter he wrote to Engin in November 1957: "One of these days, I'm going to build myself a place to live and work at the side of a mountain or at the edge of the sea."

Baldwin returned again and again to Istanbul during the 1960s, eventually moving out of Engin's place into a small flat in the neighborhood around Taksim Square. Between the fall of 1966 and the summer of 1967, he rented the Vefik Pasha Library, a red wooden waterside mansion looking out over the Bosphorus Straits toward the hills of Asia. Carole Weinstein, David Baldwin's partner, recalled sitting on the terrace of that wondrous house "to greet the day and end of the evening" and having extraordinary, hashish-aided conversations into the early hours of the morning. It was here that Baldwin entertained celebrities and threw all-night parties. But it was also here that he came to reflect upon the increasingly bitter turn of events in America. Reviewing a book of correspondence between Cezzar and Baldwin published in Turkey, Joseph Campbell wrote that by the mid-1960s, "the tone of the letters ha[d] darkened, reflecting the change in Baldwin's mood and the incendiary atmosphere on the streets of American cities."

This is borne out by a fascinating exchange I encountered in the archive at the Schomburg library in New York, between Baldwin and Hugh Downs, NBC's *Today* show anchor. Downs had written Baldwin a long letter to express his admiration and his own desire to do more with his platform to address the tumultuous times in the country. Baldwin wrote back from Istanbul in

May 1966. Already he was sounding darkening notes. "I am less sanguine, perhaps, than you are," he wrote Downs. "I may have shed too many tears already. It cannot be said that they released me, nor, since they clearly have released no one else, can I call them tears of joy. I don't have any advice to give you except the advice I give myself, which is to try to be clear, to refuse despair. But the price of change is awful and it is also extremely concrete, and one's got to be prepared, I think, to lose everything one hoped for and everything one has."

The change in Baldwin's tone would only deepen as the intensity of the brutality of American life reached a fever pitch, as King died, and then Bobby Hutton, and then as riots swept over American cities. Baldwin witnessed near-daily acts of violence against black people, from the relentless repression of Black Power by law enforcement, to shoot-outs with Black Panthers, the gagging of Bobby Seale in a Chicago courtroom, and the murder of Fred Hampton—all of it collapsed into an unimaginably short period of time.

Istanbul had been a refuge for Baldwin since he unexpectedly showed up at Engin's door, but by the mid-1960s, and especially after April 4, 1968, the city became for Jimmy a place not merely to finish his work in relative quiet but somewhere to reimagine hope itself. Here he struggled to make sense of what was happening in the United States. Here he dealt intimately with his grief.

In 1970, *Ebony* magazine published a feature piece entitled "A Love Affair: James Baldwin and Istanbul." Charles Adelsen, the author of the article, described an evening event at Baldwin's apartment. Someone asked Baldwin, "Istanbul, why?" "The Baldwin eyes fix on the visitor with a particularly attentive gaze," recounted Adelsen. "Briefly there is a smile, lips closed. Then Baldwin says, 'A place where I can find out again—where I am—

and what I must do. A place where I can stop and do nothing in order to start again.'" He went on to say that "to begin again demands a certain silence, a certain privacy that is not, at least for me, to be found elsewhere."

In Istanbul, at least initially, Baldwin's fame and the pressure to speak on behalf of black people didn't block the way of beginning anew. He could, in his own peculiar fashion, be still. Of course, Jimmy wasn't exactly rooted. As his biographer David Leeming writes, "During the Istanbul period and the months in Paris . . . Baldwin came to a decision. He could not give up on America, he could not give up on Europe. He would neither be an expatriate nor a full-time resident. He was doomed to juggle his prophetic mission as an American with his deeply complex and confused state as James Baldwin the individual. He would from now on resign himself to becoming a 'transatlantic commuter,'" and during this period he would travel from Istanbul to Los Angeles, to London, to Paris and Harlem and back again.

Despite living in Istanbul off and on for close to a decade, Baldwin never learned the language. He moved about the country, its teahouses and bookshops, in relative silence, except when he was with people who could translate conversations for him. Istanbul became Baldwin's *elsewhere:* It allowed him the critical distance from the deadly dynamics of American life. The silence enabled him to hear his own language and, I suspect, feel his own grief more deeply. That distance gave him a different angle of vision not only on the United States but on himself apart from the lie that suffocated him and much of American life.

*Elsewhere* is that physical or metaphorical place that affords the space to breathe, to refuse adjustment and accommodation to the demands of society, and to live apart, if just for a time, from the deadly assumptions that threaten to smother. Living elsewhere can offer you a moment of rest, to catch your breath and ready yourself to enter the fray once again, not so much whole and healed, but battle-scarred and prepared for yet another round. Seeking an elsewhere affords a different vantage point to assess your commitments and the depth of your loves and hatreds.

Without recourse to an elsewhere, we can be, as some of us surely are, "broken on the wheel of life." Jimmy would render this point powerfully in *No Name*, and it remains as relevant today as it was when he wrote it. It is a biting judgment of what happens to black people, to people generally, in a country committed to the value gap, where they can't escape its effects. It takes the form of a brief chronicle of the way in which we begin to read that gap into every facet of the landscape, and the accompanying sense of exhaustion:

> My desire to be seduced, charmed, was a hope poisoned by despair: for better or for worse, it simply was not in me to make a separate peace. It was a symptom of how bitterly weary I was of wandering, how I hoped to find a resting place, reconciliation, in the land where I was born. But everything that might have charmed me merely reminded me of how many were excluded, how many were suffering and groaning and dying, not far from paradise which was itself but another circle of hell. Everything that charmed me reminded me of someplace else, someplace where I could walk and talk, someplace where I was freer than I was at home, someplace where I could live without the stifling mask—made me homesick for a liberty I had never tasted here, and without which I could never live or work.

In America, I was free only in battle, never free to rest—
and he who finds no way to rest cannot long survive the
battle.

The riches of Baldwin's fame, as evidenced by his residency in the
Beverly Hills Hotel while he worked on the Malcolm X script for
Columbia, offered only a false comfort. He couldn't take the bribe,
which required him to reconcile his material success with the lie.
Instead, everything about his life exposed the contradictions of
the country and left him longing for a place where he could truly
be free.

Baldwin's longing for a place to rest reminds me of the exiled
German philosopher Theodor Adorno, who wrote in *Minima
Moralia,* "Dwelling in the proper sense is impossible. The traditional residences we have grown up in have grown intolerable:
each trait of comfort in them is paid for with a betrayal of knowledge." The plush comforts of Hollywood could not hide what
Baldwin knew of the moneyed racist interests of the country.
Freedom here could be found only in battle against those very
interests. But he needed to rest, and that required some other place
that would give him critical distance from the expectations and
assumptions of the American consensus, an elsewhere that ap-
proximated what it might mean to be free, if just for a moment,
from the American lie. Istanbul stood as Baldwin's elsewhere.

Baldwin sometimes used the language of exile when talking
about his living outside of the country. But he never used the word
in a straightforward manner. "As an exiled American . . . I am
faced with a choice of exiles," he told John Hall when asked about
his extended stays abroad. What did he mean by "a choice of exiles"? It was a way of suggesting that he, like all black people, was
*already exiled from birth,* because the country believed that white

people mattered more. We were, in a sense, *natally* exiled. Because of the lie, black people were relegated through law, public policy, and social norms to the margins of American society; they were forced to struggle daily to keep from believing all that the country said about them in order to hold off madness and rage, and to resist soul-crushing sycophancy. The fact that black people were already "in but not of" America, Baldwin believed, placed them in a state of exile, and it was from that position that he, as a black man, chose to leave the country.

Baldwin would make this point again in an interview published in the British underground newspaper *Ink,* in July 1971, but here he took it a step further. "You say I have lived the life of at least a partial exile," he said to the interviewer.

> In Harlem or Paris? You see, being an American is a very special condition, really by definition. Born already in a kind of exile. That ocean is terrifying. An American is born miles and miles and miles away from his real frame of reference. The American's real frame of reference is Europe. He has at the same time to make the world center on him. And the only way he can do that is to prove he is not a savage like me and the Red Indian. The price of being American is my flesh. My exile pays for his.

Baldwin states the point like the artist that he is. One has to fill in the gaps: "the price of being American," what he would later refer to as "The price of the ticket," is the brutal process of becoming white. For if Americans are already in exile by the very nature of their estrangement from Europe, then the resolution of that exile requires the lie about who black people are, the lie that produces the very idea of white people. Thus, to live here, or at least to think

of oneself as a black American and not succumb to madness, requires the ongoing labor of creating distance from the lie's ugly
inner working. Baldwin thought we had to resist this at all costs.
For him, that resistance took the form of repeatedly leaving the
country—of seeking an *elsewhere*.

I prefer the language of elsewhere to that of exile when talking
about Baldwin's movement around the world. It better captures
the nuances of his position in places like Istanbul and Paris. Exile
carries with it the idea of living in between a home to which you
perhaps cannot return and another place that can never quite be
home. This is not what Baldwin meant or what he experienced.
Instead, he repeatedly sought out places that allowed him to re-
orient himself toward America.

Though Baldwin often played with the word *exile* in his writing, he didn't like to describe himself as an exile or expatriate. In
"Alas, Poor Richard" in *Nobody Knows My Name,* one immediately
gets the sense that he is suspicious of the word. In the section of
the essay subtitled "Exile," Baldwin writes, "[Paris] would not have
been a city of refuge for us if we had not been armed with American passports. It did not seem worthwhile to have fled the native
fantasy only to embrace a foreign one." Richard Wright had clung
to the fantasy of France, but Baldwin, seeing the treatment of Al-
gerians there, knew that it was not the place Wright imagined it to
be. France was not free of its own lies.

Rather, Baldwin used France, and later Istanbul, as an elsewhere. In his interview with John Hall, he responded to a question
about being able "to see [his] community more clearly in exile, as
[James] Joyce was able to see Ireland."

I was driven to Europe, and my position is a misleading
one. I'm not a European. I'm not French, though I lived in

France a long time, and loved it. I learned things about France while I was there, but what I mainly learned was about my own country, my own past, and about my own language.

Hall asked about exile, but Baldwin's response was really about this country. America was always on his mind, no matter where he laid his head.

If being abroad afforded him a deeper understanding of his country, of his own past, and his own language, he wrestled no less with the struggle for his own individuality, which cut against the grain of what American individuality supposedly meant. Self-creation was a dangerous and radical act for an American, so fixed from birth in this country by the American fantasy of the unfettered individual, who was white, decidedly male, and heterosexual. Conceding to those terms about who one is would mean living an empty life, as Baldwin saw in white southerners when he traveled south and feared for in the black students he met at Howard. We had to struggle against the terms the country imposed on us. And in that struggle for individuality, Baldwin saw the need to distance himself from the categories and fantasies that trapped all Americans: "If one is trying to become an individual in that most individual of countries, America, one's really up against something," he said.

To try to think for oneself, and act for oneself, and have as little regard as I was forced to have for the architecture of my prison . . . to go into battle with all of that is to be very lonely. It's a sort of exile, and if you're lonely enough, you can perish from being lonely.

It is a wonderful concept Baldwin sketches here, the loneliness inherent in the process required to create oneself apart from the assumptions of who one is *supposed* to be in America. This supposition is a prison, containing the assumptions held by both black and white Americans. In this light, the very act of self-creation within this prison involves rejecting those suppositions, and that act, in turn, creates the distance that allows us to think of ourselves differently.

As a transatlantic commuter, constantly in search of an elsewhere, Baldwin observed and bore witness to "the workings of U.S. society." That movement back and forth, especially in moments of profound trauma and grief like that after the murder of Dr. King, gave him an ability to see both the ruins and the glimmers of possibility still left here. His elsewhere also afforded him the space to experiment with language and form as evidenced in *No Name,* and to create himself anew in the shadow of the after times.

It is important to understand Baldwin's use of an elsewhere as a critical feature of his social criticism. He never turns his back on America, even in these darkest of hours in his life and in that of the country. He refused to cede the argument over the country to those who wanted Dr. King dead and cleaved to the idea of being white. After King's death, he admitted that his strategy had to change, but he never tossed the country aside. Instead, Baldwin criticized America, as he wrote in *No Name,* "out of a passionate love, hoping to make the kingdom new, to make it honorable and worthy of life."

In May 1970, over a period of three days, Sedat Pakay, a young Turkish photographer and graduate of Robert College (now known as Boğaziçi University), filmed Baldwin in the last year of his stay in Istanbul. The translation of *Another Country* into Turkish and his successful staging of John Herbert's play *Fortune and Men's Eyes* in December 1969 had robbed Jimmy of the relative peace the ancient city afforded him. He was famous there now, in the troublesome sense of the word, and it had become difficult, if not impossible, for him to get his work done.

Pakay offers a beautiful black-and-white portrait of Baldwin in the most intimate of settings. Whether we see him sprawled out in his bedroom wearing only his underwear, or moving around the city in Taksim Square looking at books at the antique bookstore in Beyazit, or feeding pigeons at Misir Çarşisi, one gets a sense of how important the elsewhere of Istanbul was to Jimmy in this difficult time in his life. This wasn't exile—it was something much more intimate. Baldwin is heard in voice-over in many of the scenes, together with the haunting jazz compositions of Sonny and Linda Sharrock. He reflects on his presence in Istanbul, on how he understands himself as a witness, and on how he views his own sexuality and how it is perceived by others.

The short film, *James Baldwin: From Another Place,* opens with a close-up shot of Baldwin's hands as he handles Muslim prayer beads, or *tespih.* In the background are shadows that reveal that Baldwin is not quite alone, but yet he is in a larger sense, even with the camera lens pointed at him. The image and the sound of Baldwin's elegant fingers moving between the beads, two at a time, frame the film as a prayer of sorts. What follows is a recitation.

We find ourselves in Jimmy's bedroom as he awakens and opens the curtains, revealing an American warship in the Bosphorus. His baritone contrasts with the slenderness of his barely dressed body, and he offers those of us with our voyeuristic eyes looking in on his morning routine the reason why he was resting in this place.

> I suppose that many people do blame me for being out of the States as often as I am. But one can't afford to worry about that, because . . . you do what you have to do, the way you have to do it. As someone who is outside of the States, you realize that it is impossible to get out. The American power follows one everywhere. But I'm not, any longer, worried so much about that. I am worried about getting my work done, getting on paper, which is the best way for me, a certain record, which hopefully would be of some value to somebody, some day. In any case, I have to do it and it's part of the symptoms of this century that I can't do it very easily at home or, probably by this time, not at all. And, in a way, being out, even temporarily, and with a perfect awareness that one is not really very far out of the United States . . . one sees it better from a distance . . . from another place, from another country.

The anxiety around the writing is palpable. One can hear it in the urgency of Baldwin's voice. But he also reveals that he desperately needs the distance to see America for what it is—not to escape the country but to bear witness on the page to what has happened in the after times. As he says in the film, "I leave and I go back. I leave and I go back. . . . My whole effort is to try to bear witness to something which will have to be there when the storm is over. To help us get through the next storm."

The urgency of the political moment is enveloped in the deeply personal visual landscape of the film. Pakay shoots scenes in such a way that Baldwin's words merge seamlessly with the intimacy of his private life. In this sense, it works as a visual companion piece for *No Name,* collapsing the landscape with the personal. Jimmy sits at his desk with his typewriter and a glass of scotch. The prayer beads lie underneath his hands as he toys with a lit cigarette, and an article in *Life* magazine about the Black Panthers lies open on the bed. He speaks powerfully about the privacy of his sexuality, about the fact that he has "loved some men and some women," and that the challenge is to "say yes to life" and to know that "love saves."

The haunting voice of Linda Sharrock transitions the scene to Taksim Square. Jimmy stands on the balcony looking out at the busy square only to abruptly turn around and face the camera, to face us. Behind him, as the camera zooms in, the square turns into shimmering lights and shadows. The bustling sounds of the city give way completely to the voice of Linda Sharrock. Baldwin's brow is furrowed. He seems puzzled, only to slowly reveal an astonishingly beautiful smile and a full laugh. Joy erupts. Although he is alone in the shot, Jimmy's face expresses a joy that signals a community of love in Istanbul off camera that nurtures him. But even that love is shadowed by the battle to come.

Baldwin still struggled to put his thoughts on the page at the time of the filming of *From Another Place.* But, like Jacob who wrestled an angel, he saw the beginning of daybreak. The time was near. The prayer was almost finished, though he remained profoundly fragile. Near the end of the film we see Baldwin riding in a boat on the Bosphorus, his gaze fixed on some distant idea, on another place, and glancing, every now and again, backward or admiring the remnants of the old city. Pakay leaves us with the image of Jimmy staring into a distant future, his eyes watery and full of pathos, declaring, "I got to move and I got to finish the book."

As in Jimmy's times, in our own the storms come daily. It is not uncommon to find that one day a police officer has been acquitted of murdering an unarmed black person, the next day Trump has inflicted some new torture on the people coming to the United States to escape violence in their countries. Like so many people I have talked to—writers, scholars, activists, and many others—I often find myself struggling to locate a space to breathe and to think, but it is hard to find that space apart from the distractions and anxieties produced by today's politics. One of the more insidious features of Trumpism is that it deliberately seeks to occupy every ounce of our attention. In doing so, it aims to force our resignation to the banality of evil and the mundaneness of cruelty. To invoke T. S. Eliot's *Burnt Norton*, Trump aims to "distract us from distraction by distraction." He greedily intrudes on our time, seeking our adoration or our scorn. It becomes, at least for me, next to impossible to turn him off, but I know I am not alone in feeling trapped.

Trump's followers are all too often consumed with a debilitating anxiety about the current trajectory of the country, as they are told repeatedly by Fox News and in Trump rallies that America has been overrun by those who don't look like them. That anxiety seeps into every nook and cranny of our politics and demands everyone's attention. We are told constantly we must remedy this anxiety: Who is speaking for the white working class? Who represents rust-belt America? Who is talking to the so-called forgotten American? Every time I hear the question asked, especially by white liberals, I sink deeper into a kind of depression or rage, because these are just nice ways of saying that white people matter more than others. Nice ways of saying that the only way we can defeat Trumpism is to leave behind, or put aside, concerns about justice with regard to black and brown people or women or the LGBTQ community because all of that is just bad identity politics.

As I watch the vitriol of Trump's rallies, listen to the deafening silence of Republicans in the face of his racist demagoguery, and navigate my own anxieties about living in a place where white hatreds and fears are at a fever pitch, I can't help but think, as Jimmy did after the disaster of 1968, of an *elsewhere,* a refuge to get myself together, because all of this shit can drive you mad. The work we must do of seeing ourselves and America anew can seem overwhelming in the face of our demands to respond to these day-to-day assaults. But it strikes me that the lesson Baldwin's time in Istanbul after King's assassination holds for our own resides in his approach to elsewhere. We have to create spaces to accomplish this work without succumbing to the depression and exhaustion produced by the onslaught of the reassertion of the lie in Trump's America.

For a time Baldwin found his space in Istanbul, but to seek an elsewhere does not necessarily mean one has to physically leave the United States. For most of us that's neither possible nor preferable, and in any case, Jimmy was clear that there was no real *escape;* today, more than ever, American power follows you everywhere. I suspect Baldwin would not find Istanbul as hospitable a place today as he did in the 1960s; Recep Tayyip Erdoğan would have reminded him of the loveless strongmen that he was all too familiar with. But Jimmy would insist that we find our elsewhere in these after times. He was right in so many ways. The storms keep coming, and we are expected to keep moving and to endure no matter what.

I believe an elsewhere can and must be found *here:* in our efforts to refuse to accommodate and adjust to the status quo and in those very small moments when we make choices that place us outside of the norms and expectations that confine us, when we cultivate the capacity to say no. In both instances, we stand askance to the way things are. That affords us the critical distance to imagine our lives and, hopefully, the country differently.

When I began working on this book, I thought that I had to get out of the craziness of the day-to-day grind that is Trumpism, so I rented an apartment overseas, far enough away to escape the demands of the news cycle. But then Charlottesville happened. And then Hurricane Maria happened. The storms kept coming. There was no escape. I found myself back home, and I had to find a space *here* to breathe. But where? How? I needed an elsewhere-in-place, so to speak, but wasn't sure how to get there.

Then I remembered working on my last book and traveling to Ferguson, Missouri, and to Raleigh, North Carolina, to bear witness to what happened there. In those spaces, I saw and heard people saying no. In their pursuit of a more just America, they made a choice to not adjust themselves to the status quo and to put their bodies on the line for a different America where black people and those on the margins of this society might flourish. (It reminded me of the declaration of individual defiance by Herman Melville's Bartleby the Scrivener—"I prefer not to"—but on a collective level.) To embrace this vision and to take this stance often put one at odds with America. It was similar to that more individual moment of rejecting the suppositions that imprisoned one in an empty and morally dubious American individualism and, in doing so, creating the distance necessary for a different way of being in the world.

The future isn't set, but we can say, based on our current condition, that the future will damn sure be hard. Trump has revealed the ugly underside of America. And the work that needs to be done to defeat the forces that strangle American democracy will be painful and will require, as Baldwin said, "an overhauling of all that gave us our identity." We have to muster the moral strength to reimagine America. We have to risk everything now, or a choice will be made that will plunge another generation into that unique American darkness caused by the lie. The moral stamina to fight this fight requires that we cultivate our own elsewhere, because the one "who finds no way to rest cannot long survive the battle," and this battle of ours isn't going to end soon. Baldwin's time in Istanbul taught me that.

We have to find and rest in *a community of love*. That community doesn't have to take any particular shape or form; it simply has to be genuine. It can be made up of family or people who hold similar commitments or those who make us laugh with full-belly laughs and those without whom we could not imagine living. Here genuine mutuality serves as the basis for a broader, more collective expression of mutuality necessary for a vibrant democracy. Ralph Ellison was right: "The way home we seek is that condition of [one] being at home in the world, which is called love, and we term democracy." Baldwin sought refuge among those who weren't concerned about his fame or his political standing, but who offered him a place of nurturance to heal his wounds and an intellectual space to think creatively. They gave him space to enjoy his pleasures of cooking, of drink and company, a space to express his rage and vulnerability. They loved him. Love takes off the mask and when experienced deeply, it fortifies the soul and offers a cure for what ails our living together.

In our time, with so much hatred and venom in our politics and our culture, we must actively cultivate communities of love that allow us to imagine different ways of being together. That means pulling people we love closer; opening ourselves to the un-expected pleasure of meeting and knowing someone new; and re-treating into the comfort of their company as a material counterweight to the ugliness of our politics. We must try as best as we can to find the space, however fleeting, that makes possible the utter joy expressed in Jimmy's face on the balcony looking out on Taksim Square.

We also have to engage in *a critical inventory* of who we take ourselves to be and to make a decision to choose life. I do not mean this only in some collective sense. Baldwin referred to the individual and the torment of one's private life. He insisted, again, that the unexamined life was not worth living. To live and move about the world without questioning how the world has shaped and is shaping you is, in a way, to betray the gift of life itself, Bald-win argued. In our after times, in the full light of the country's latest betrayal, we have to find the courage to confront honestly the lies that rest in us, if we are to confront and change the lies that confound the nation. Baldwin remained committed to the idea that the disaster of our private lives shaped our public witness. We have to work on ourselves, if we are to live up to the kind of world we want to create. The props and crutches that have sup-ported our individual identities in this country have been knocked from under our arms and feet. We have to make of ourselves a new creation without them.

In the face of his elegant despair, Baldwin discovered in him-self that he could act. But this required looking back on his life, understanding as best as he could the choices he had made that brought him to that point of desperation and possibility. We have to do the same in our individual lives if we are to call the nation to be otherwise. It is the only way we can become the kinds of people that a genuine democracy requires.

In the end, *finding space at the margins* of the society helps us see this country more clearly. What might it mean to stand with those who are demanding real change in the country? How might it shift or change our angle of vision? My brief time in Ferguson and in North Carolina showed me the transforming power of solidarity with those who fight from the margins. This may necessitate risking one's status and forgoing the awards and recognition of the powers that be. Or, as the late cultural critic Edward Said put it, it entails moving "away from the centralizing authorities toward the margins, where you see things that are usually lost on minds that have never travelled beyond the conventional and the comfortable." Jimmy understood the risks when he decided that he had to change his "we"; he fully grasped the implication of what it meant for him to tell the truth in the after times. People would turn on him. Critics would dismiss him. He wrote *No Name in the Street* anyway. He experimented with form to find a way to express what he had experienced. He stood with those advocates of Black Power who were full of rage, and with whom he may have disagreed, because he told those young people in 1963 that he would never betray them. He worked to the point of collapse to understand and bear witness to the forces that made their rage necessary. Always the poet, Baldwin struck at the heart of what the country held sacred, no matter the costs. And in the midst of it all he loved hard, he found time to laugh, he cherished his family, and he found the space to rest in order to get up and fight again.

It seems to me that a large portion of white America today, especially white men, has lost its mind—figuratively, of course. These are the "troubled Americans" that Baldwin referred to in 1969.

Still, they are not going to listen; they don't want to know or hear the truths about the situation of black people. Theirs is a narrow concern, a familiar conceit: For them, this country must remain white. To face this kind of thinking again, in 2020, is profoundly depressing; to see its deadly consequences is frightening. You have to work hard to hold off what W.E.B. Du Bois called the temptation of despair, as we find ourselves fighting this battle over and over again. One can easily say, as my great-grandmother once told me, "You know white folks ain't gon' change." No matter. That fact should not resign us to our fate. We must search for an elsewhere to start anew—to love, to critically assess who we are and who we aspire to be, and to seek refuge in the margins in order to fortify our imaginations so that we can rejoin the battle.

In one of his darkest hours, living through one of the more shameful moments in the country's history, Baldwin found the resources to begin again. He held off despair and chose life. In that 1970 *Ebony* interview, the reporter asked him, "What then, about hope?" Baldwin's response is instructive for us as we live through another shameful period in the life of the nation: "Hope is invented every day." And, God be my witness, we desperately need hope today. If we are not able to summon it, we may find ourselves where Jimmy found himself only a few years later—at the end of the after times, with the vicious cycle about to begin once more.

# CHAPTER SIX

# Ruins

In 1979, James Baldwin wanted to write an essay about the South for *The New Yorker*, a retrospective about his first journey to the region in 1957 and what had happened in the intervening years. He would call it "Remember This House." Baldwin had witnessed and experienced so much since that first trip. America had changed dramatically. Jim Crow segregation was no more. The election of black mayors and a growing black middle class suggested that life in the United States was much better or, at least, different from what it was before the 1960s. Women were entering the workplace in droves. The gay liberation movement brought the issue of sexuality out of the closet. Cities like Atlanta, a place supposedly too busy to hate with its growing class of black political elites, signaled the rise of the so-called New South and the possibility that the nation might be ready to leave the ugliness of its recent past behind. The election in 1976 of Jimmy Carter, a peanut farmer from Georgia, signaled that promise, or so many black leaders initially believed.

But despite the changes, the country struggled to bounce back from the scandal of Watergate as distrust of government and politicians spread like an aggressive cancer. Economically, the post–World War II boom had come to a startling halt as stagnation and deindustrialization shattered the American dream for many white Americans. Jobs at the local factory, which once provided a wage sufficient to take care of a family and send children to college, were disappearing at alarming rates. Once-vibrant cities and towns in what would become known as America's "rust belt" were transformed into monuments of national decline. Factory doors shuttered and landscapes from Ohio to Maine were filled with abandoned buildings with broken windows and tattered cloth swaying in the breeze, ghostly reminders of what had been. A new service economy was taking hold as manufacturing moved abroad in search of cheaper labor and larger profits. Financialization started to shift the emphasis of the economy from stakeholders to shareholders, and immediate profits, a symptom of the narcissism of the times, mattered more than anything else—especially more than workers. The "American Century," as *Time* publisher Henry Luce declared it in 1941, had come to a premature end. And many white Americans who suffered, whether they lived in cities or in the suburbs, blamed the troubles of the nation on the tumult of the sixties revolution and the black people who were at the center of it all.

Baldwin had changed too. He had experienced literary fame and had emerged, even more so than during the civil rights movement, as a leading moral voice in the country. Even as critics continued to find his work lacking, his books hit *The New York Times* bestseller list. He now faced the inevitable distance between his life as a world-famous writer and the community about whom he cared so much and for whom he fought so ferociously. By the decade of the 1970s, as Michael Thelwell, the writer and SNCC activist, wrote, "The man became the 'personality,' the personality became the story, and the story became the myth." Going back home to Harlem, or to the United States generally, would always be fraught and fitful, especially now. Celebrity made it so. "The way the cards had fallen meant that I had to face more about them [black people] than they could know about me," Baldwin wrote in *No Name in the Street* in 1972, a statement that became increasingly true as years went by.

Baldwin worked hard during this period to describe the severe storms he saw engulfing black America and the country. Mass incarceration had flourished with calls for law and order beginning in the 1960s, and the reactionary forces of American conservatism continued to gather across the country. By the end of the 1970s, Baldwin had become what he would call in his last interview before his death a "despairing witness." He had always borne witness, but now he saw white America reorganizing its defenses, and Black Power organizations splintering and collapsing under the pressure of ideological differences and state surveillance. He had watched something similar happen to the Nation of Islam in the 1960s, culminating in the murder of Malcolm X, and now he saw J. Edgar Hoover's FBI brutally destroy the Black Panther Party. People he knew were going into exile or being thrown in jail. He continued to reach for the possibility that the country could be better while desperately trying to "avoid a certain estrangement," as he put it, "between myself and my generation."

The way he saw and rendered the world had changed; he was no longer, nor had been for some time, the person who wrote *Go*

*Tell It on the Mountain* or *Notes of a Native Son. No Name in the Street* announced that. His writing in the 1970s—the novels *If Beale Street Could Talk* and *Just Above My Head,* and his book of essays, *The Devil Finds Work*—transformed the themes of those early works in the full light of his ascent to fame and the ruins of the after times. These works also saw him reaching for new techniques that could capture it all on the page in an innovative way. Baldwin drew on black English, disrupted linear narrative in his fiction, and drew on the resources of black music to experiment with form. And yet critics, for the most part, reacted negatively to much of his writing during this period. The after times had hardened Baldwin's vision, they believed. But, for Jimmy, those times required of him different aesthetic choices and a different language to render his private anguish and to engage in his public witness.

The story that Baldwin and Dr. King had both told in 1968 about the bitter failures of the civil rights movement had not taken a turn for the better. America had not listened. Despite the passage of the Civil Rights Act of 1964 and the Voting Rights Act of 1965 and the bold declarations of the Great Society, by the mid-seventies the heroic and tragic efforts of the black freedom movement to transform the country had fallen apart. Deepening poverty engulfed large segments of black America as social scientists now talked about a black underclass. A raging carceral state, with its police often menacing black communities in the name of law and order, seemed to swallow communities whole, and the belief that white people still mattered more than others continued to choke the life out of American democracy. The black freedom movement had, in some significant ways, transformed America. But, as historian Vincent Harding wrote, "the soul of America had not been redeemed. As a matter of fact, its deepest character had only been fully revealed and all the long-held suspicions of black people concerning the nature of racism North and South were confirmed." The nation had brazenly refused to give up the lie, and in the growing energy of reactionary conservatism, actually seemed to be working harder than ever to secure it.

It was in this context that Baldwin pondered revisiting his trip to the South. "I don't want to say that nothing has changed. Something is always changing," Baldwin said in 1979. But, "the spirit of the South has not changed. . . . The spirit of the South is the spirit of America." On one level, America and the South are one and the same, both are haunted and vexed by the macabre reality of the dead, the suffering beneath the country's and region's feet, and by the lie of their innocent role in it all. That innocence allowed the bodies to continue to amass.

The seventies involved a confrontation with a frightening truth: that despite the sacrifices and costs of the black freedom struggle, the country remained profoundly racist and, no matter its proclamations to the contrary, white America was perfectly comfortable with that fact. For Baldwin, the reality of death, grief, and "all that rhetoric which betrayed so many people" jutted out among the rubble. The country lied, once again, and we were left with the consequences. "The horror is that America . . . ," Baldwin wrote, "changes all the time, without ever changing at all."

This was brought into stark relief by the 1980 presidential campaign of Ronald Reagan, the former—and, for some, notorious—governor of California. The major-party candidates presented a clear choice between the liberalism of old—though President Carter's economic policies of austerity turned out to be a grave disappointment that hurt black communities—and the allure of modern conservatism. Reagan declared, "Let's make America great again," and the majority of white America got in

line. The consolidation of a new age, in which a certain conservative economic and political philosophy would dominate the imagination of the country for decades, was fast coming to seem like
common sense. Small government, marked by the dismantling of
the so-called welfare state, deregulation, privatization, being tough
on crime, tax cuts for the wealthy, and a strong military were features of this view. The culture wars gave it all added fuel. Meanwhile, the modest gains of the black middle class and the end of
legal segregation in the South led some to believe that sufficient
progress had been made in the country with regard to race matters.

Baldwin wanted to strip the illusions bare. "Remember This
House" aimed to ask how one might measure the meaning of
progress in that region where Dr. King, with his memorials and
named streets, lies buried.

Although Baldwin had made arrangements with *The New Yorker*
to travel south, he never wrote the essay. It was one among a number of titles and ideas in his head or his journals that never came
to fruition. But he ended up pursuing the idea in a different way,
one that would lead to an important and underappreciated docu-
ment in his oeuvre.

During the time he was kicking around the idea for "Remember This House," he met an English filmmaker named Dick Fontaine at Mikell's, a jazz club at the corner of Ninety-seventh Street
and Columbus Avenue in New York City. Fontaine and his partner, Pat Hartley, initially suggested making a film about the whole
of Baldwin's corpus, revealing the relationship between the work
and the shifts and permutations in Baldwin's witness. Fontaine
wrote a script and brought it to Saint Paul de Vence, but when

Baldwin read it, he was enraged. According to David Leeming, Baldwin shouted, "I am not going to let you define me!" Instead, he offered to let Fontaine and Hartley film his trip to the South. They were to follow him as he retraced his steps from 1957 and met with some of the people and friends who survived the civil rights movement with him. He hoped they might capture on film, as best as they could, the terrible effects of the after times in light of the stakes of the 1980 presidential campaign.

The complex relationship between history and memory preoccupied Jimmy as he witnessed the country's zealous embrace of Reaganism. So much was being willfully forgotten at a breathtaking pace, and just as much was being relived through the emotions and experiences of black people who remembered Reagan's tenure as governor of California. Baldwin later expressed the interaction between time and history in a stanza in his 1983 poem "Staggerlee Wonders."

> Lord, History is weary
> of her unspeakable liaison with Time,
> for Time and History
> have never seen eye to eye:
> Time laughs at History
> and time and time and time again
> Time traps History in a lie.

The passage of time between 1975, when Reagan left the governorship, and the 1980 election allowed the majority of the country to forget his negative reaction to the black freedom movement. That forgetfulness made a lie of history, as Reagan became simply the genteel actor who declared "morning in America." And yet for the majority of black people, he was the face of a choice made by

white America to turn its back on the movement of the 1960s—
he embodied the lie. In Baldwin's last interview in 1987, he put it
this way: "Ronald Reagan represent[ed] the justification of [white
America's] history, their sense of innocence."

But many black people did not forget, and carried that sense of
history experienced in the moment when something triggers the
recollection that collapses past and present. History and time blur
as the traumas of the present call forward a litany of past betrayals.
Slavery, Jim Crow, lynching, police killings, prisons, black ghettos,
failed schools, and the people and politicians who sanctioned it all
packed into one pile of American shit. This is what the late poet
Amiri Baraka called, in his classic work *Blues People,* "the changing same"—that sense of alienation rooted in terror and trauma,
which remains no matter the shifts and permutations in our lives,
and is exacerbated by the country's forgetfulness. For many, Reagan's presidential campaign was that trigger.

Jimmy saw the deaths and betrayal of the sixties movement as
moments linked to the devastation of a ghastly century that left
human beings caught between the carnage of gas chambers and
ovens in Europe, the charred bodies in Nagasaki and Hiroshima,
and the horrors of Vietnam on the one hand, and the election of
the likes of Ronald Reagan and Margaret Thatcher as supposed
remedies to our postmodern malaise on the other. As he wrote in
an unpublished draft of an essay initially titled "The Price of the
Ticket":

I believe something has happened to the nature of time, in
this century, because something unprecedented, and, for
me, unnameable, has happened to human beings in this
century. It means something, I think, to observe that, with
artists, the century begins with the smashing of the clock—

Proust, Joyce, Stein, for example, and even, in fact, Henry James—and the violent rearrangement of space—Picasso, for example—and reaches its terrifying climacteric with the smashing of the atom. So far as we can now know, no age before this one has been so relentlessly cataclysmic— the very word, cataclysmic, in the face of our enormities, fades into a weird nostalgia.

A nostalgia for what exactly I am not sure. Less menacing problems than our complete annihilation, perhaps, or a simpler time when our stories cohered. But something about what it meant to be modern and the spiritual malaise that came with it, Baldwin maintained, had metastasized into something even more horrific as we threatened ourselves with annihilation. Instead of confronting what we have done to bring us to such a moment, we forget, or as Baldwin put it, retreat into a "weird nostalgia," a longing for a time that never was. What was needed, he believed, was an unflinching confrontation with the ruins. That included confronting the ongoing terror and brutality of white supremacy. The smashing of the clock *and* the smashing of the dream left us all at life's bitter edge.

*I Heard It Through the Grapevine* opens with an older Baldwin seated at a desk in his brother David's apartment at 209 West Ninety-seventh Street, looking pensively at a book of photographs of the civil rights movement. Such photographs always present, especially for someone like Baldwin, a certain kind of peril. These are relics of the past, and for him, of lived and intimate experiences. The images cannot be arrested on the page, cannot be reduced to their aesthetic content. One can see the slight smile on

Baldwin's face or the furrow of his brow as he pauses to look at a photo. He *feels* the images. His face reveals a mix of emotions as he looks at history while his cigarette-coated baritone speaks these words in voice-over:

> It was 1957 when I left Paris for Little Rock. 1957. This is 1980, and how many years is that? Nearly a quarter of a century. And what has happened to all those people— children I knew then, and what has happened to this country, and what does this mean for the world? What does this mean for me? Medgar, Malcolm, Martin dead. These men were my friends. All younger than me. But there is another roll call of unknown, invisible people who did not die, but whose lives were smashed on the freedom road. And what does this say concerning the morality of this country or the morality of this age?

The danger in these photographs is that they can easily preempt such questions. They can be seen as powerful, beautiful images of a heroic time and of America's promise, not as traces of what has happened and is happening in this country. But Baldwin keeps turning the pages and sets the stage for a reckoning with the reality of lives shattered amid the lies about progress and the willful ignorance of the carnage left in its wake. The photographs frame his return to the South, and his repetition of the names of "Medgar, Malcolm, and Martin" sounds like a dirge that calls us to the tragedy of the times and the forgetfulness of the after times.

Baldwin's return to the southern ruins serves as a primal scene of instruction for the nation: He attempted to make explicit the perils of the illusion of progress and what it meant for the country at the dawn of the Age of Reagan. In *No Name,* Baldwin invoked

Dante by way of T. S. Eliot to describe the tragic inner lives of southern white people suffering from the sickness of racism: "I would not have believed that death had undone so many." Eliot comes to mind again as Baldwin returned south in the after times, not so much to describe the inner lives of white southern men but to account for what has happened to *all of us* in the years that followed the end of the civil rights movement, when the world refused to see the horrors of the age. "These fragments I have shored against my ruins," Eliot wrote. Baldwin aimed to walk among the ruins and to bear witness.

Baldwin began his journey south in Washington, D.C., by visiting Sterling A. Brown, the noted Howard University professor of literature who had served as his initial guide when he first went south in 1957. Brown understood, better than most, the rhythms of the South—especially the black South, and it is easy to see why Baldwin, who in 1957 had never been to the South, would seek him out. Brown's first book of poetry, *The Southern Road*, explored with sensitivity and sophistication the intricate contours of black southern dialect and the beauty and simplicity of the country folk of the region. Sitting in an office as Brown smoked his pipe, Baldwin listened like an attentive student. "I'm very glad that you're taking this trip," Brown said. "I'm gon' take a trip after you. I'mma visit where you've been. See your tracks. If you haven't done right, I'mma tell you."

After a bit more banter, Brown gets to the heart of the stakes for Baldwin's journey. "You're getting back to some roots," he says. "What you see and how you render what you see. That's very important for us." Baldwin's face reveals the seriousness and burden of what Brown just expressed. He nods in agreement, and his eyes are suddenly distant, like his eyes at the end of Pakay's *From An-*

*other Place.* Then Brown, who knows more about the South than almost anyone, says to Baldwin: "I'm going to learn a lot about the South from you." For a second, Baldwin thinks about the meaning of Brown's words. Finally, he chuckles with surprise and says, "Well, turnabout is fair play."

The scene in Brown's office ends with the sound of Brown reading his haunting poem "Old Lem," as the visuals transition to images and footage of the civil rights movement—of members of the Klan and of George Wallace, of the violence of the police, the tears of a young Ben Chaney at James Chaney's funeral in Mississippi, of Medgar Evers in the coffin.

*I talked to old Lem*
*and old Lem said:*
*"They weigh the cotton*
*They store the corn*
*We only good enough*
*To work the rows;*
*They run the commissary*
*They keep the books*
*We gotta be grateful*
*For being cheated;*
*Whippersnapper clerks*
*Call us out of our name*
*We got to say mister*
*To spindling boys*
*They make our figgers*
*Turn somersets*
*We buck in the middle*
*Say, 'Thankyuh, sah.'*

*They don't come by ones*
*They don't come by twos*
*But they come by tens. . . ."*

Later in the film, after Baldwin has been to Atlanta, he describes the city to his brother David by saying, "You wouldn't recognize it." For Baldwin, Atlanta represented the illusion of the New South and, by extension, the lie: The changes that promised revitalization were only on the surface and not at the heart of the city, the region, or the nation. In this sense, the contradictions around Atlanta and how Dr. King was represented by those in the city become the essential frame for what follows in the film.

By 1979, the decade-long congressional push for a national holiday to celebrate Dr. King had gained enough steam to reach a vote in the House, though it did not yet succeed. But Baldwin worried that tributes to King served to obscure a deeper truth. People could ignore what was happening in black communities across the country and instead celebrate the so-called legacy of Dr. King. They could pin King's wings to the page. In this sense and for that purpose, Baldwin lamented, the memorials and the named streets perfumed the carnage. They hid in plain sight what actually happened to many of the movement's survivors and their children. All one had to do was look down from the street signs for Dr. Martin Luther King Jr. Avenue and see the poor neighborhoods along it to get the point. As Baldwin said to David, his words slurring slightly from a bit too much drink:

The monument [Dr. King's memorial] in Atlanta is absolutely as irrelevant as the Lincoln memorial. It is one of the ways the Western world has learned or thinks it has learned to outwit history, to outwit time—to make a life and a death irrelevant, to make that passion irrelevant, to make it unusable for you and for our children. There is nothing you can do with that monument, someone said to the widow.

The film makes plain the lessons about the domestication of King's witness and the broader insight gained from the failures and losses of the sixties revolution. "[The sixties] clarified, once and forever and in the sight of all the world," Baldwin maintained, "the real intention of our co-citizens towards us. When Martin's head was blown off we learned something." The scales fell from our eyes and our faith in American democracy, so Baldwin believed, was profoundly shaken. King's murder and the tragic consequences for those who survived it was not the work of some lone madman; indeed, this *was* America.

One exchange in particular between Baldwin and Dave Dennis, the Mississippi director of CORE and one of the leaders of Mississippi's Freedom Summer in 1964, drives home this point about the consequences of the betrayal. The conversation is framed by grainy footage of a Neshoba County jail cell and people searching for the bodies of Andrew Goodman, Michael Schwerner, and James Chaney, the three civil rights workers killed in Philadelphia, Mississippi. Dennis is heard in voice-over, and then we see him, eyes gray and sullen, as he recalls a gruesome revelation made during the search. As local and national law enforcement looked for the three civil rights workers, they kept discovering other black bodies. "Sometimes, I mean, two and three and they found three bodies floating in the Mississippi one day," Dennis remembers. "They had all been decapitated. Heads were gone. Cut up and everything else. All of sudden it hit us . . . what difference does it make?" he asked as he looked at Baldwin, who was off camera. "If it's not Chaney, Goodman, and Schwerner. They were finding black people buried under trees, floating in rivers and everything else. . . . People were being killed because they were attempting to get the right to vote."

The three civil rights workers were eventually found. One pathologist described the body of James Chaney, the only black man of the three volunteers, as so brutally tortured that in his twenty-five years of experience he had "never witnessed bones so severely shattered." The camera then turns to the photograph of a white man staring directly at us as Dennis describes the farce of the attempt to hold the men who committed the murders accountable years after the horrible act. (None of the men served more than ten years.) We see the footage of James Chaney's mother, her eyes distant and full of grief, and the young Ben Chaney, all of twelve years old, weeping as he sings "We Shall Overcome." She pulls him close to her side.

Dennis recalls the funeral, then turns his attention to Ben. "Ben loved his brother," he says,

> Ben believed in the system. And Ben felt that something should have been done about his brother's death. . . . But the whole thing about Ben Chaney is that he was a good kid who believed in the system that . . . you might say betrayed him and told him, "Nigga, you're a fool for believing in it." And what they did was create a very angry young man.

After James Chaney's murder and the circulation around the world of the image of Ben bent over at the funeral, crying so hard that his little body shuddered, the Chaney family had to leave Mississippi. In Meridian, the Chaneys continued to receive death threats over the phone. People randomly shot at their home. Finally, Fannie Lee Chaney, Ben's mother, decided to move the family to New York.

Resettled in Harlem, Ben received the first scholarship of the Andrew Goodman Foundation, an organization founded by the family of the civil rights worker murdered alongside James Chaney, and he attended the Walden School, a private day school in Manhattan committed to progressive education. He felt out of place, one of only twenty-five black students in a student body of about eight hundred. "It was like going to a foreign land," he said.

Ben found some comfort in Harlem. He joined the Black High School Coalition, which fought for the inclusion of black history and black studies in schools. By October of 1969, though, he had dropped out of Walden. One of Ben's sisters said, "He just seemed to lose interest." That same year, he participated in a protest of the YWCA because it refused to house the Black Panther Party's breakfast program for children. As one of his friends put it, "We were all moving away from the ideology of the civil rights movement toward examining the philosophy of the Black Panther Party and things like the writings and philosophy of Mao Tse-tung, Malcolm X and others involved in the struggles of oppressed people." Ben, like so many of his generation, had been radicalized by the country's latest betrayal and his tragic experience of it.

In April 1970, a friend asked Ben to drive with him to Florida. He said it was to visit family. It turned out to be a trip to pick up guns for an Ohio unit of the Black Liberation Army, an underground Black Nationalist/Marxist organization made up of former members of the Black Panther Party. The BLA was, perhaps, the most radical response to the after times. Its members decided to wage war against the United States.

On the road trip, Ben found himself in the middle of what would become a murder spree. Four white people would be killed and two wounded on the road between Florida and the Carolinas. The two teenagers with Ben, Martin Rutrell and Lindsey Lee Thompson, robbed and killed an insurance collector in Ft. Lauderdale. They murdered two coeds in Boca Raton, Florida, and killed the proprietor of a fireworks stand in Hardeeville, South Carolina. In Durham, North Carolina, they robbed and shot two white youths and left them for dead. The young people in Durham survived and identified Ben's friends. They also identified Ben near the scene in a stolen Buick. Once captured, Ben and Martin Rutrell, under separate questioning, told the police that Thompson had done all of the killing. Ben said that Thompson was "a guy just back from Vietnam who liked to kill for the pleasure." He told the police exactly what he told his mom, "that he had only driven the car."

The young, bright-eyed Mississippi boy who loved his big brother dearly and, after his brutal murder, wanted to follow in his footsteps, now, at the age of eighteen, was sentenced to life in prison for murder. He served thirteen years. Eventually, Ben returned to Mississippi, only to find his brother's grave site riddled with bullet holes.

For Dave Dennis, Ben's story illustrated the tragic after times of the black freedom struggle. Sitting in a wicker chair against floral wallpaper in the Mississippi heat, Dennis looked tired and angry as he recounted what had happened to Ben. He told Baldwin,

> What they did was to create permanent enemies of this country . . . I use Ben as just an example, because God knows with the Vietnam War and the corruption that has happened in this country and what they've done to people—not just Blacks but to poor people as a whole—

how many enemies have they created? This country had its opportunity to choose the right road, but they've decided over and over again to take the wrong road. . . . I don't know if it can ever come back again, 'cause I don't think it will have that opportunity again to make that decision of whether . . . to take the right road or the wrong road.

Baldwin listened intently as he dabbed at the sweat dripping from his head. He thought of August 1963 and the promise and hope of the March on Washington as Dr. King and others petitioned the government for redress of grievances, and said to Dennis:

The bombing of the four little girls in the Birmingham Sunday school . . . that was the first answer that we received to our petition. I thought then what you've just said now. There will be no more marches on Washington. No more petitions of the government. No one will ever trust the government again.

For both men the civil rights movement offered the country the chance to reject the lie and take the road toward a truly multiracial democracy. And both believed that its refusal to seize the moment may have fully closed the door on the possibility that the country could ever be otherwise.

On one level, *I Heard It Through the Grapevine* chronicled the collapse of a particular political order shaped by the New Deal and the emergence of another based in the conservatism of Barry Goldwater and Ronald Reagan. Baldwin stood in the interregnum

("Lord, they know not what they do"), and his return to the South aimed to make it all explicit. He implicitly surveyed the ruins of the New Deal consensus, with its optimistic faith in human freedom and its belief that government policy could affect profound changes in the quality of people's lives. He saw what was to take its place in the charming mean-spiritedness of Reagan, a B-list Hollywood actor, all too willing to feed the country's fantasies.

Just twelve years after the last major legislation of the Great Society—the Fair Housing Act of 1968—aimed, however clumsily, at addressing inequalities produced by generations of racist policies, the country elected a president whose charge was to dismantle it all. It would do us good to remember both how remarkably little time passed *and* to recall the way Reagan drew on racial resentment to usher in this new age. Reagan's campaign was clear about his loyalties. One of his first events after his nomination was at the Neshoba County Fair in Mississippi, just a few miles away from the place where civil rights workers Goodman, Schwerner, and Chaney were murdered. (Ben Chaney was still in prison.) Some fifteen thousand people turned out to hear Reagan declare, among other things, his commitment to "states' rights" and his promise "to restore to states and local governments the power that properly belongs to them." This was the language of the racist South spoken with Hollywood charm, but the charm didn't fool black people. Black America, as Representative Mickey Leland of Texas said at the time, "believe[s], whether he denies the allegations or not, that he is racist."

Reagan's attack on affirmative action, his calls for constructive engagement with apartheid South Africa, his eventual evisceration of the Equal Employment Opportunity Commission (EEOC) and the U.S. Commission on Civil Rights, all in the name of color blindness, signaled a hard change in the tone and substance of racial politics in the country. Calls for law and order (and the war on drugs it would unleash), demands for smaller government, and pleas for personal responsibility as a replacement for government "welfare programs" became part of an arsenal of code words and dog whistles for white resentment and racist retrenchment.

If Black America knew exactly what Reagan and the Republican Party were doing, so did white America. Republicans passionately defended themselves against claims that they were racist, maintaining that one could make arguments for "states' rights" without being a committed racist. When Jimmy Carter accused Reagan of injecting hatred and racism into the campaign after the Neshoba County Fair speech, Reagan, in a move all too familiar to many of us today, dismissed Carter's "unfair" attack as "shameful." *Washington Post* reporter Richard Harwood wrote that "there is nothing in Reagan's record to support the charge that he was a racist." *The New Republic* said Carter's statements were "frightful distortions, and bordering on outright lies."

Reagan was exactly the kind of president that allowed white America to be secure in its commitment to the value gap. His smile, his down-home charm, exuded exactly the opposite of the vitriol of loud, southern bigots. Reagan's was genteel racism and, politically, he knew exactly what he was doing: playing on the fears and hatreds of some white people, especially in the South, the West, and the suburbs, for political gain. Throughout his career, Reagan subtly exploited the resentments of white Americans who resisted the black freedom movement of the sixties and seventies. In 1966, in his race for the California governorship, he denounced open housing and civil rights laws. In his 1976 campaign for the Republican presidential nomination, he invoked the image of the "welfare queen" who bilked the federal government out of hundreds of thousands of dollars. What happened in Neshoba County was not a political misstep, but a tactical decision by Reagan and his operatives to exploit racism for political purposes, and it reveals how that decision, along with a host of other choices, gave modern conservatism its dark, racist undertones. This is the soil in which Trumpism grows.

In the end, Reagan's election carried deep symbolic significance. For white America, he inaugurated the end of milquetoast liberalism and the beginning of an economic and political epoch that would guarantee prosperity and liberty for Nixon's not-so-silent majority and Reagan Democrats. For them, Reagan was making America great again.

But for black America, Reagan triggered traumas. He stood for what the spoken-word artist Gil Scott-Heron called "Winter in America." He represented a treacherous betrayal of the promises of the second Reconstruction. Baldwin put it this way in his 1980 essay "Notes on the House of Bondage":

> I lived in California when Ronald Reagan was governor and that was a very ugly time—the time of the Black Panther harassment, the beginning (and the end) of the Soledad Brothers, the persecution and trial of Angela Davis. I saw all that, and much more, but what I found unspeakable about the man was his contempt, his brutal contempt, for the poor.

Ronald Reagan was as notorious to proponents of Black Power as George Wallace was to those who participated in the civil rights movement. To elect Reagan president of the United States and declare him as some kind of redeemer-in-chief amounted to a hard backhand slap on the face for black America. The fact that Ralph Abernathy, Dr. King's closest confidant, and Hosea Williams, one of King's lieutenants, endorsed him only underscored for many how far we had fallen. To Baldwin, it showed the depth of our own madness. Reagan's appearance on the national stage signaled the door slamming shut on the window of possibility opened by the civil rights movement twenty-five years earlier. Reagan was a captivatingly sinister representative of the new world born in the aftermath of the betrayal of the black freedom struggle.

Baldwin does not explicitly address Black Power in *I Heard It Through the Grapevine,* but it hovers in the background as an unspoken response to the collapse of the civil rights movement. Only when he visits Newark, with the footage of the Newark riots, do we get a glimpse of that moment. Amiri Baraka drives him and David around to see the rot that remains in the city some twelve years after the riots. It is a depressing scene. Baraka, who once harshly criticized Baldwin, now saw in him a visionary figure. The two had moved closer to each other's thinking, as Baraka gave up the cultural nationalism of his early days and Baldwin changed the nature of his "we." Now together they surveyed an example of the devastation of the after times.

The film cuts from Newark to Baldwin and his brother David sitting at the bar at Mikell's. Just above their heads is a black-and-white television beaming the image of Ronald Reagan being interviewed on ABC News. The scene is shadowed by the previous footage of the desolation of Newark. Baldwin speaks with venom. "I would like to indicate to the President-elect who says you can vote with your feet in this country . . . I dare him to go to Newark and tell the people in Newark they can vote with their feet in this country."

Reagan had argued that Americans could escape poor living conditions if they so chose. All they needed to do was to "vote with their feet." They could just move along. Those who remained, he seemed to suggest, did so because they wanted to or were too lazy to aspire to something more. This was the lie. The film cuts from the footage in Newark to a pianist playing a deep blues in Mikell's, and Baldwin's words continue in what turns out to be a poem of sorts delivered over a blues, an echo of the poetic style of Amiri Baraka: "I dare him to tell all of those trumpet players, honky-tonk pianists, all those gospel singers, and their mammas and their papas that you can vote with your feet in this country. That day in Newark."

No matter. *I Heard It Through the Grapevine* did not reach theater screens until 1982. By then, the Age of Reagan had begun.

Baldwin understood the limits of elections. As he said in the film as he crossed the Edmund Pettus Bridge in Selma, Alabama, black people had clamored for the right to vote only to end up in the intolerable situation of not having very much to vote for. It was one of the tragic ironies of the movement. Voting was not, by any stretch of the imagination, freedom. But Baldwin understood the instrumental value of the vote. In "Notes on the House of Bondage," he put it this way as he pondered the election that would give us President Reagan:

> My vote will probably not get me a job or a home or help me through school or prevent another Vietnam or a third

world war, but it may keep me here long enough for me to
see, and use, the turning of the tide—for the tide has got to
turn. And . . . if Carter is reelected, it will be by means of
the black vote, and it will not be a vote for Carter. It will be
a coldly calculated risk, a means of buying time.

I wish I had learned that lesson: that voting, as much as it is a
democratic duty, for black people, can also be a means to buy some
time when the choice is as stark as it was between Carter and
Reagan.

In 2016, I could not bring myself to vote for Hillary Clinton.
I had grown tired of the Democratic Party and its failure to deliver
substantive policies to remedy black suffering. We had experienced eight years in power, according to Ta-Nehisi Coates, supposedly because a black man was in the White House, but the
police were still brutalizing black people, the collapse of the housing market had devastated black communities, and the country
seemed as divided around race as it had been in generations. Much
more was required than the Clinton name, or the endorsement of
her bid for the presidency by President Obama or by some celebrity, or the brandishing of hot sauce in a handbag. I urged black
voters to leave the presidential ballot blank ("blank out") if the
Democratic Party failed to propose substantive policies to address
the lingering impact of the Great Recession on black communities. Black people had to wake up from the sleepwalking induced
by the Obama years. Something dramatic had to happen. Then the
Republicans nominated Donald Trump.

In an essay in *Time* magazine co-authored with Fredrick Har-
ris, a political scientist at Columbia University, I amended my
view. If you were a Democrat who lived in a battleground state like
Wisconsin or Pennsylvania, we argued, you should vote for Hil-

lary Clinton. But if you lived in a decidedly red state (to Fred's horror, I extended the view to overwhelmingly blue states as well), then you could blank out or vote your conscience. Our idea was to organize the electorate to push the Democratic Party to the left on racial issues, to impact the delegate apportionment for the 2020 Democratic Convention, and to break open the political silence around race imposed by those seeking to protect Obama from racist claims that he was, in all matters, a black president.

With the nomination of Donald Trump, who by every estimation was woefully ill-equipped to be president of the United States, I believed we had an opportunity to break the stranglehold of the corporate wing of the party. We needed to refuse to play the old political game around race matters in which Democratic candidates pandered to a facile idea of identity politics (with no serious policy content) and black political elites jockeyed for position by promising to deliver black voters to them as if we were cattle chewing cud. The "carnival barker" nominated by the Republican Party offered a chance to upend the rules of the game, so I believed, because white America would never elect such a person to the highest office in the land. I was wrong, and given my lifelong reading of Baldwin, it was an egregious mistake.

The 2016 election was a referendum on the direction of the country and on who we took ourselves to be. It was an election about the substance of the American Idea as the possession of white people. And I was stupid enough, in that context, to overestimate white America. I did not realize it then, but I needed to *buy more time* to fully grasp the fact that we were living in the after times.

As Reagan had in his 1980 campaign, Trump represented a full-throated reassertion of a particular vision of the country as decidedly white and forever committed to the principles of Reagan and his inheritors. For his supporters, to suggest a different political vision amounted to heresy or revolution. A coalition of forces—Tea Party radicals, Republican partisans, and white suburbia—made Trump possible. In the end, his election was, like Reagan's, a backhand slap on the face of those, especially African Americans, who after eight years of having a black man in the White House and renewed faith, imagined the country otherwise.

It is funny, at least to me, that pundits and scholars identify Trump with a distinctive political lineage that excludes Reagan. The explicitness of his racism and the brazen way he has discarded the post–civil rights consensus about how to talk and not talk about race has led some to liken him to Strom Thurmond of the Dixiecrat Party in 1948 or to the racist campaign of George Wallace in 1968 or to Patrick Buchanan's runs for president in 1992, 1996, and 2000. These are clear racist demagogues, and Trump stands among them. But in some ways, and perhaps it is intentional, such classifications are too easy. They suffer from the limits of melodrama, where good and evil are clearly discernible and heroes always come to the rescue as in the cowboy movies of old or the blockbuster Marvel films of today.

But human beings are much more complicated than these stories suggest. Trump cannot be cordoned off into a corner with evil, racist demagogues. We make him wholly bad in order to protect our innocence. He is made to bear the burdens of all our sins, when he is in fact a clear reflection of who we actually are. As with Reagan in 1980, with Trump white America reached for an image—a Hollywood-generated fantasy—on which to project their hatreds and fears. In this sense, Trump is best seen as a child of Reagan.

After what Dave Dennis experienced in segregated Mississippi and what he witnessed after the demise of the movement, he doubted the country would have another opportunity to choose the right road. Baldwin echoed that sentiment: Black people would never again march or trust the government. In 1979, Baldwin could not have imagined the euphoria surrounding Barack Obama's election or Michelle Obama's declaration that "for the first time in my adult life, I am really proud of my country, because it feels like hope is finally making a comeback." He could not foresee all of the future marches on Washington and their market and symbolic value. He could not have imagined the "illusion of safety" Obama's presidency provided for us. In this sense, Baldwin did not anticipate a moment of profound disappointment such as ours, because he didn't believe—and why would he?—that we would ever trust these people again.

But here we are, bookended by the likes of Reagan and Trump with, of all things, a black president pinched in the middle, and wondering what will happen next. We stand in the ruins. Modern conservatism has collapsed. Its claims about the value of small government, the importance of tax cuts for the rich, and the benefits of deregulation and privatization have resulted in most Americans drowning in profound uncertainty about their future and their children's future and have left the planet mortally wounded. All that is left of this once-vaunted ideology are appeals to our lesser angels in order to divide Americans along the fault lines that have been a part of this democratic experiment since the very beginning: "We must keep the proverbial niggers and those like them in their place." It worked.

I can imagine my conservative friends crying foul, saying that I am too harsh and bitter, that Trump's election was not simply about race and that economics were more important, and they would be genuinely sincere. But sincerity can often be a mask for cruelty, especially the cruelty of conscious disavowal. To agree with me entails much more than condemning Trump. It necessitates an honest confrontation with and condemnation of one's complicity with a way of life that insists that some people matter more than others and with a society organized to reflect that belief. Baldwin has it right when he says:

> Americans are always sincere, it is their most striking and appalling attribute. . . . Nixon was perfectly sincere when lying about Watergate, the military were perfectly sincere when lying about Vietnam and Cambodia, Helms is perfectly sincere when he says that he is not a racist, and the late J. Edgar Hoover was sincere when he called the late Martin Luther King, Jr. the biggest liar in America. This sincerity covers, and pardons all, [and] is the very substance of the American panic.

Baldwin cuts to the heart of the matter here. Our sincere commitments to democracy have always been shadowed by the lie evident in our practices. Sincerity, ostensibly, requires that we not mislead or deceive ourselves or others—that we, at least, seek to be true to ourselves. But in matters regarding race, sincerity comes with the lie, for the very heart of American identity is at stake. White America has to believe this stuff. Like the drunken southern gentleman who sincerely, and greedily, grabbed Baldwin's cock, the emptiness is revealed in knowing that a lie undergirds it all. Panic ensues when crises reveal the truth, because we are snatched from our fantasies and forced to confront who we really are.

To understand this is to see why the desire to distance oneself from Trump fits perfectly with the American refusal to see ourselves as we actually are. We evade historical wounds, the individual pain, and the lasting effects of it all. The lynched relative; the buried son or daughter killed at the hands of the police; the millions locked away to rot in prisons; the children languishing in failed schools; the smothering, concentrated poverty passed down from generation to generation; and the indifference to lives lived in the shadows of the American dream are generally understood as exceptions to the American story, not the rule. Blasphemous facts must be banished from view by a host of public rituals and incantations. Our gaze averted, we then congratulate ourselves on how far we have come and ruthlessly blame those in the shadows for their plight in life. Gratitude is expected. Having secured our innocence, we feel no guilt in enjoying what we have earned by our own merit, in defending our right to educate our children in the best schools and in demanding that we be judged by our ability alone. To maintain this illusion, Trump has to be seen as singular, aberrant. Otherwise, he reveals something terrible about us. But not to see yourself in Trump is to continue to lie.

*I Heard It Through the Grapevine* confronts the country with its abject failure. Baldwin bears witness among the ruins and, in doing so, opens up the possibility that we might reach for another way of being in the world together. But the reality we must see is hard and coarse, like untreated white oak. We cannot shrink from the difficult work it demands of us if we are to make it beautiful.

Mikell's jazz club, the wondrous place at the corner of Ninety-seventh Street and Columbus Avenue where Baldwin and his brother David chopped it up about the past and the future in the film, no longer exists. It has been replaced by a sprawling Whole Foods supermarket. Those who lived in the suburbs are returning to cities now, and they need their shrines. Baldwin anticipated the impact of all of this in his unpublished draft initially titled "The Price of the Ticket" as he assumed the voice of white people moving back to cities:

> We are sorry . . . but we really must, for our own peace of mind, dismiss you. We refuse to be intimidated by your insistent presence, your endless demands on our integrity, your bottomless reproaches. As soon as we get you out of here, we'll fix the streets and re-build the houses and raise our children as we see fit—without you.

As white people have made their way back, we have been accused of "barbecuing while black," "moving in while black," "trying to enter our own apartments while black," "playing go-go music while black." We have been accused of being in spaces where we are obviously not wanted. In the end, Americans will have to decide whether or not this country will remain racist. To make that decision, we will have to avoid the trap of placing the burden of our national sins on the shoulders of Donald Trump. We need to look inward. Trump is us. Or better, Trump is *you*.

Our after times are indeed hard and rough, like untreated white oak. But if we aren't resigned to our fate, we *must* believe that we can still make our world beautiful. We must cling to hope, but it is a hope drenched in blood and disappointment—what W.E.B. Du Bois described as "a hope not hopeless but unhopeful." With that in mind, we have to gather ourselves to fight and to begin again.

# CHAPTER SEVEN

# Begin Again

I ARRIVED IN BIRMINGHAM EARLY WEDNESDAY MORNING ON A surprisingly cool day for Alabama in July. It was the summer of 2019, a summer of cruel immigration policies and cries of Russian collusion, and I had decided to fly to Birmingham-Shuttlesworth International Airport and drive to Montgomery to visit the new Legacy Museum and the National Memorial for Peace and Justice. The museum and memorial were the brainchild of the Equal Justice Initiative (EJI) and its founder and executive director, Bryan Stevenson, whose work on behalf of death-row inmates had long captured my attention. I admired Stevenson's dedication and his sense of moral clarity. The way he framed the need for the museum and the memorial fit perfectly with the way I read James Baldwin. "Memory is powerful, it is a powerful force in the way a society evolves," Stevenson said in his documentary *True Justice*.

We have a constitution that talks about equality, liberty, and justice for all and for decades, for centuries we tolerated enslavement of other human beings. We tolerated abuse and violence against people. We tolerated bigotry and discrimination. . . . I think there is a kind of smog in the air that's created by the history of slavery and lynching and segregation, and I don't think we're going to get healthy, I don't think we can be free . . . until we address this problem. But to get there we're going to have to be willing to tell the truth.

Stevenson understood that his work within the criminal justice system required telling a different story, one that did not begin with the lie. For him, if we are to face honestly what is happening in the country, and specifically what is happening in our criminal justice system when it comes to race, it requires that we see the connection between slavery, Jim Crow segregation, the violence of lynching, and mass incarceration. We must recognize the relationship between devaluing black people, seeing them as inherently criminal, and our willingness to cast black people aside and to lock them up in alarming numbers. Since the election of Ronald Reagan in 1980, we have witnessed a 500 percent increase in the number of people in America's prisons and jails. More than two million Americans are incarcerated, and 67 percent of that population are people of color. Our history corrupts the soul in such a way that we have stood by in relative silence as this happened.

Baldwin had a remarkably prescient view of the incarceration problem. Over the course of his life, he had experienced the brutality of American police in Harlem and saw up close the country's peculiar brand of justice. In *No Name in the Street*, he used the case of Tony Maynard, an aspiring actor whose family lived close to Baldwin's when he was young and who worked as Baldwin's personal assistant for a time, to show that the criminal justice system crushed black people with intention. In 1967, Maynard had been falsely accused of murdering a twenty-one-year-old white marine sergeant named Michael Kroll. Maynard rejected an offer of a plea bargain and was tried three times. After a hung jury and a mistrial, he was finally convicted in December of 1970 and sentenced to ten to twenty years in prison. Baldwin wrote about this period and his attempt to win Maynard's release. In the epilogue of *No Name,* Baldwin mentioned that he was still "waiting to hear the fate of Tony Maynard, whose last address was Attica." Two years after the publication of the book, in April 1974, a judge released Maynard on bail when it was revealed that prosecutors had suppressed information about a key witness. The district attorney dismissed the case altogether later that year.

Baldwin devoted a number of pages in *No Name* to describing the details of the case and recounting his efforts to exonerate Maynard. In doing so, he offered, perhaps, one of the first accounts of what would become known as carceral studies, putting into stark relief the systemic racial bias in the American criminal justice system. As Baldwin put it,

> If one really wishes to know how justice is administered in a country, one does not question the policemen, the lawyers, the judges, or the protected members of the middle class. One goes to the unprotected—those, precisely, who need the law's protection the most!—and listens to their testimony. Ask any Mexican, any Puerto Rican, any black man, any poor person—ask the wretched how they fare in the halls of justice, and then you will know, not whether or

not the country is just, but whether or not it has any love
for justice, or any concept of it. It is certain, in any case, that
ignorance, allied with power, is the most ferocious enemy
justice can have.

In the wake of the passage of the civil rights and voting rights acts,
Baldwin had seen the emergence of a different kind of law, one
that did not take aim at the value gap but rather worked to en-
shrine it. One of the Johnson administration's last major pieces of
legislation was the Omnibus Crime Control and Safe Streets Act
of 1968, which Johnson signed that June, two weeks after Robert
Kennedy was assassinated in California. Ostensibly prompted
into motion by the murder of John F. Kennedy five years earlier,
the law was nonetheless more correctly viewed as a response to
white fear over the perceived threat of black violence; it was probably not a coincidence that it was first introduced in the House in
July of 1967, less than two months after the Black Panthers occupied the state capitol in California.

The law established the Law Enforcement Assistance Administration (LEAA), which provided local police departments support in the form of weapons, surveillance, and research about
criminality—much of which targeted black communities to prevent crime and riots. The act resulted in the increased militariza-
tion of police departments, which had a direct impact on how
black communities were policed. A 1969 *New Yorker* article described the legislation as "a piece of demagoguery devised out of
malevolence and enacted in hysteria," and a harbinger of what was
to come. Black people were no longer sources of wealth to be exploited, Baldwin argued. Now they were disposable, and their
idleness posed a threat to the Republic. "Some pale, compelling
nightmare—an overwhelming collection of private nightmares—is

responsible for the irresponsible ferocity of the Omnibus Crime Control and Safe Streets Act," he wrote, as monies flowed into local police departments to deal with "riot control." Those nightmares were rooted in a host of assumptions about who and what black people are, the same assumptions that shaped the rhetoric of people like Richard Nixon and Ronald Reagan.

The problem of criminal justice in this country, Baldwin maintained, was bound up with the disastrous consequences of the lie the country told itself. And Baldwin understood that if anything substantive was to be done about it, we would finally have to tell the truth about what we had done to put all those people behind bars. Stevenson, insofar as I could see, agreed with Baldwin, and he helped build a museum and a memorial to tell the truth in order that we may *begin again*. I had to see it all for myself.


As I walked through the Birmingham airport, I couldn't help but think of Reverend Fred Shuttlesworth, the courageous minister and SCLC co-founder who led the Birmingham movement. Shuttlesworth's courage and faith were the stuff of legend. He survived beatings and stabbings and multiple assassination attempts while working to bring equality and justice to Birmingham. Images of him being viciously attacked by white racists came to mind as I collected my bags. So did the dogs and fire hoses Commissioner Bull Connor unleashed on children in Kelly Ingram Park in May 1963. I thought about the monuments to heroes like Reverend Shuttlesworth and to those heroes of the civil rights movement like Dorothy Counts in Charlotte or the Little Rock Nine in Arkansas that fill the southern landscape and are now integral parts of civil rights movement tourism. The monuments memorialized the movement and the heroism of the people. But as I walked through the airport, I couldn't square the meaning of their sacrifice with the reality of America today. I imagined Shuttlesworth confronting Donald Trump and chuckled to myself.

In *I Heard It Through the Grapevine*, Baldwin returned to Birmingham to witness the trial of J. B. Stoner, one of the men who bombed the Sixteenth Street Baptist Church in 1963 and killed those four little girls. Another one of the bombers, Bobby Cherry, had years earlier been part of a mob that attacked Shuttlesworth and his wife when they tried to enroll their children in a newly integrated Birmingham school. Shuttlesworth told Baldwin that much more could have been done if the country had held the men to account at the time of the murders. The trial was a bit too late, and the symbolism, even if justice was served, wasn't enough. "I think, first of all, it's a miscarriage of justice. Not to have tried somebody at the time. . . . It would have slowed up the climate of violence," Shuttlesworth told Baldwin as they walked down the steps of the courthouse. Leaving the airport, I thought of what Baldwin said in the film about the monument to Dr. King in Atlanta and wondered if it applied here: if these gestures, these memorials, aimed to make the past unusable, and if there was "nothing you can do with that monument." The airport was nice, though.

Montgomery was just a little over an hour and a half drive from Birmingham, a relatively straight shot south along Highway 65. I loved driving that road; it reminded me of the days I used to travel from Morehouse College in Atlanta to my hometown in Mississippi. That drive took about six hours, heading southwest along Highway 65 until it intersected with Interstate 10 just outside of Mobile. From there, I-10 would take me to the eerie beauty of the Gulf Coast and to my momma's home cooking.

Driving Highway 65 again brought back a flood of memories, but on this trip I found myself drawn to surrounding details on the way to Montgomery that I had not noticed before. I saw that if you took exit 205 and traveled east on U.S. Route 31, it would take you to Confederate Memorial Park in Marbury, Alabama, a 102-acre expanse that once housed poor or wounded Confederate war veterans. Just a few more exits down, a large Confederate battle flag towered over the highway, with a billboard next to it in bold red letters against a white background that read "Property of the Sons of the Confederacy, Alabama Division." Around exit 181 or so, near the last rest stop before Montgomery, a part of Highway 65 had been renamed the War on Terror Memorial Highway. It took me a minute to process that one. I couldn't understand what would motivate anyone to memorialize, of all things, the war on terror.

During a pit stop at the rest area right outside of Montgomery, I saw two rather old sheriffs of Winston County, Alabama, one slumped with age, his gun hanging loosely at his side like Barney Fife's on *The Andy Griffth Show*, the other sporting a bushy mustache, sandy red hair, and a classic beer belly. They escorted to the bathroom a white prisoner in handcuffs dressed not in an orange jumpsuit, but in a gray-striped prison uniform. The scene looked like something straight out of the nineteenth century or an old Little Rascals short film. I was at once amused and afraid. In moments like these, going home always felt like stepping back in time. I hurried up, used the bathroom, and got back on the highway. I didn't want to linger here.

All these evocative details of American life in the South stood between the Birmingham-Shuttlesworth International Airport and the Legacy Museum and National Memorial for Peace and Justice. As I drove Highway 65, it all passed by like snapshots, or a montage from a film. I couldn't help but wonder about the significance of renaming the Birmingham airport after a civil rights ography of the Con-

*True Justice.* "When I look around and I see the iconography of the glory of enslavement and the era of lynching, I say we're not in a very healthy place." The drive along Highway 65 gave me a sense of that, and of the scale of the task before us. Progress, in this country, is always freighted with lies. "We have lived through avalanches of tokens and concessions but white power remains white," Baldwin wrote in the introduction to *The Price of the Ticket.* "And what it appears to surrender with one hand it obsessively clutches in the other."

I arrived a bit early for my timed ticket at the Legacy Museum, so I decided to walk around Montgomery. I realized, and was a bit shocked to admit to myself, that for all those trips passing by the city on the way to and from college, I had never actually stopped to visit. I had never seen the Dexter Street Baptist Church or visited the Rosa Parks Museum. So from the museum I headed southwest along Coosa Street, winding my way past the Rosa Parks bus stop and turning down Dexter Street, which dead-ends a few blocks down at the state capitol, its white dome rising up above the low-lying surroundings. I imagined hearing George Wallace's words "segregation now, segregation tomorrow, segregation forever." I read signs that described the grandeur of the five-day Selma-to-Montgomery march in 1965 and how it ended in front of the steps of the capitol building with King narrating a

SNCC, and all o...

white clergymen and lab...

get out of our community and let Alabama return to normalcy?" But I have a message that I would like to leave
with Alabama this evening. That is exactly what we don't
want, and we will not allow it to happen. For we know that
it was normalcy in Marion that led to the brutal murder of
Jimmy Lee Jackson. It was normalcy in Birmingham that
led to the murder on Sunday morning of four beautiful,
unoffending, innocent girls. It was normalcy on Highway
80 that led state troopers to use tear gas and horses and
billy clubs against unarmed human beings who were simply marching for justice. . . . It is normalcy all over our
country which leaves the Negro perishing on a lonely island of poverty in the midst of a vast ocean of material
prosperity. . . . The only normalcy that we will settle for is
the normalcy that recognizes the dignity and worth of all
of God's children.

As I thought about Dr. King's words and about how the cry for
normalcy still rings out today, I found myself standing in front of
Dexter Street Baptist Church, a quaint and unassuming red brick
building with a classic steeple and a signature pair of symmetrical
turned staircases leading up from the street to the church's entrance. Here a young Martin King, fresh out of seminary, stepped
into history. All of those powerful and courageous black women

helped organize the Montgomery bus boycott here. It was a bit overwhelming.

Montgomery has many markers along streets and buildings, suggesting what feels like a civil rights movement trail, and as I kept coming across them, I wondered about the story they told of sacrifice and faith. I was curious as to whether other plaques and markers told of the moments of doubt, of the riots right after the bombing of the Sixteenth Street Baptist Church, or of Dr. King's often debilitating depression in the face of the country's recalcitrance. I suspect the story of a movement on the precipice of failure in 1968 that Baldwin and King talked about in Los Angeles—a story that takes seriously the after times—has little to no place in the narrative of civil rights tourism.

In old cities, it's not uncommon to find a lot of history packed into a small expanse of land, and Montgomery is no exception. The Dexter Street Baptist Church itself is built on the site of an old slave pen and sits just a block away from the house where Jefferson Davis lived and led the Confederacy during the Civil War. Three blocks south on Decatur, a marker calls out the former site of the house of Warren Reese, a Confederate colonel who later became the mayor of Montgomery and persuaded Davis to tour the South in 1886, a kind of post-Reconstruction victory lap. Dexter had just come into being then, and the fruits of Reese's mayorship would exist forever in ironic juxtaposition with the church. From Dexter's staircase, the platform from which King and generations of black preachers and parishioners would have emerged each day, one can see poking through the trees to the northeast a figure extending upward from a column next to the state capitol. This is the top of the Alabama Confederate Monument, an eighty-eight-foot-high monument to the soldiers of the South. Mayor Reese helped raise funds to erect it, and its cornerstone was laid on April 29, 1886, three years after work began a block away on the brick building that now houses Dexter. For almost the entire history of the church, then, its congregants have had to confront a white supremacist memorial on the horizon.

As I walked back toward the Legacy Museum, I saw a quotation from Maya Angelou emblazoned across the side of the building: "History, despite its wrenching pain, cannot be unlived, but if faced with courage, need not be lived again." It gave me the sense, before I had even set foot inside, that whatever this museum aspired to do, one of its aims was to disrupt a standard narrative of the country that had become a part of the civil rights movement tourist industry of the city. This wasn't a triumphalist story of redemption of a racist South by the moral courage of black people. Presumably, Stevenson and his curators wanted to linger on the memory and consequence of what Dr. King referred to during the Selma march as the normalcy of violence in the South. In a way, the subject of the museum—the violence of white America and its traumas—refused to be assimilated into that traditional story, where the courage of ordinary people and the redemption of America mattered more.

The museum building is only about eleven thousand square feet. When you enter the front door, after you pass through security, you walk into a dark area and are immediately introduced to the scale and violence of the slave trade and to Montgomery's role in it. Data, maps, and video footage cover the wall. As a result, the foot traffic stops. I had to squeeze through the groups watching the videos to walk into the space that held re-creations of slave pens. The path from the initial video leads you down a narrow, dimly lit hallway. The wall is sectioned into individual pens. People stop to look through bars that foreshadow the bars of prison cells, and to listen to holographic images that describe the horror of the slave trade and the auction block.

It becomes immediately clear that the Maya Angelou quotation had announced the museum's purpose: This is a narrative museum, and its story is one of the continuous and vicious strands of racial violence that characterize this country's history; it is what Stevenson describes as the "untold cruelty that hides in silence." Here that violence is front and center. As you move into the major part of the museum, you are introduced to a wide-ranging story that reaches from slavery to mass incarceration. The words and sounds tend to run together.

I decided to stand in the middle of the room. I wanted to see and feel what was happening on this unusually comfortable summer day in Alabama in a museum that challenged America's innocence. I saw young black students with their smartphones typing information from a table that listed the Supreme Court decisions around race. I noticed people crying as they looked at a wall full of the signage of the era of segregation. On one sign the town of Ozark, Arkansas, prided itself on not having any Negroes. I watched people watch footage of Ross Barnett, son of a Confederate soldier and the notorious governor of Mississippi from 1960 to 1964, declare his commitment to racial segregation and his pride in being a member of the white citizens' council. A young white woman pushing an elderly white woman in a wheelchair spoke loudly as they read the time line along the wall of the museum. The young woman shouted, "Brown versus Brown!" and then corrected herself. The older woman said, "I guess they had to leave and go west and north to avoid all the violence."

Two women, one black and one white, sat close to each other on a bench watching Technicolor video footage of Dr. King speaking about the legacy of slavery and segregation and how it affected black people. In the video, King questioned the demand that black people should pull themselves up by their own bootstraps. "It is a cruel jest," he said, "to say to a bootless man that he ought to lift himself by his own bootstraps." The women watched King intensely, slightly bent forward. Both were crying. The black woman, in fact, was weeping. I thought they were together because of the intimacy of their grief. But then they got up and walked their separate ways. The white woman looked at me as she passed by and said, "This is rough." The black woman simply walked away shaking her head.

One wall in the museum had shelves full of bottles of soil from the places where people were lynched. The bottles were large, at least a foot tall, and each one contained a unique shade of earth, running from deep browns to umbers to sandy tans. The distinctive colors and textures of the soil made each jar like a signature of land, with dark histories written into the composition. They revealed the geography of the violence. Names and counties were listed on the labels. A few just listed the county, when the person remained unknown. I stood beside a black woman as she looked at each bottle. She leaned back onto the heels of her feet to look at the bottom shelf, as if she was searching for something or someone—perhaps the soil of the place where she lived, or where someone she loved lived—on the wall.

The museum's story isn't necessarily a linear story, at least not in the organization of the space. One can wander about. Once you move away from the wall telling the story from slavery to mass incarceration, there is no attempt to suggest how you take in the details of the four eras of slavery, segregation, lynching, and mass incarceration that make up the museum. Sounds and sights bleed from one exhibit section into the next, and if you stand in the center of this small museum, as I did, you can hear the voices of King and Barnett, the sounds of freedom songs and the screams of people being overrun by the police in Selma. You can hear people taking in the violence of it all with deep sighs and hushed groans. It is the cacophonous song of America.

As I stood and listened, I thought of Baldwin's view of American history. The past is not past; "history is literally *present* in all we do," he wrote in "The White Man's Guilt." People carried that history with them as they moved about the museum—as they saw the relationship between slavery, Jim Crow, and mass incarceration. Perhaps more to the point, I got the sense that what was happening as people confronted the violence was an attempt to give voice to the trauma at the heart of the American experience— not just an attempt to depict the scars and bruises endured by black people, but to show what that violence had done to the soul of white Americans. Confronting the trauma and giving it language offered an occasion for those in the museum to confront what our history has made of all of us, shorn of any preordained American story of a more perfect union or the burden of black suffering as the basis of white salvation. There were no happy endings here. No feel-good stories or catharsis of overcoming. Looking unflinchingly at what we've done was enough.

The National Memorial for Peace and Justice (often called the Lynching Memorial), the other half of EJI's Montgomery project, is a little less than a mile south of the museum. A shuttle bus ferries visitors between the two, and once my bus had pulled out, our driver began an impromptu guided tour. He showed us where ground had recently been broken for a new memorial to Rosa Parks at Court Square Plaza and pointed out an elegant fountain on the site where a slave auction block once stood. He mentioned where the Selma to Montgomery march ended, pointed out the state capitol, and asked if we could imagine George Wallace on the steps shouting "segregation now, segregation forever," as I had done not hours before. We all had just stepped out of a museum that eschewed the traditional focus of the civil rights story, but now it suddenly felt as though that story had snapped back into place.

When we got off the bus, though, I had a different sensory experience. We had moved from the cramped space of the museum, where words guided our eyes and thoughts, to the six-acre open space of a memorial to the lynched black body. Nestled between Caroline Street and Holcombe Street, overlooking the state capitol and just down the road from the Alabama State Board of Pardons and Paroles, was a monument to our dead and to the countrymen who killed them. I looked up a beautifully landscaped hill and saw the elegant symmetry of the memorial against a backdrop of a clear blue sky. The architects had been inspired by the Holocaust Memorial in Berlin and the Apartheid Museum in Johannesburg. With sculpture, art, and design, they had aimed to build a place to heal. It felt like sacred space.

As I walked into the memorial, I saw walls featuring text blocks that told the story of the violence, but no one lingered as they did in the museum. The words weren't the story here. Instead, my eyes turned to the *Nkyinkyim Installation* by Ghanaian artist Kwame Akoto-Bamfo, a haunting sculptural representation of slaves chained together in agony, defiance, and unimaginable grief. The sculpture stands on the side of the path that leads you up an ascending walkway to the monument, the physical structures that commemorate the dead. With each step you make your way up the hill. Before you reach the memorial, you can see lined up across the lawn duplicate monuments that can be claimed by the individual counties where the lynchings occurred. It looked like a prairie full of rusted, brown coffins.

Eight hundred monuments, which look like vertical headstones made of corten steel, sit at eye level, and as I walked I could read each county and count the number of dead. Some had one or two or three people listed. Others had many more. I started taking photos of those counties that had more than ten lynchings, imagining these places as haunted by ghosts. Had anyone in any of these counties acknowledged the carnage? Had anyone atoned? I kept taking photos, but it became too much. I had to stop. I was overwhelmed with grief.

As I kept walking, the floor slanted downward, but the monuments remained level. Before long their bottoms were above my head. As I looked up at them, it was as if I were witnessing bodies swaying from poplar trees—except these were stiff. "Black bodies swinging in the southern breeze," Billie Holiday sang in *Strange Fruit*. In contrast to my experience in the Legacy Museum, where the space was crowded and the experience could take on a nearly communal feel, as I moved through the memorial I wasn't fully aware of others around me. This was a solitary experience. On the walls were descriptions of some of the reasons for the lynchings. One man was murdered for having a photo of a white woman in his hat; another had been falsely accused of peeping at a white woman through a peephole; another refused to buy seed from a white man. An entire wall, black and shimmering, which stretched the length of the side of the memorial, was also a wall of tears, with water streaming for the dead memorialized here. Underneath the water, etched into the wall, were these words: "Thousands of

African Americans are unknown victims of racial terror lynchings whose deaths cannot be documented, many whose names will never be known. They are honored here."

The experience was only intensified when I saw the monument of Jackson County, Mississippi, the place where I was born and raised. Eight people had been lynched there. Throughout my childhood, I never heard that such a horrendous thing had happened, never mind happened eight times, anywhere near my home. I knew none of the names. Staring at the monument, I understood a bit better my dad's claim that he doesn't "do white people." Why would he? As the jars of dirt at the museum had made plain, the places we live are often, though not always, landscapes layered with the violence of generations. It is in the soil that nurtures us even when we can't see it on the surface.

The German philosopher Friedrich Nietzsche wrote that in order for human beings to live full lives we must cultivate our ability to forget. "It is possible to live with almost no memory," he said, "but without forgetting, it is quite impossible to live at all." He was referring to history. But the National Memorial for Peace and Justice represents a *traumatic* history, and it isn't easily forgotten, if at all. Our bodies carry the traumas forward. The history of racial trauma lives on and moves us about in ways we often don't realize. It grounds our fears and, whether we know it or not, it affects our dreams. In places all over the South and the country, the legacy of this terror and trauma continues to haunt. The memorial confronts the trauma directly and offers us, in its own way, a chance to begin again. Stevenson put it this way,

> I want there to be repair in this country not just for communities of color that have been victimized by bigotry and discrimination, I want it to be for all of us. I don't think we

can get free until we are willing to tell the truth about our history. I do believe in truth and reconciliation. I just think that truth and reconciliation are sequential: That you can't have reconciliation without the truth.

Fundamentally, Stevenson and the Equal Justice Initiative have built a museum and memorial in the heart of the Confederacy that not only bear witness but tell a history that provides a foundation for the even harder work we still must do. Their story counters the lies on offer in the surrounding city; it both rebukes the still-standing Confederate monuments, with their explicit claims to superiority by white people, and at the same time counters the triumphalist narrative of the civil rights movement stamped into markers on every corner. Taken as a whole, the project can be seen as part of the work Baldwin called for in the after times. In its depiction of the tenacity of the lie and the brutality of its consequences, and in its unsparing look at how terror and violence have undone us all, the museum and memorial perform the work that establishes the precondition for a new way of imagining America.

Of course, there are no guarantees. Just down the road a bit, a large Confederate flag still towered over Highway 65 as I drove back to Birmingham.

I have taken the title of this book from a passage in James Baldwin's last novel, *Just Above My Head*. In light of the collapse of the civil rights movement and the consolidation of the after times with the election of Ronald Reagan, Baldwin offered these words for those who desperately sought to imagine a way forward: "Not everything is lost. Responsibility cannot be lost, it can only be abdicated. If one refuses abdication, one begins again." *Begin again* is shorthand for something Baldwin commended to the country in the latter part of his career: that we reexamine the fundamental values and commitments that shape our self-understanding, and that we look back to those beginnings not to reaffirm our greatness or to double down on myths that secure our innocence, but to see where we went wrong and how we might reimagine or recreate ourselves in light of who we initially set out to be. This requires an unflinching encounter with the lie at the heart of our history, the kind of encounter that cannot be avoided at places like the Legacy Museum.

Irony abounds. The National Memorial for Peace and Justice opened in 2018, in the middle of Donald Trump's first term. As I have argued, Trump's election represents *our* after times; all that he stands for reasserts the lie in the face of demographic shifts and political change represented by Obama's election and the activism of Black Lives Matter. Every day Trump insists on the belief that white people matter more than others in this country. He has tossed aside any pretense of a commitment to a multiracial democracy. He has attacked congressmen and women of color, even telling four congresswomen "to go back to the countries they came from"; scapegoated people seeking a better life at our borders; and appealed explicitly to white resentment. On top of the racist rhetoric, his judicial appointments and his policies around voting rights, healthcare, environmental regulations, immigration law, and education disproportionately harm communities of color. In every way imaginable, Trump has intensified the cold civil war that engulfs the country.

But to view Trump in the light of the lynching memorial in Alabama is to understand him in the grand sweep of American history: He and his ideas are not exceptional. He and the people who support him are just the latest examples of the country's ongoing betrayal, our version of "the apostles of forgetfulness." When we make Trump exceptional, we let ourselves off the hook, for he is *us* just as surely as the slave-owning Founding Fathers were us; as surely as Lincoln, with his talk of sending black people to Liberia, was us; as surely as Reagan was us, with his welfare queens. When we are surprised to see the reemergence of Klansmen, neo-Nazis, and other white nationalists, we reveal our willful ignorance about how our own choices make them possible. The memorial confronts both Trumpism and those who would never imagine themselves in sympathy with it, with the truth and trauma of American history. It exposes the lie for what it is and makes plain our collective complicity in reinforcing it.

In his introduction to his 1985 collection of essays, *The Price of the Ticket*, Baldwin noted that America had become quick to congratulate itself on the progress it had made with regards to race, and that the country's self-congratulation came with the expectation of black gratitude. (This was particularly the case with the election of the country's first black president.) As Baldwin wrote, "People who have opted to be white congratulate themselves on their generous ability to return to the slave that freedom which they never had any right to endanger, much less take away. For this dubious effort . . . they congratulate themselves and expect to be congratulated." The expectation was that he should feel "gratitude not only that my burden is . . . being made lighter but my joy that white people are improving."

Baldwin viewed this demand for gratitude from the vantage point of someone who had lived through and was deeply wounded by the betrayal of the black freedom movement, someone whose recollection or remembrance of that moment involved trauma. In

1979, on the eve of the election of Ronald Reagan, for example, in a short piece for *Freedomways,* Baldwin wrote of the difficulty of recalling the past. "Let us say that we all live through more than we can say or see. A life, in retrospect, can seem like the torrent of water opening or closing over one's head and, in retrospect, is blurred, swift, kaleidoscopic like that. One does not wish to remember—one is perhaps not *able* to remember—the holding of one's breath under water, the miracle of rising up far enough to breathe, and then, the going under again. . . ." Here Baldwin captures beautifully the cycles of the after times that illustrate how horrific the white expectation of gratitude is.

Baldwin believed the after times required that we look back in order to understand the choices we've made that have brought us to the moment of crisis. We don't begin again as if there is nothing behind us or underneath our feet. We carry that history with us. In the introduction to *The Price of the Ticket,* Baldwin formulated his point about beginning again a bit differently. "In the church I come from," he wrote, "we were counselled, from time to time, to do our first works over." Here Baldwin invokes Revelations 2:5: "Consider how far you have fallen! Repent and do the things you did at first. If you do not repent, I will come to you and remove your lampstand from its place." In the mode of poet-prophet, Baldwin called the nation, in his after times, to confront the lie of its own self-understanding and to get about the work of building a country truly based on democratic principles. As he wrote:

> To do your first works over means to reexamine everything. Go back to where you started, or as far back as you can, examine all of it, travel your road again and tell the truth about it. Sing or shout or testify or keep it to yourself: but know whence you came.

White America in the generality, he argued, refused to do such a thing because the exploration itself would reveal that the price of the ticket to be here in the United States was in fact to leave behind the particulars of Europe and become white. That transformation "choked many a human being to death," because to become white meant the subjugation of others, an act that disfigured the soul by closing off the ability to see oneself in others, and to see them in onself. Our task, Baldwin maintained, was to understand the history of how that disfiguring of the soul happened and, in doing so, to free oneself and the country from the insidious hold of whiteness in order to become a different kind of creation— a different way of being in the world.

The call to "do your first works over" is a distinctive feature of Baldwin's later work, one that emerged only as he reckoned with the after times. Earlier in his career, for example, during a 1960 speech at Kalamazoo College, when he took up the question of the early beginnings of the country, he did not invoke Revelations or the phrase "begin again." He told the story of early America as a melting pot of sorts, with racial hierarchies that enable a certain definition of white America over and against black people; for "the Negro tells us where the bottom is: because he is there, and where he is, beneath us, we know where the limits are and how far we must not fall." Even so, we, black and white, Baldwin believed, remained inextricably linked ("bound together forever") with love, and together, we would bring forth a new majority. This is the tone of Baldwin before the murders of Medgar, Malcolm, and Martin, before the ascent of Black Power and the election of Ronald Reagan. This isn't the tone of a critic of the after times.

Later, Baldwin came to see the early history of America as the site of our Fall. In February 1969, Baldwin wrote in *The New York Times,*

For the sake of one's sanity, one simply ceases trying to make them hear. If they think that things are more important than people—and they do—well, let them think so. Let them be destroyed by their things. If they think I was happy being a slave and am now redeemed by having become—and on their terms, as they think—the equal of my overseers, well, let them think so. If they think I am flattered by their generosity in allowing me to become a sharecropper in a system which I know to be criminal—and which is placed squarely on the backs of nonwhite people all over the world—well, let them think so. Let the dead bury their dead.

The concern here is not with the intimate bonds between black and white. In the after times, Baldwin concerned himself with imagining what was necessary for a different understanding of who we are and, by extension, a broader concern for creating the conditions for a new beginning for the country. A New Jerusalem was still on his mind, and those who opted to be white would either leave their idols behind or be left behind.

By 1985, Jimmy had little patience with the residual traces of white America's willful ignorance. Instead, the phrases "begin again" and "do your first works over" reflect a more serious encounter with the past that we carry with us as the grounds for a radical reimagining of the country. "When I speak of doing one's first works over," he wrote in his last book, *The Evidence of Things Not Seen*, "I am referring to the movement of the human soul, in crisis, which, then, is forced to reexamine the depths from which it comes in order to strike water from the rock of the inheritance." We had to understand the beginnings of the lie and its effects— that would release us into a different and more genuine way of living. It would also be an indication of our maturity as a nation; we would look back on the life of the country, just as we might look back and assess our youth, and learn the lessons of our journey as we step into a new phase of living. We would put the childish things behind us.

Eleven months before his death from cancer, Baldwin appeared at the National Press Club. He seemed exhausted and frail, and coughed as he stepped to the podium. In fact, he coughed throughout the hour. Baldwin offered a sweeping history of how we arrived at that moment in 1986 with what he devilishly called "a post-adolescent who is almost eighty years old" in the White House. He offered what he thought of as "the view from here," a narrative of the choices and experiences that brought us to the then-current crisis. Close readers of Baldwin would have heard before many of the themes of his talk. In some ways, the speech illustrated what Jimmy told Quincy Troupe a month before he died, "You're a running motor and you're repeating, you're repeating, you're repeating . . ." He spoke about America's aversion to history and how the stories the country told itself about its past corrupted any genuine understanding of the present. "In the effort to deny from whence we came," Baldwin declared, "we've had to make up a series of myths about it."

Baldwin ended his talk with a powerful admonition, a preface as it were to a last will and testament:

> We are living in a world in which everybody and everything is interdependent. It is not white, this world. It is not black either. The future of this world depends on everyone in this room. And that future depends on to what extent and by what means we liberate ourselves from a vocabulary which now cannot bear the weight of reality.

Liberation from the languages and categories that box us in requires that we tap the source of it all, free ourselves of the lie, and start this whole damn thing over.

We, too, have to go back to our first works. Doing so will involve much of what Baldwin called for, and will entail an honest reckoning with what the Age of Reagan has wrought. Jimmy was there at its beginning and warned us; we have lived in its shadow. Obviously, an important step in these after times, as it was in Baldwin's, is to tell a story of our trauma. What is happening today isn't unprecedented; it's just uniquely of *our* times. We have to understand our own anger and disappointments and figure out for ourselves how to pick up the pieces, to hold off the temptations of hate and despair, and to fight the battle once again.

Baldwin offers us resources. He struggled mightily after the murder of Dr. King. He admitted that he went to pieces. Twelve years later, he watched the country elect Reagan, a clear indication, if there ever was one, that white America had no intention of changing when it came to matters of race. Less than a month before Jimmy took his last breath, he said that Reagan represented "the justification of . . . being white." Of the choices that led to Reagan's election and caused so much pain, he had little sympathy to offer. "I don't care who says what," he said. "I watched it happen. And all this, because they want to be white. And why do they want to be white? Because it's the only way to justify the slaughter . . . —they're trapped." Until the end, Jimmy never stopped being a disturber of the peace.

Beginning again or doing one's first works over involves concrete efforts and stories to bring into reality a new America. I mentioned in the introduction that we have previously reached in our history two critical moments of moral reckoning where we faced the daunting challenge of beginning again; both times we failed. The first was during the Civil War and Reconstruction and the second was the black freedom struggle of the mid-twentieth century. These moments are connected insofar as the black freedom struggle, what scholars call the Second Reconstruction, sought, among other things, to complete what was left of what the historian Eric Foner describes as the unfinished revolution.

In this framework, we can think of the Civil War and Reconstruction as constituting a second founding of the country—a moment when the fabric of the country was woven anew after fraying almost beyond its ability to hold. Reconstruction led to the formation of the modern U.S. nation-state. With expanded federal power, the passage of the Civil Rights Act of 1866 and the Civil War amendments—the Thirteenth, Fourteenth, and Fifteenth—Congress, led in many respects by House Ways and Means chairman and radical abolitionist Thaddeus Stevens, put forward an idea of citizenship untethered to the issue of race. Almost immediately forces sought to undermine the promise of the second founding, but the point here is that Stevens and others sought to radically transform the country's understanding of itself as they grappled with the very question of equality, the right to vote, and the role of government in protecting the rights of all of its citizens.

On one level, what Stevens and others did was exactly what Baldwin calls us to do: They went back to where we started. They understood that the three-fifths clause and the fugitive slave clause had tilted the balance of power to the slaveholding states; that the Constitution did not live up to the Declaration of Independence's promise of equality; that the actions of states and of the courts consolidated a view of black people that mandated their inferior place in American society. With the Civil War amendments, they aimed to begin again. But the country, just as it did with the Second Reconstruction, turned its back.

Now we find ourselves facing a moral reckoning of the same magnitude. We should have learned the lesson by now that changing laws or putting our faith in politicians to do the right thing are not enough. *We* have to rid ourselves, once and for all, of this belief that white people matter more than others, or we're doomed to repeat the cycles of our ugly history over and over again. George Santayana, the Spanish-born American philosopher, was right to point out that "those who cannot remember the past are condemned to repeat it." But what he didn't say is that those who willfully refuse to remember become moral monsters.

What we need is a third American founding, to begin again without this insidious idea of the value gap that continues to get in the way of a New America. We need an America where "becoming white" is no longer the price of the ticket. Instead, we should set out to imagine the country in the full light of its diversity and with an honest recognition of our sins. As the Lynching Memorial seeks to do, we have to confront our national trauma honestly if we are to shake loose from the political frame of Reaganism and Trumpism with its racial dog whistles and foghorns, its greed and selfishness, and its idealized version of America as the shining city on the hill, where the country's sins are transformed into examples of its inherent goodness. This will demand of us a new American story, different symbols, and robust policies to repair what we have done. I don't yet know what this will look like in its details—and my understanding of our history suggests that we will probably fail trying—but I do know that each element is important to any effort toward beginning again. And as Samuel Beckett wrote in his 1983 novella *Worstward Ho,* "Try again. Fail again. Fail better."

A new story doesn't mean that we discard all of the elements of the old story, nor does it mean that we dwell only on our sins. Instead, we narrate our national beginnings in light of our contradictions *and* our aspirations. Innocence is left aside. But who we aspire to be, without the safety of the lie, should always organize the stories we tell ourselves about who we are. I say this because our stories carry moral weight. Who and what we choose to exclude exposes the limits of our ideas of justice. Our stories can make some people the center of the plot and make of others latecomers and objects of charity and goodwill or of scorn and derision. Ours should be a story that begins with those who sought to make real the promise of this democracy. Put aside the fairy tale of America as "the shining city on the hill" or "the redeemer nation," and recast the idea of perfecting the Union not as a guarantee of our goodness but a declaration of the ongoing work to address injustice in our midst.

In 2019, Nikole Hannah-Jones and *The New York Times Magazine* launched the 1619 Project. They set out to tell a different story of the country by focusing on Jamestown instead of Plymouth Rock. As they did so, the messiness of our national beginnings came into clearer view. Slavery became a central part of the story, as did our relationship with the land and with Native peoples, and the complicated pursuit of profits is seen as interwoven into the very texture of what would become the country. Here neat perfectionist tales are cast to the wind, and out of that complex history we weave a consensus story that binds us one to the other because we no longer have at the center of our national imagination the value gap—the belief that has distorted and deformed our democracy from the beginning. With a different story, our national greatness will not reflect some grand lie that hides our evils and protects us from shame but will be a consequence of our acknowledgment of what we have done and the ongoing work to be better.

But this story requires a different symbolic landscape. In moments of profound national transition, the symbols of the old order have to be removed. In our case, the statues of the Confederacy have to be torn down and some placed in museums. They do not represent who we are and who we aspire to be. Our built environment should reflect the brilliant diversity of the people that make up this country. We are a mosaic of people, and our symbols should reflect that. But the shift in our symbolic landscape goes beyond statues. The value gap is experienced and lived as we move about in this country. It is evident in the very spatial organization of towns, villages, and cities in this country. The monuments of ghettos, housing projects, and highways that cut off and isolate communities all reflect an age shaped by the lie. We have to build a different America.

All of this—the stories and the symbols—presuppose the importance of policies. For generations, we have lived according to the lie, and it has had tangible, material consequences for the lives of so many Americans. We have to begin a serious conversation about what form and shape repair will take. That can start with something really basic: passing H.R. 40, which establishes a commission "to study and consider a national apology and proposal for reparations for the institution of slavery, its subsequent de jure and de facto racial and economic discrimination against African-Americans, and the impact of these forces on living African-Americans, to make recommendations to the Congress on appropriate remedies, and for other purposes." In a way, such a panel could function as our truth and reconciliation commission. We could finally get out in the open all of that gunk that mildews in our national cellar. Hearings in open sessions, town hall meetings across the country, an organized effort to tell a different story about who we are (something like a national civics week to tell our story), and the scholarly study of the policy impacts of repair would position the country to take that bold step toward beginning anew. Then we must take bold steps to change how we live and govern: What is clear to me is that we have to end, no matter the costs, the policies that breathe life into the lie.

This third American founding must happen in the context of a political transformation. It must involve a complete rejection of the way we have conducted politics up to now. Otherwise, we will succumb to the temptation of safety and find ourselves trapped once again. It is worrisome that there is deep sentiment in some quarters of this country for nothing more than a return to American life before Trump. I find this feeling dangerous, because often it is not merely a response to the damage that Trump has wrought on the country—and on the American psyche—but also more subtly a reaction to all the long-standing and difficult questions Trump's presidency has brought into view. The way he treats black people prompts open discussion of the way black people are treated in America generally; it makes the painful confrontation with the value gap unavoidable. The horror he visits on immigrants at the border necessitates a broader conversation on the role of immigrants in American life. Trump makes it impossible to turn away. And for as many people who find his conduct abhorrent, there may be just as many who simply do not want to experience daily reminders of suffering and injustice. It explains the seductive appeal of Democrats whose sole promise is to steer toward calmer waters.

Trumpism presents us with a choice. We can either double down on the lie and reelect him or find comfort in reaching back to an idea of normalcy and elect someone "safe," or we can decide to untether our politics from the insidious assumptions of race that have guided our choices for generations. If we now choose Trump or choose to be safe, we should prepare ourselves for even darker days ahead. But if we decide to be otherwise, as difficult as that may be, we will finally make possible the birth of a new America.

Baldwin did not call for a third American founding. Instead, he worked tirelessly for what he called the New Jerusalem. To my mind, there is little difference between the two. Both call for a world and a society that reflect the value that all human life, no matter the color of your skin, your zip code, your gender, or who you love, is sacred. In his after times, Jimmy understood that something new was desperately trying to be born, but the old ghosts had the baby by the throat. He wrote in the epilogue to *No Name in the Street:* "An old world is dying, and a new one, kicking in the belly of its mother, time, announces that it is ready to be born. This birth will not be easy, and many of us are doomed to discover that we are exceedingly clumsy midwives. No matter, so long as we accept that our responsibility is to the newborn: the acceptance of responsibility contains the key." That was 1972. The labor has been long and hard, and the new world has yet to be born. We are now in our after times, but responsibility has not been lost. Whatever happens next will be up to us.

# A New America

On the day the National Memorial for Peace and Justice and the Legacy Museum first opened its doors, the editorial board of the *Montgomery Advertiser,* a newspaper founded in 1829 as *The Planter's Gazette,* published an op-ed entitled "Our Shame: The Sins of Our Past Laid Bare for All to See." The op-ed was a stunning mea culpa rarely seen in this country and especially in the South. The board apologized for the newspaper's "shameful place in the history of these dastardly, murderous deeds," acknowledged its role in perpetuating the lie that dehumanized African Americans, and pushed back against some of its readers who "wish we would leave the past in the past."

Part of our responsibility as the press is to explore who we are, how we live together and analyze what impacts us. We are supposed to hold people accountable for their wrongs, and not with a wink and a nod. We went along with the

19th and early 20th century lies that African Americans were inferior. We propagated a worldview rooted in racism and the sickening myth of racial superiority.

With an extraordinary clarity about the moral role of the press, the editorial board of the *Advertiser* did exactly what the Legacy museum called for: They admitted the paper's complicity in the wrongs and stated a commitment that "we must never be as wrong as this again." This wonderful first step must now be joined by an effort to call attention to the effects of the lies on the actual lives of black people in Montgomery, Alabama, today, to challenge the symbols of the Confederacy that dot the landscape of the city, and to advocate for policies at the local and state level that will help remedy the historic wrongs.

First steps are always important. We have to exhibit the courage and the willingness to take the risk and step out on faith with the hope that our rocky start will give way to more confident strides. The country needs to take such a step. We stand at a critical crossroads with the lie of the American idea in full view. Our after times confront us with a choice, and a decision has to be made. We cannot stand pat where we currently are, or the political superstorms will tear us apart. Either America will turn its back and embrace the value gap as Trumpism demands, or we will risk everything, finally, to become a truly multiracial democracy and the first of its kind in the West. In the past, white America has chosen the safety of its illusions. No matter. We go on, together.

This was one of the lessons I learned digging through the rubble Baldwin left behind. We don't have to save *white* people. We just have to keep working to build a better world where the color of one's skin matters little in the quality of life one chooses to live. Baldwin's words can sound harsh, as if he is throwing away millions of Americans and declaring them irrelevant to the life and future of our democracy. It's easy to read him that way, and sometimes, when his rage boils, he might actually mean it. But, in the end, he wanted us to see that whiteness as an identity was a moral choice, an attitude toward the world based on ugly things. People can, if they want to, choose to be better. We need only build a world where that choice can be made with relative ease.

If we, and I mean *all of us* who are committed to a new America, organize and fight with every ounce of energy we have to found an America free from the categories that bind our feet, implement policies that remedy generations-old injustices, and demonstrate in our living and political arrangements the value that every human being is sacred, we can build a New Jerusalem where the value gap cannot breathe.

This requires an imaginative leap beyond the limits of our present lives. We cannot let the current political moment strangle our imaginations. We hear politicians and pundits recoiling from bold visions: "No big ideas about healthcare; no revolutionary ideas about education or about a living wage for workers." They say: "Don't press the issue of white supremacy. You'll alienate white voters. Don't overreach." Safety, for them, is found in the comforts of the familiar, in an incremental approach to our problems. But our after times require big ideas and bold visions, or we will find ourselves stuck right where we are. Our history tells us as much because we have been stuck here before.

I have spent a career as a scholar of African American religion. My first book sought to explain how enslaved black people in this country used the Exodus story to imagine their freedom and to imagine themselves differently. Nothing about their condition as slaves would suggest to them that they could be anything other than slaves. The system was brutal and thorough in its dehumanization. Despite all of this, the enslaved found a way to see beyond the brutality of slavery. They found a way in the love seen in the eyes of someone who held their heart or in the fleeting smile of their beautiful child. Some found in Christianity a language to imagine themselves as children of God, beholden to the Master in Heaven. They broke free from the world as it was, because *they imagined the world as it could be*. If the enslaved gave over that power to white masters, especially the power to imagine and to love, black people would not have survived this place. There is a lesson here, and Baldwin understood it clearly.

Even in the darkest moments in his life and in that of the country, Jimmy always believed we could be better than what we are. He also understood that the battle to choose life was fought every day, and imagination was one of his most potent weapons. But he had to fight for that insight. Fight against the country's repeated betrayals. Fight his own rage and sense of despair. And fight for generations yet unborn. It made for a lonely life, but the fight was his choice.

The image on the cover of this book comes from Sedat Pakay's short film *From Another Place*. It captures Baldwin's loneliness. His eyes look distant, as if he sees something we do not, and his face reveals a level of concentration that makes him feel at once distant and present as he puzzles over what to say about what he sees. In the film, Baldwin actually sits next to two men dressed in suits and ties (what Pakay called penguin suits) at a teahouse in Bebek, Istanbul, in 1970. They sip tea and are surrounded by a group of men and boys staring at Baldwin and the camera. As the camera zooms in for a close-up of his face, Baldwin winks and smiles a coquettish smile at one of the men staring at him. His voice is heard over the visual: "I am generally very alone . . . I've got a lot on my mind. Not exactly alone. But not really present."

That sense of loneliness was necessary for his work, especially for his writing about America. Over a lifetime, Jimmy left us with a road map to travel toward a better country, a better world. When you read him, no matter the intensity of his anger, he keeps you from free-falling into despair in the face of the country's betrayals (even as he struggles with despair). He holds off the conclusion that you should throw your hands up in defeat and accept the world as it is. Baldwin didn't stick his head in the sand. Hope isn't found there, only our peril. Instead, he ran toward the trouble— the terror and fear—because he understood that facing it honestly was our only possible path to salvation. "If you're scared to death, walk *toward* it," he said.

Americans must walk through the ruins, toward the terror and fear, and lay bare the trauma that we all carry with us. So much of American culture and politics today is bound up with the banal fact of racism in our daily lives and our willful refusal to acknowledge who benefits and suffers from it. Underneath it all is the lie that corrupts American life. It corrupts how we imagine governance; how we think about our private lives (constraining even who we can love); and how we imagine community and the broader public good. It even tells us which voters matter. The lie is the lifeblood of Trumpism. Anything that does not corroborate its reality is dismissed as "fake news." Anyone who doesn't fit the view of America as a white nation or refuses to submit to it is cast as a traitor or as someone who hates America.

As we confront this latest iteration of the lie, we cannot hide in the comfort of an easy identity politics or revel in the self-righteousness of a moralism that announces our inherent goodness and the obvious evil of our opponents. This is too simplistic a moral picture. We should all remember that we are at once miracles *and* disasters. Demonizing others isn't the point. Failing to realize this springs the trap again. Baldwin wants us to imagine ourselves without need for enemies. He wants us to be *a new creation,* a reflection of a new America.

This place, as I imagine it, would be a country where black children are not born in exile, where they don't have to endure a thousand cuts and slashes that wound their spirits and require their parents to engage in daily triage to protect their souls. A new America, no longer tethered to the value gap, would make it possible for millions of black people like myself to finally feel at home without the concern that the nation's contradictions might very well drive us mad. That unsettling feeling of being "in but not of" this country would be no more. Everyone could rest for a while, because we would no longer need the lie to hide our sins. This is the America I imagine coming into being. This is the idea of America that Trumpism has by the throat. What we decide to do in our after times will shape another generation. The choice is that momentous. I pray we don't choose safety, again.

I likened Jimmy's writings after 1963 to John Coltrane's "Pursuance" on his classic album *A Love Supreme,* where Coltrane takes the same notes and, using a different tonal framework, frantically pursues enlightenment. Even when he sounds most dissonant, one gets the feeling that he is playing the same song. Baldwin reads like that. Even when his rage overwhelms, one gets the sense that he is shouting the same thing. Repeating himself. Repeating himself. But the last section of *A Love Supreme,* "Psalms," is the moment when Coltrane's pilgrim revels in the presence of the Divine and offers a "wordless recitation" of the poem "A Love Supreme," printed in the liner notes on the album. It is, at once, a beautiful and moving ode to the love of God.

Reading Jimmy until the end leads one to his understanding of the power of love. No matter how vague his invocation of love may be, love remains the one force that transcends the differences that get in the way of our genuinely living together. In one of his last essays, "To Crush a Serpent," published in *Playboy* magazine in January 1987, he recounts his journey with and through religion and, along the way, casts aside the hypocrisy of white evangelicals like the Moral Majority, who had thrown their moral weight behind Reagan. Jimmy offers an understanding of salvation that reads like his "Psalms," his poem to love. "Salvation is not flight from the wrath of God," he declares, "it is accepting and reciprocating the love of God. Salvation is not separation. It is the beginning of union with all that is or has been or will ever be." Love opens up the rusted lid of the heart.

> There is absolutely no salvation without love: this is the wheel in the middle of the wheel. Salvation does not divide. Salvation connects. . . . It is not the exclusive property of any dogma, creed, or church. It keeps the channel open between oneself and however one wishes to name That which is greater than oneself. It has nothing to do with one's fortunes or one's circumstances in one's passage through this world. It is a mighty fortress, even in the teeth of ruin or at the gates of death.

In the end, we cannot hide from each other. When we imprison our fellows in categories that cut off their humanity from our own, we end up imprisoning ourselves. We can't hide behind the mask either. We have to run toward the trouble that makes us afraid of life. We have to choose life, Baldwin repeatedly said. Salvation is found there: in accepting the beauty and ugliness of who we are in our most vulnerable moments in communion with each other. There, in love, a profound mutuality develops and becomes the basis for genuine democratic community where we all can flourish, if we so choose. This was his prayer, and it is my own.

On a hot summer day in June, I decided to visit Jimmy's grave site at Ferncliff Cemetery in Hartsdale, New York. Carole Weinstein, who became a cherished friend over the course of my work on this book, agreed to drive me there. She knew the grave site, and it would make things much easier—at least that's what we thought. The grave is located in the Hillcrest A section of this sprawling graveyard. Headstones and flowers lined up one after the other. Sections were named like gated neighborhoods. Elegant buildings housed the remains of loved ones. I stood on a hill and saw the dead everywhere, like droves of people in New York City but buried underground.

Carole remembered particular landmarks, and we found the Hillcrest section. We saw Hillcrest Garden and Hillcrest Terrace. We walked past Willow and Knollwood. We kept walking back and forth, but we couldn't find Jimmy. Carole went to one side. I chose another. As I walked I thought about how writing this book has changed me. My eyes aren't as bright. I am a bit grayer. I feel a bit wiser, like I have gone through a gauntlet and made it to the other side. I thought about my dad: how it feels when I tell him "I love you" and the joy of hearing him say "I love you too." Some wounds and scars heal. I once jokingly told a colleague that every time I worked on the book, I found myself with a glass of Jameson in hand, desperately trying to hold everything together. Reading Baldwin's writings in this moment demanded a level of honesty *in me* that threatened to crack the foundation of the world I had created. The very thing I feared about him in graduate school, I experienced as a fifty-plus-year-old man. He exposes your private lies and forces you, because of his own relentless commitment to the examined life, to confront your deepest wounds as a precondition for saying anything about the world. As I walked up and down the cemetery, I chuckled as I thought to myself that my refuge from the betrayal of the country and the craziness of Donald Trump was the storm of Jimmy's life. Made sense to me.

As I laughed, I noticed an Asian man and woman standing over several grave sites. He was dressed in khaki pants and a casual floral-print shirt that hung down over his waist; she wore something more solemn. She cleaned the plots and replaced the flowers. He stared. I nodded hello and kept looking for Jimmy's grave. He came over and asked if we needed help, and tried to sell me his plots.

Carole said we should drive over to the main office of the cemetery and ask for help finding Jimmy. She murmured that she was getting old and apologized for not remembering. I noticed two people standing beside a parked car on the side of the road, a mother and daughter perhaps. The older woman's face was swollen from crying. The daughter stared. She wasn't looking at anything in particular; it was a stare of grief like the look on Fannie Lee Chaney's face. I hadn't thought to bring Jimmy flowers or a gift. Maybe I should have brought potted lilies or a few roses to add to what was there. How could I come to him empty-handed? I wasn't even sure what I would say or think when, or if, I found the grave. We drove off.

A group of young men stood along a certain section of the cemetery facing one of the mausoleums. The men were black, white, and Latino. I didn't know if they worked there or were just hanging out. I asked Carole to stop, and I rolled down the window. The strong smell of marijuana wafted through the window. I asked if they knew where Jimmy's grave was. A young black man turned to me, his eyes glazed over. He said he didn't know where Baldwin's grave was. "But maybe he's buried near Malcolm X," he offered. "I know where Malcolm is. He's over in that section," he said, pointing over the top of the car. Carole immediately shook her head and said that Jimmy was not buried near Malcolm.

We found the main office. The woman, apparently accustomed to guiding lost tourists, pulled out a map and with a yellow highlighter traced the path to Jimmy. We drove back to the Hillcrest section. I took out the map, and it led us right back to where we were. Carole began to walk in a different direction, back toward the tree she remembered from the funeral. The young men were still there. The smell of weed was still strong. I walked right behind them, and there was Jimmy. I shouted to Carole. The young men turned around, and one of them said, with amazement, "He is right there?" I smiled and said, "Yes, he's right here." He was right here all along. Hidden in plain sight.

We need to gather ourselves, for we are in the eye of the storm. We must find the courage to make the bold choices necessary for these after times. And we cannot shrink from our rage; it is the fire that lights the kiln. We have to look back and tell a different story, without the crutch of our myths and legends, about how we have arrived at this moment of moral reckoning in the country's history. We must do our first works over, and this requires an imaginative leap of faith. I reached out for Jimmy to help us.

The late Toni Morrison said these words at his funeral at the Cathedral of St. John the Divine on December 8, 1987, and they capture the power of Baldwin's witness:

Yours was the courage to live life in and from its belly as well as beyond its edges, to see and say what it was, to recognize and identify evil but never fear or stand in awe of it.

It is a courage that came from a ruthless intelligence married to a pity so profound it could convince anyone who cared to know that those who despised us "need the moral authority of their former slaves, who are the only people in the world who know anything about them and who may be, indeed, the only people in the world who really care anything about them."

Yours was a tenderness, of vulnerability, that asked everything, expected everything, and like the world's own Merlin, provided us with the ways and means to deliver.

I didn't say much at the grave site. I kneeled down and quietly said, "Thank you," as I touched his grave. I stood up and thought to myself, I've been reading Jimmy for thirty years. He has been waiting for us. Waiting to see what this history of ours, once we pass through it, has made of us all. He still waits.

My work on this book began with James Baldwin's words. "You must understand that your pain is trivial except insofar as you can use it to connect with other people's pain," he wrote in "The Artist's Struggle for Integrity" in 1963, "and insofar as you can do that with your pain, you can be released from it, and then hopefully it works the other way around too; insofar as I can tell you what it is to suffer, perhaps I can help you to suffer less." Those words framed how I approached the writing of this book; they gave me a sense of the personal stakes. The task, in part, was to understand Baldwin's intent here and to enact it in my own writing and in this political moment.

I also read Baldwin as one of the great American writers. To my mind, he takes Ralph Waldo Emerson across the proverbial tracks and the result is a fuller and more tragic vision of the country. Emerson shows up in this book, explicitly and implicitly. I am particularly taken with his essay "The American Scholar, an Oration delivered before the Phi Beta Kappa Society, at Cambridge, August 31, 1837" and with "The Poet" from *Essays: Second Series*. The quotations "shall draw us with love terror," "chaunt[s] our own times and social circumstances," "America is a poem in our eyes," and "the poets are thus liberating gods" all come from "The Poet" essay. I also utilize his journals and notebooks to draw a contrast between his understanding of the American Idea and Baldwin's.

I have been teaching a seminar on Baldwin for the last few years that has defined my approach in this book. At the heart of the class is an implicit comparison of *The Fire Next Time* and *No Name in the Street*. The idea is to get my students to track the continuities and breaks in Baldwin's nonfiction writing—to understand how the sentiment in "The Artist's Struggle for Integrity" shapes his oeuvre and how he responds to Emerson's imagining of the country. There is a lot of material to wade through. The edited collections, *The Price of the Ticket* (1985) and *James Baldwin: Collected Essays* (1998) edited by Toni Morrison, and his books *A Rap on Race*, co-authored with Margaret Mead, and *The Evidence of Things Not Seen* have been indispensable to that effort. Randall Kenan's edited book, *James Baldwin: The Cross of Redemption*, changed everything for me. I was able to see the development of Baldwin's thought with these fugitive essays. Most of the quotations in *Begin Again* can be found in this collection. The slender volume *James Baldwin: The Last Interview and Other Conversations* was also a wonderful resource to get a sense of Baldwin's thinking in the latter days of his life. The interviews in *Conversations with James Baldwin*, edited by Fred Standley and Louis H. Pratt, also helped me understand the arc of his thinking.

Of course, Baldwin's biography matters. His movement across the globe, his personal relationships, his immediate family, his dealings with publishers, his personal disasters and triumphs, his volatility and gentleness play a critical role in how one reads his work. Baldwin's pain and joy drip from the page; they shape his craft. His life deserves the extensive scholarly treatment that, for example, David Levering Lewis gave W.E.B. Du Bois and Arnold Rampersad gave Langston Hughes. I anxiously await that book. My initial reaction to James Campbell's biography, *Talking at the Gates: A Life of James Baldwin*, wasn't very positive. I disagreed with his declension story about Jimmy post-1963. But like David Leeming's *James Baldwin: A Biography* and W. J. Weatherby's *James Baldwin: Artist on Fire*, Campbell provided much needed context. Douglas Field's *All Those Strangers: The Art and Lives of James Baldwin*—particularly the second chapter, "Radical Baldwin and the FBI: From the Civil Rights movement to Black Power"—influenced how I read Baldwin's shift after the murder of Dr. Martin Luther King, Jr. Although Baldwin did not care very much for his first biographer's work, Fern Marja Eckman's *The Furious Passage of James Baldwin* is a treasure trove of first-person reflection. Quotations like "I didn't have to walk around with one half of my brain trying to please Mr. Charlie and the other half trying to kill him. Fuck Mr. Charlie!" and "fantastically unreal alternatives to my pain" are found throughout the book. No matter her attempts to psychoanalyze Baldwin, the interviews that make up the heart of the book are especially helpful in understanding his response to the changing political landscape of the United States.

On a whim and with the help of Imani Perry, I found a phone number for Fern Marja Eckman in New York and I called her. Amazingly, she was still alive, but not in good health. She couldn't speak. I eventually met her niece, Leslie Freeman, and talked with her about her aunt's amazing life. Leslie was moving Eckman out of the apartment she had lived in for over fifty years and placing her in a home. Ms. Eckman died on May 7, 2019, at the age of

103. I was able to see her amazing collection of letters, signed copies of original editions of important books, and her many interviews with thinkers and celebrities over her years working at the *New York Post*. Leslie told me that they could not find the tapes of the Baldwin interviews, but she had five transcripts. I was able to see two of them and the material blew me away. "Interview with James Baldwin, Oct. 9, 1963, 4 pm at 320 E. Third Street" and "Interview with James Baldwin, Part III, Nov. 9, 1963, 3 pm at 320 E. Third Street" are quoted here in the introduction and in chapter two, "Witness." I was particularly taken with his explicit description of what the role of bearing witness involved.

The James Baldwin papers at the Schomburg Center for Research in Black Culture were absolutely essential. With every visit, I found something new. Luckily, the particular framing of *Begin Again* winnowed down what could be included in the book. But it was here that I found Baldwin's handwritten note to Robert Kennedy and the fascinating exchange of letters between Baldwin and Hugh Downs. In the personal collection of Carole Weinstein and David Baldwin, I found the unpublished draft of an essay initially titled, "The Price of the Ticket." Actually, Carole handed it to me and said it was a first draft of the introductory essay to *The Price of the Ticket*. I remember reading the essay as I walked down Nassau Street with my mouth wide open when I realized what I had in my hands. The essay contains elements of Baldwin's unpublished novel, *No Papers for Muhammad*, and clearly shows his engagement with modernist themes (hence my repeated references to T. S. Eliot). Carole also allowed me a glimpse into the activity in the house in London with Rudolph Kizerman's "A Letter to Myself," written in April/May 1968.

There has been a veritable explosion in work on James Baldwin. The journal *James Baldwin Review* (*JBR*), with its editors, Douglas Field, Justin A. Joyce, and Dwight McBride, is just one indication of the scope and depth of interest in Baldwin's work. Consuela Francis's "Reading and Theorizing James Baldwin," in *JBR*, vol. 1 (2015), Lynn Orilla Scott's "Trends in James Baldwin Criticism," in *JBR*, vol. 2 (2016), and Ernest L. Gibson III's "Trends in James Baldwin Criticism 2013–2015," in *JBR*, vol. 4 (2018) provide an exhaustive list of secondary literature on Baldwin. I drew on some of this work for *Begin Again*. Joseph Vogel's *James Baldwin and the 1980s: Witnessing the Reagan Era* was particularly helpful. Ed Pavlic's *Who Can Afford to Improvise? James Baldwin and Black Music, the Lyric and the Listeners* and his essays in the *Boston Review*, especially "The Lonely Country," and Harold Bloom's *Modern Critical Views: James Baldwin* helped me clarify my own position about the later Baldwin. My overall reading of Baldwin has been greatly influenced by George Shulman's *American Prophecy: Race and Redemption in American Political Culture* and Lawrie Balfour's *The Evidence of Things Not Said: James Baldwin and the Promise of American Democracy*. Both books, along with Jack Turner's *Awakening to Race: Individualism and Social Consciousness in America*, have brought Baldwin into the center of academic discussions of American democracy.

I reached for older books too: Ekwueme Michael Thelwell's classic essays on Baldwin in his book of essays, *Duties, Pleasures, and Conflicts: Essays in Struggle*, are stunningly brilliant. I also found an often overlooked book, Horace A. Porter's *Stealing the Fire: The Art and Protest of James Baldwin*, particularly helpful in understanding the somewhat standard criticism of Baldwin's later works. It was in this book that I discovered Albert Murray's rather harsh criticism of Baldwin. I also quote a small phrase, "simultaneously conspire[d] and corroborate[d] one's fate," from Porter's insightful essay "The Significance of 'Notes of a Native Son'" in Harold Bloom's edited book on Baldwin.

So much of *Begin Again* presupposes the historical context of the period between 1963 and our contemporary moment. In chapter one, for example, I draw on Ekwueme Michael Thelwell's powerful biography, *Ready for Revolution: The Life and Struggles of Stokely Carmichael [Kwame Ture]*, for the description of the NAG meeting. The quotation of Malcolm's thoughts about Baldwin is cited in that book, as well as the quotations of what Jimmy said to the Howard students that night. I used Peniel Joseph's biography, *Stokely: A Life*, to draw the picture of Carmichael's radical transformation. Carmichael's words about Vietnam are cited in Joseph's biography. Throughout *Begin Again*, Carol Anderson's *White Rage: The Unspoken Truth of Our Racial Divide*, Kevin Kruse and Julian Zelizer's *Fault lines: A History of the United States Since 1974*, Elijah Anderson's *The Cosmopolitan Canopy: Race and Civility in Everyday Life*, and Jon Meacham's *The Soul of America: The Battle for Our Better Angels* influenced how I generally described the context.

I also read everything I could get my hands on about trauma. But Serene Jones's *Trauma and Grace: Theology in a Ruptured World* and, oddly enough, Bessel van der Kolk's *The Body Keeps the Score: Brain, Mind, and Body in the Healing of Trauma* (thanks to Imani Perry for the reference) really helped me understand how to read trauma in Baldwin's writing and witness.

In chapter three, David Garrow's *Bearing the Cross* and Taylor Branch's *Pillar of Fire* and *At Canaan's Edge* inform the narrative. The description of the young black woman who accused Dr. King of selling out and the challenge Dr. King and William Rutherford faced in organizing the Poor People's campaign is indebted to

Garrow's book. I was able to listen to both Baldwin's introduction and Dr. King's speech in the Pacifica Radio Archives. Dr. King's speech honoring W.E.B. Du Bois can be found in Cornel West's important edited book of King's speeches, *The Radical King*. The quotations from Billy Dee Williams and the account of Baldwin hearing of Dr. King's death on the phone can be found in W. J. Weatherby's biography. The quotation attributed to Nixon that "minorities were undercutting America's greatness" can be found in Meacham's *The Soul of America*. Carol Polsgrove's *Divided Minds: Intellectuals and the Civil Rights Movement* situates Baldwin in the intellectual environment of the civil rights movement. She also noted that the FBI caught King on tape expressing a deep suspicion of Baldwin. Although I decided not to use the material, Willam J. Maxwell's *F.B. Eyes: How J. Edgar Hoover's Ghostreaders Framed African American Literature* and his edited book, *James Baldwin: The FBI File*, provide a sobering view of the scale of government surveillance of Baldwin.

In chapter four, the quotation about the Oakland police's "head-knocking brutality" comes from the 1974 KRON-TV program on the history of police violence in the city. Joshua Bloom's extraordinary book, *Black Against Empire: The History and Politics of the Black Panther Party*, influenced my thinking in writing this chapter. I also found Reginald Major's book, *A Panther Is a Black Cat*, odd and interesting. The quotation describing Eldridge Cleaver as "cowering in the back room" when meeting Baldwin comes from a conversation between Major and his daughter, Devorah Major. She posted it on her blog.

Chapter five, "Elsewhere," relies heavily on the work of Magdalena J. Zaborowska. Her book *James Baldwin's Turkish Decade: Erotics of Exile* has influenced how most scholars understand Baldwin's years in Istanbul. She certainly shaped my own. The quotation of Cezzar that begins, "Let's face it—I saved Jimmy in a very, very bad period of his life," comes from her interviews with him. Carole Weinstein also provided an invaluable roadmap to help me navigate the argument of the chapter. Suzy Hansen's wonderful book, *Notes on a Foreign Country: An American Abroad in a Post-American World*, offers a fascinating account of Baldwin's time in Istanbul and his influence on her. Although Hansen doesn't explain "elsewhere" in the way that I do, her essay, "The Importance of Elsewhere" in *The National*, inspired me to think about the limits of the word *exile* in describing Baldwin's time abroad. Cezzar's quotation of Baldwin telling him, "I'm broke, baby. I'm sick," comes from that essay as well. Also, the images and essays in *James Baldwin in Turkey: Bearing Witness from Another Place*, a retrospective of the photography of Sedat Pakay, are stunning and insightful. That book, along with the film, gave me a sense of the intimacy of Jimmy's time in Istanbul. Two important books loom in the background of chapter five: Edward Said's *Representations of the Intellectual* and Michael Walzer's *Interpretation and Social Criticism*. Walzer says "critical distance is measured in inches." Said agrees, but insists "never solidarity before criticism." For years, I have taught a course exploring the subtle differences between their views of social criticism. How I think about Baldwin and elsewhere has been shaped by their work.

In chapter six, Ekwueme Michael Thelwell brilliantly captures the difficulty of fame for Baldwin. The quotation "The man became the 'personality,' the personality became the story, and the story became the myth" can be found in his article, "A Prophet Is Not Without Honor," in *Transition*, No. 58 (1992). Vincent Harding's underappreciated book, *The Other American Revolution*, helped me to understand the decade of the 1970s. The quotation "The soul of America had not been redeemed" comes from chapter twenty-nine of that book. In working on chapter six, I had an opportunity to visit the Dick Fontaine Paper and Film Outtakes Collection housed at Harvard University. I wanted to see what went into the making of *I Heard It Through the Grapevine*, and what was left on the cutting floor. I read the full transcripts of the interviews. Baldwin's interviews of John Lewis and Ben Chavis were left out of the film. The interview with Chavis was of particular interest. It could have provided a kind of bridge in the film between the Newark riot, Black Power, and the election of Ronald Reagan. Chavis was part of the Wilmington Ten, nine young men and a woman wrongly convicted of arson and conspiracy in Wilmington, North Carolina, in 1971. Chavis was released from prison in 1980. As Chavis described what happened to him and the others, Baldwin's rage leaps from the page. It could have easily overwhelmed the entire film. What I read gave me a sense of the depth of his anger.

I used newspaper accounts and interviews throughout the book to add color to the historical moment. Newspaper accounts from *The Charlotte Observer* informed my description of Dorothy Counts's efforts to integrate Harding High School and *The New York Times* shaped my description of what happened to Ben Chaney. Baldwin himself gave hundreds of interviews and received an extraordinary amount of press coverage, especially at the height of his career. Many interviews are still in need of translation. The *JBR*, for example, published the first English translation of the 1969 interview with Baldwin conducted by Nazar Buyum.

Toni Morrison passed away while I was finishing the last chapters of *Begin Again*. I had already visited the Toni Morrison Papers at Princeton and found a wonderful poem, echoing Robert Frost, that Jimmy wrote to her reflecting on his life. The letters between them—as well as the ones housed in the Schomburg collection—are simply beautiful. I also noticed an explicit connection between them in the work. In chapter two, I write about trauma and memory. I had Morrison in mind and I explored implicitly the ways the two agree and disagree. The quotation "pitched battle between remembering and forgetting" comes from Morrison's "Rememory," in *The Source of Self-Regard*.

In the end, I could not have written this book without the extraordinary and brilliant work of so many people who have dedicated their lives to understanding the complex and beautiful vision of James Baldwin. My task has been to channel that labor, to let it all be my guide as I reached for Jimmy's delicate hands to help us in these after times.

## ACKNOWLEDGMENTS

I first started reading James Baldwin seriously in graduate school at Princeton University. Albert Raboteau, Jeffrey Stout, and Cornel West helped me, in their distinctive ways, to understand Baldwin's fiction and nonfiction. Cornel's reading of Baldwin in *Prophesy Deliverance!* as an exemplar of radical humanism still sticks with me. Once I returned to Princeton as a faculty member I co-taught a course on Ralph Waldo Emerson and James Baldwin with Jeffrey Stout. In so many ways, that class laid the foundation for *Begin Again*. Traces of Jeff's influential reading of Emerson can be found throughout this book. I am immensely grateful and blessed to have had all of them as teachers and still have them as friends.

My colleagues in African American Studies at Princeton offer an amazing environment for the incubation of ideas. I am excited to walk into Stanhope Hall every day. The joy of working with Chika Okeke-Agulu, Wallace Best, Wendy Belcher, Ruha Benjamin, Reena Goldthree, Joshua Guild, Tera Hunter, Anna Arabindan-Kesson, Naomi Murakawa, Kinohi Nishikawa, Keeanga-Yamahtta Taylor, and Autumn Womack helped make this book possible. I am especially grateful to Imani Perry, my writing partner. She listened to me ramble on about obscure references in Baldwin's writings and, as always, she read the draft of each chapter and offered detailed feedback. Thanks also to the department staff: April Peters, Dionne Worthy, Elio Lleo, Jana Johnson, and Anthony Gibbons, Jr. April Peters, our department manager and a close friend, knows how to give me space to write and knows when to force me to pay attention to my duties as chair. Also, my life would be a mess without my assistant, Dionne Worthy. I could not have finished this book without her.

The Princeton students in my James Baldwin seminars inspired me with their fresh and imaginative readings of Baldwin's nonfiction. In 2016, we read Baldwin during the presidential election. We struggled together to makes sense of what we were witnessing as the country elected Donald Trump. Their anxieties and insights shaped how I approached *Begin Again*. In 2018, we read Baldwin amid the chaos of the Trump administration. They found resources in Baldwin's work to speak to the ugliness of our current political moment. Every class was a source of inspiration.

I am also thankful to Andrina Tran at Yale University for her work in the Beinecke collection of Baldwin's papers in the early stages of the project. I am particularly grateful to my research assistant, Shelby Sinclair, here at Princeton. She is a brilliant historian. The mistakes in this book are my own, but she worked really hard to limit them.

A special thanks goes to Carole Weinstein. Carole contacted me out of the blue when she heard that I was working on a book about James Baldwin. Her close relationship with the family and her intimate knowledge of so many of the events that I write about helped me in the early stages of the book. She read every chapter and offered extensive, typed responses. I have come to cherish her presence in my life, and I am forever grateful for her faith in my reading of Jimmy and her faith *in me*. I am also grateful to Ekwueme Michael Thelwell. He opened his home to me, cooked an exquisite seafood dinner, and brazenly demolished the early versions of the first four chapters of the book. As we reasoned through the night, he gave me the hook—Baldwin changed his "we"—that framed my revisions. Thanks to Jeffrey Robinson, my first interview for *Begin Again*. He told me marvelous stories about Baldwin and Saint-Paul de Vence, and helped me understand the various pressures of Baldwin's later years. The great Angela Davis graciously sat down with me in Princeton and talked about her first meetings with Baldwin. I can still see the way she lit up when she talked about him, his faith *in us*, and how in many ways, as she put it, he was out there fighting all alone. And David Leeming met with me at the Princeton Club in New York. His quiet grace and attention to detail offered a wonderful example for me as I began the project.

So many scholars of James Baldwin have influenced this book. Too many to name. I am delighted by the work of Dwight McBride and the editors of the *James Baldwin Review*. I learn something with every volume. Thanks also to Ed Pavlic. His work on Jimmy has inspired my own in so many ways. He graciously shared an unpublished manuscript on Baldwin with me. It is an inspired book and I can't wait to see it in print.

A number of others were kind enough to read some version of the book or offered comments on the introduction. Thanks to Kiese Laymon, Cornel West, Edwidge Danticat, Jon Meacham, Walter Isaacson, Tracy K. Smith, Paul C. Taylor, Melvin Rogers, Kevin Wolfe, and Clifton Granby for their support and responses to an early version of the manuscript.

I am especially grateful to my amazing editor, Kevin Doughten. Kevin has this uncanny ability to force me to say what I mean more clearly. His curiosity makes him a masterful reader—asking questions at every turn. At times, he can be maddening, but without him and his belief in me, this book would have never been written. Kevin, we are doing this work together to bring about the New Jerusalem, one sentence at a time. I also owe an enormous debt to my agent, Gail Ross. Gail's confidence and faith are contagious. I couldn't ask for a better advocate.

Without a close group of friends and my family I honestly could not survive the demands and pace of my life. My golf partners, Larry and Charlie Upshur and Robert Langley, provide a respite from the demands of the world. We laugh. We smoke cigars. Talk trash. And Charlie, Bob, and I watch Larry score in the seventies! I am blessed to have the support of my mother, Juanita Glaude, and my dad, Eddie S. Glaude, Sr., my brother, Alvin Jones, and my sisters, Bonita Glaude and Angela Glaude-Hosch. They kept me grounded as I worked on the book. My mom kept reminding me that I had to slow down and "write that book." My in-laws, Doreen Brown and Wilfred Brown, have been a stalwart source of support as well.

I am especially thankful to Dr. Winnifred Brown-Glaude and our son, Langston Glaude. Whenever I am writing I am not really present; I am always in the throes of the ideas moving around in my head. Writing this book has been particularly challenging. Jimmy made it so. I found myself wrestling with him in ways that disturbed everything around me. I am thankful that she gave me the space to work it out and get it all on the page and loved me still—something she has been doing for over twenty-six years.

In the end, I am thankful to Jimmy. I burned candles as I wrote and revised. I called up his image and his spirit to shape my thoughts and to guide my hand. I am thankful for his witness . . . for his example of what it really means to love.

# INDEX

JB = James Baldwin

# CONTENTS

# SARAH JANE AND THE

# TEMPLE OF EYES

· · · • • • · ·

## BY JACQUELINE RAYNER

'Have you ever heard the phrase "Caesar's wife"?' the Doctor asked Sarah Jane, as they strolled through the marketplace.

All about them, stallholders in tunics exhorted them to buy pastries, bread, silks and jewellery. Some stalls boasted rows of amphorae containing oil or wine; others displayed baskets of figs, dates and raisins. If Sarah closed her eyes, the smell of cinnamon and cloves from the spice stalls transported her to a twentieth-century English Christmas with mulled wine and mince pies. The heat of the day, however, gave the lie to those imaginings.

Julius Caesar might have been as far in the past for the

people at this market as Queen Anne was to Sarah, but the
Doctor had nonetheless been inspired by the surroundings to
regale Sarah with various nuggets of Ancient Roman trivia.

'Yes, I have,' Sarah replied. 'It means someone who's
pure, perfect. Above suspicion.'

'That's how it's used, yes, but it doesn't actually mean
that at all,' the Doctor said, to Sarah's annoyance – she
prided herself on her wide-ranging knowledge (an essential
asset, she believed, for a good journalist). The Doctor looped
his scarf round his neck a couple of times. 'Caesar's wife,
Pompeia, was hosting a festival of the Bona Dea – cakes, fizzy
pop, no men allowed – and a man called Clodius sneaked in.
So Caesar divorced his wife.'

'What? Why?'

'Because gossips would have been able to say anything
they liked about what had gone on at the party, and Caesar
wouldn't have been able to prove otherwise, so she was for
the chop. It didn't matter whether she'd done anything or
not, because, as Caesar himself said, his wife must be "above
suspicion".'

Sarah drew herself to her full height – which, owing to
the flat Roman sandals she was wearing, brought her up to
about the Doctor's shoulder. 'Of all the male chauvinist pigs –'

The Doctor raised his hands. 'You don't think he had a

point, then? Some of the things I've seen at parties – pass the parcel, musical chairs, blind man's buff . . .'

Sarah gave an involuntary shudder and pulled her Roman cloak tighter round her, although she didn't need it for warmth. The Doctor immediately noticed, of course. That was just like him, Sarah thought: he'd be completely oblivious when she was sure her feelings were as obvious as the nose on her face, then immediately pounce upon the thing she was trying very concertedly to keep hidden.

'Nothing. It's nothing,' she said, defending herself before he could even ask. He was looking so intently at her that she couldn't help elaborating, although staying silent might have been more sensible. 'It's silly. You'd laugh.'

'Well of course I'd laugh! If it's a joke. Is it a joke?'

A sharp shake of her head.

He was staring right into her eyes, no smile, and she knew that he was already well aware it wasn't funny to her. How did he know her so well? How did her tiniest gesture give away the unspoken fear that lay beneath her smiles?

'Blind man's buff . . .' he repeated, his eyes boring into hers.

And she did it again. She shuddered! It made her angry, and even more defensive. 'Well, if you already know, why ask?' she said, crossing her arms defiantly and ignoring the fact that he hadn't asked her anything at all.

During her travels with the Doctor, Sarah had been nearly killed a dozen or more times – actually, definitely more, now she came to think about it. Recently, an attack that had been meant to kill her had instead blinded her, and it had scared her more than she wanted to admit. The powerlessness, the sudden tearing away of one of her senses, had left her terrified. She hadn't said anything about it to the Doctor, but it seemed she didn't need to.

'Look, everyone has silly little fears,' she went on. 'Mine happens to be going blind. Well, that and snakes,' she added after a second, remembering a horrifying experiment involving a the illusion of a snake that she'd been put through during another adventure with the Doctor. Going blind and snakes were now two of her top-three fears, but she would never admit the third to the Doctor, not even under duress – and she knew he would never guess what it was, either.

'You're not scared of Daleks, or Sontarans, or giant spiders?' the Doctor asked her.

'No.' She paused, trying to find the right words. 'Those are all . . . *extraordinary* things. Of course they're terrifying – really terrifying – but they're extreme. It's the little things, the things that could still happen when I'm back home and there are no aliens for a million miles. Things like going blind, or being bitten by a snake – an ordinary Earth snake.

'Look, tell me more about the – what was it? The Bona Dea,' she said, desperate to change the subject.

'The Bona Dea? It means the Good Goddess. Most of the details of her and her cult – including her real name – are lost to history, though. Do you know why?'

'Seeing as I hadn't heard of her until three minutes ago, no,' said Sarah.

'Go on.' The Doctor showed all his teeth, his eyes inviting her into the game. 'Have a guess!'

A challenge to her journalistic reasoning! Sarah couldn't resist.

'Oh!' She concentrated hard for a moment. 'Of course! Because hers was a women-only cult, but all the Ancient Roman historians were men, so they didn't have any information to pass on for posterity.'

'Good girl!' said the Doctor. It was a pretty patronising comment, but the Doctor was about 719 years older than her and probably the cleverest person ever to walk the Earth, so she'd let it be; anyone else – the Brigadier, say, or Harry Sullivan – would have known her wrath.

'Maybe we could investigate the Bona Dea cult while we're here,' Sarah suggested. 'Cause a storm in historical circles when we get back to the twentieth century.'

The Doctor gestured down at himself. 'I don't think they'd let me in.'

'Oh, come on. With a ribbon in your hair, maybe . . .' Sarah tried to look serious, but couldn't help herself — a laugh burst out. 'Okay, fair point. Not exactly your look. I'll just have to do it myself, then.'

'Well, yes, if you want to visit a temple or two. Of course, the Bona Dea is not only a goddess of women. She's also a goddess of healing, and the symbol of healing —'

'Is a snake. Great. Thanks for the warning. She'll just have to remain a mystery for ever.'

The Doctor grinned. 'Have I ever told you about the time I met the three-headed serpent of Orestian Major — oof!'

They'd been so intent on their conversation that neither of them had noticed the woman running towards them until she cannoned into the Doctor, knocking him into a basket of cabbages. Hooking his scarf round the stall's corner post, the Doctor pulled himself up. As he did so, one flailing arm caught the door of a wicker birdcage and burst it open. The stallholder shouted furiously as a dozen tiny birds hopped tentatively towards liberty, then took to their wings and flew out in a single, joyful mass, twittering gleefully.

'Are you all right?' Sarah said, helping the woman, who had also fallen, to her feet. Then she gasped. The woman's eyes were solid white and blank. *Unseeing.* 'I'm sorry,' Sarah said hurriedly, embarrassed at having reacted so obviously. 'Has someone hurt you? Is someone chasing you?'

By now a crowd had gathered around them, eager for the slightest touch of drama to colour their workaday lives. The stallholder even stopped shouting about his fly-away profits and came round the front of his booth to see more clearly what was going on.

'I need a doctor,' the woman said desperately, panicky breaths punctuating her speech. 'Please, someone, find me a doctor.'

Sarah nudged the Doctor hard in the ribs.

'I'm not that sort of doctor,' he hissed under his breath, but the woman realised he was talking and turned towards his voice.

'Are you a doctor? Can you help me? Please.'

'I'm sorry,' said Sarah, as the Doctor shook his head at her. She spoke softly, trying to calm the woman. 'Can you tell me what happened to you? Are you lost? Were you attacked?'

The woman's breathing only grew more frantic. 'I . . . I can't *see!*'

Sarah and the Doctor exchanged a look.

'Do you mean you suddenly went blind? Just now?' Sarah said.

'Yes!' A bewildered expression crossed the woman's face. 'But I don't . . . I don't know what happened,' she said. 'I can't remember. Why can't I remember? Oh, Fortuna, what has happened to me?'

Sarah helped the woman to a nearby seat and put a hand on her arm. 'It'll be all right,' she said soothingly. 'Try to keep calm.'

Sarah could tell that the Doctor's mind had already moved on, that rather than worrying about caring for this woman he was trying to work out what was going on. No, that wasn't quite right. He *did* care; he just didn't see the need for small gestures. No cups of tea or sympathy from him when he could be out there, fighting the monsters, instead. It made perfect sense, pragmatically – anyone could offer a drink and a shoulder to cry on, but very few people could defeat an invasion from another world. Therefore, his time was more profitably spent on the latter. This clinical approach to any crisis or problem only served to emphasise his alien nature. The Doctor was Sarah's best friend, and she was his, but sometimes she wondered how she'd feel if she were one of the people he left behind. How unbearable that would be.

The stallholder, standing nearby, pointed at the woman. 'I know who you are!' he said in a smug tone. 'You're Titus Fabius's wife! Lucilla, that's it. He's offered five denarii to anyone with information on your whereabouts.' Then he added, in an aside to Sarah, 'Missing for a couple of days, she's been.'

It was a foolish thing to say if he'd been hoping to get the reward for himself. Suddenly the crowd swarmed in even closer, each person determined to be the one to claim the bounty. People grabbed at the woman's sleeves, trying to pull her to them.

Sarah slapped their hands away, putting herself between Lucilla and the mob. Her eyes fell on a boy loitering near the edge of the horde. 'Hey! Do you know this Titus Fabius?'

He nodded eagerly.

'Then go and find him, and tell him his wife is here.'

The boy slipped away.

'And that means none of you will be getting the reward, so you might as well make tracks,' Sarah told those who remained. Grumpily, they moved off, although they didn't go far, possibly hoping there might still be more entertainment to come.

Sarah turned back to Lucilla, whose milky-white eyes were wet with tears. 'Your husband will be here soon to take you home,' Sarah said. She paused, knowing her next words wouldn't be so comforting. 'Look –' she winced at the careless phrasing – 'I mean, I know something terrible has happened to you and you probably don't want to think about it, but please try. See if you can remember something. *Anything*. It might help.'

'I can't remember anything. I can't!' Lucilla's breath became fast and shallow again, and Sarah spent a few more minutes calming her down. When she was breathing normally once more, Sarah tried a different tack.

'Think back. Were you at home? Or outside?'

A tiny nod from Lucilla.

'Outside. Right. Here, in the market?'

A shake of the head.

'Somewhere in the town?'

Again, the tiniest of nods, then a sudden cry. 'The harbour!'

'The harbour?' echoed Sarah. 'Tell me about that.'

A deep breath from Lucilla. 'I had been . . . visiting. Yes, that was it. And I walked back home by the water.'

'What do you remember about that? Put yourself back there. The sounds, the smells . . .'

'There was the sound of the seagulls, the smell of the sea. I went on a boat once – one of my husband's merchant ships – and it made me feel ill, so at first I thought the gulls and the ocean were bringing back those memories, but then I realised I was actually feeling ill. I felt pain. A lot of pain.'

'In your eyes?'

'No. In my stomach.'

'What happened then?'

Lucilla's breathing grew agitated again. 'I don't know! I just don't know. I can't remember anything else before I found myself here . . . and I don't even know where I am now! Is this even Ostia?'

Realising she had no idea either, Sarah jumped up and dragged the Doctor off to one side. 'Is this Ostia?' she whispered.

He took a deep sniff of the air. 'Yes, it smells like Ostia to me. Spices, fish and salt. A port just south-west of Rome,' he added. 'Important port. Like Dover. But without the white cliffs. Or the bluebirds.'

Sarah hurried back to Lucilla. 'Yes, this is Ostia,' she said.

They were interrupted by the arrival of a tall, rather pompous-looking man accompanied by a retinue of slaves. 'Lucilla! Is it true?' he cried. 'Have the gods struck you blind?'

Sarah felt her anger rise. 'Ooh, don't you get all Caesar's wife and use this as an excuse to divorce her,' she said, jumping up and waving a finger in the man's surprised face. 'The gods aren't punishing her. She hasn't done anything wrong!'

As Lucilla rose wearily, she stumbled. Her husband

dashed forward and caught her in his arms, then turned to look at Sarah as he held his wife close. 'I have no intention of divorcing my wife. She cannot and will not be blamed for the whims of the gods.'

'Oh,' said Sarah, slightly cowed. 'Well, that's good. Goodbye, Lucilla. I hope —' She broke off. What to say? 'I hope you get better soon' hardly felt appropriate.

'Thank you for helping me,' said Lucilla, cutting across Sarah's stumbling words. 'I will be forever grateful.'

The Doctor and Sarah watched the couple and their entourage walk away. After a second, Sarah realised the stallholder was still standing with them. He clicked his tongue. 'Who'd've thought it?' he said. 'Another one.'

The Doctor rounded on him. '*Another* one? You mean this has happened before?'

'Might have, might have,' said the man.

'Well, has it or hasn't it?'

The man took a deep breath, then let it out with a sigh. 'So hard to remember the details, when all I can think of is that five-denarii reward slipping through my fingers. Not to mention watching my profits fly away . . .' He moved back behind his stall, looking pointedly at the empty birdcage.

The Doctor stared at him, unsmiling. 'How much do you charge for a cage of birds?'

'Two sestertii.' The trader looked down at the large coin that landed on the counter in front of him. 'That's not a –'

'Golden Delphonian mega-dollar. Solid gold. Now talk.'

The man's hand shot out and grabbed the coin. 'Well, it's been happening all over – people turning up blind. At least three others I've heard of, could be more. Probably looked at something they shouldn't have. Weak minds, women have. Can't handle stuff.'

'I'll give you weak minds –' Sarah began, then felt the Doctor give her arm a restraining squeeze.

'Do you know who these others are? Where they live?' he barked at the stallholder, who looked slightly alarmed at the ferocity of the Doctor's voice and took a step back.

'Well, I might do,' he began, clearly trying to regain control of the situation. 'If I thought hard.'

Another Delphonian mega-dollar landed in front of him.

'Yeah, I think I can remember.' Names and addresses spilled from his lips. Then, his fingers stroking the two huge coins, he added, 'For another one of these, I could even take you there.'

'We can find our own way,' said the Doctor. His eyes swept the stall. 'I've already paid more than the information was worth. In fact, I think I've paid enough for all these birdcages too . . .'

As the stallholder watched in dismay, the Doctor moved along the stall, opening all of the birdcages and shooing out the little creatures within.

Sarah clapped her hands in delight, ducking as a cloud of chaffinches swooped over her head.

'I don't like things in cages,' the Doctor said.

The Doctor and Sarah went to visit the homes of the people the stallholder had named: Lucius Sestius, a silk importer; Gaius Helvius, a grain trader; and Manius Salvius, an ivory supplier. At every house they found a blind woman – each time, the merchant's wife – and all their stories were the same: pain, then a sudden awakening to blindness, with no knowledge of what had happened in between. Each woman had come to herself alone, frightened and sightless, somewhere in the streets of Ostia, and on her arrival home had discovered she'd been gone for days.

'Could it simply be an illness?' Sarah suggested, as she and the Doctor walked back towards the marketplace. 'There are diseases that can cause blindness, aren't there? Measles and things like that? Or – oh! I know! There's river blindness. Flies that live near water pass that on, and Lucilla did say she was near the harbour when she became unwell.'

'An impressive fly, to ignore everyone who works at the waterside in favour of a few merchants' wives.'

Sarah shrugged. 'All right, I didn't claim it was *plausible*. So let's accept that someone's deliberately targeting these women. Who, or what? And why? We don't have a lot of leads.'

'We need to work out who the next victim could be,' said the Doctor.

'Okay, so let's find other women who are in similar positions to the previous victims,' Sarah said, eager to start digging and already drawing connections. 'We know they were all married to Ostian merchants – and, going by their houses and their clothes, pretty successful ones too.'

'I know just the person to ask,' said the Doctor.

As soon as they were back in the market, the Doctor headed straight for their old friend, the stallholder. It would be a lie to say the man looked happy to see them.

'You again,' he snapped.

'Ah, good, you remember me,' said the Doctor.

'How could he forget you, Doctor?' Sarah said with a smile.

'Doctor? Doctor! Well, that makes sense. A foreigner.'

'Are you a foreigner, Doctor?' asked Sarah, wide-eyed and mock surprised.

'Ah, most of the doctors in Ancient Rome were Greeks, you see,' the Doctor explained. 'So were most of the philosophers and mathematicians, of course, so, well –' he smiled at the stallholder – 'it's not *that* surprising that I'd be mistaken for one.' He pulled an empty box from under the stall and stood on it, one hand holding his coat lapel and the other stretched out to an imaginary crowd, as he declaimed, 'I think, therefore I am the sum of the squares on the other two sides. Take 3.14159265 tablets before meals with a glass of water.'

Sarah burst out laughing, and the Doctor climbed off the box. The stallholder didn't seem to find it quite as funny, but he sulkily gave the Doctor the information he asked for. Titus Fabius, Lucius Sestius, Gaius Helvius and Manius Salvius were undoubtedly some of the most powerful and important merchants in Ostia; according to the stallholder, there were only four others who could come close to matching them. He gave the Doctor their names and addresses.

'You take two. I'll take two,' the Doctor said to Sarah. 'Talk to the wives, find out their plans for the next few days. See if anything leaps out at you. See if they have any connection to the other women, besides being merchants' wives. I'll meet you back here.'

At the first house Sarah visited, she was granted an audience with Aulus Pumidius's wife, Marcia. As they sat drinking honeyed wine, Sarah did her best to explain the situation. Marcia was older than the other women they'd met that day, and didn't seem inclined to take Sarah's warnings seriously.

'Yes, I'd heard that Lucilla and the others had met with misfortune – my slaves keep me well informed – but are you seriously trying to tell me I might be in danger too?' she drawled, incredulity clear in her voice. 'Sweet of you to advise me, but I think I'll take my chances. Besides, my husband is away in Carthage, carrying out some very important business negotiations, and I am kept extremely busy in his absence. I've no time to go gadding about Ostia, waiting for someone to strike me blind.'

Sarah persisted. 'We don't know what happened to the other women. Whatever it is could just as easily happen to you here, at home.'

Marcia rolled her eyes. 'I'm surrounded by slaves at all times. Nothing and no one can get in to my house without my knowledge.'

Sarah realised Marcia wasn't going to take the threat seriously, no matter what she said, so she took a different angle. 'Do you know the four victims socially?' she asked.

'Yes, we meet from time to time.'

'Well, can you think of anything they all have in common? Perhaps something that's relevant to you too? Apart from the fact you're all married to merchants.' This was just the sort of thing Sarah enjoyed: interviewing sources, searching for that tiny scrap of information that might make a story, that little clue that might link one thing to another and bring about a breakthrough.

'Apart from our husbands, and apart from the fact we are all women, no. I can think of nothing.'

*All women.* A switch suddenly flicked in Sarah's mind. It was probably nothing. No more than the merest hunch . . . but a journalist had to follow her hunches. 'Is there a temple of the Bona Dea in Ostia?' she asked.

'Yes, down by the harbour. Why do you ask?'

'It's just that it's the only place I've heard of here that's for women only, and as you say all the victims have been women,' said Sarah. 'Sick women. Women who might be taken to a place of healing.'

'Oh, that seems very far-fetched,' said Marcia, with a supercilious air. 'More wine?'

'No thanks,' said Sarah, still caught up in her hypothesis. 'I'd better be going. It probably is far-fetched, but I think I'm going to ask a few more questions of the other women.'

She drained her cup and stood up. 'Thank you for your
hospitality. And please – stay safe.'

Meanwhile, the Doctor was finding Caelina, the wife of
Sextus Icilius, an ivory merchant, much more willing to talk.
In fact, he could barely get her to *stop* talking. She was half
his height, twice his width and full of pity for the four women
who had been blinded.

'That *poor* Lucilla,' she said. 'And to think I was only
sitting chatting with her the other day and she had no idea
what the gods were about to visit upon her. And with her just
having had a little boy too. Imagine never seeing his chubby
little cheeks again! I don't like to think of it, that's a fact.'

By this point, the Doctor had been listening for twenty
minutes to tales of all the misfortunes that had been visited
upon Caelina, her children, her friends, her friends' children
and pretty much anyone else she'd ever come across. 'You
don't know of anyone who might have wished harm to these
women?' he asked, trying to steer her back to the topic at
hand.

'There's not a single person who'd want to hurt a hair
on any of their heads,' Caelina informed him. 'If we were
talking about their *husbands*, though . . .'

The Doctor leapt on this. 'Someone might want to hurt their husbands?'

'Well, not actually *hurt* them – I'm not saying that – but that Aulus Pumidius, he's right jealous of the lot of them, and that's including my Sextus. All more successful than him, and he doesn't like it. He'd do them a bad turn if he could. But he can't have had anything to do with this, because he's been gone for, ooh . . . about ten days. Off trying to undercut someone else's deals, probably.'

'Aulus Pumidius? My friend's gone to speak to his wife.'

Caelina snorted. 'I wish your friend joy. That Marcia's a stuck-up one and no mistake. Lording it over us at our little gatherings when she's got nothing to be superior about.'

The Doctor's ears pricked up. 'Little gatherings? You and the other merchants' wives meet up?'

'Well, wasn't I telling you only now how I was sitting with Lucilla just the other day? Every few days we have a little get-together – a bit of a gossip and a few honey cakes. Only with those from our own sphere of life, of course.'

The Doctor questioned her urgently, and learned that every single one of the victims had vanished shortly after one of these get-togethers – but none of them had mentioned it. Why? Were they too traumatised to put two and two together? Or was he the one who was leaping to conclusions?

The Doctor jumped up abruptly. 'I need to find my friend,' he told Caelina.

'Well, good luck to you. And don't you worry about me. I'm not going to let anyone blind me, the gods' will or no.'

*

Sarah was trying to find the house of the second merchant on her list. Marcia had told her about a shortcut, but it didn't seem to be taking her where she wanted to go. She was hardly an expert in Ostian geography, though, so she shrugged and carried on hopefully.

She winced at a twinge of pain – a brief dart across her stomach. Then another twinge, not as brief. She stumbled forward, looking for a place to sit down. As the noise of gulls filled her ears and she breathed in the smell of salt, she realised she was near the harbour. The pain was getting worse, her stomach cramping so much she couldn't take another step. Then a hand grabbed her arm, and a familiar voice said, 'You look ill. Let me take you to find help.'

As she was dragged away, the tiny part of Sarah that was still conscious sobbed inside her head, *Not me. Don't let me go blind. Oh please, don't let me go blind.*

*

The Doctor thumped his fist against the wall of Aulus
Pumidius's house. He was too late. Sarah had already left, the
young slave on the door had informed him, and Marcia, the
mistress of the house, had gone out shortly afterwards. The
Doctor was frustrated, and he was worried.

'Did you hear anything of their conversation?' the
Doctor asked the slave.

The boy shook his head, but the Doctor wasn't
convinced. He knew the Ancient Romans treated their slaves
like furniture; it wouldn't have crossed Marcia's mind to keep
quiet in front of this boy.

'Come on, you can tell me,' he said, with a winning
smile, hypnotic eyes boring into the slave's nervous ones.
'Have a jelly baby.'

The boy shook his head again, both at the question
and at the offer of the strange green sweet. 'I dare not,' he
whispered.

'Because you'd be punished,' the Doctor said. 'I
understand, but I need your help. It's critical. My friend could
be in great danger, and any information you give me could
save her life.'

'They talked of the Bona Dea,' said the slave, still
whispering. He was staring down at his bare feet, as though
by not looking at the Doctor he could pretend he was telling

his secrets to the air. 'The mistress put herbs in the lady's cup. After the lady left, the mistress followed her.'

'Thank you,' said the Doctor. 'Oh, and here's something for you.' He held out another of the golden coins. 'For caring more about my friend's safety than about your own. That should be enough to buy your freedom. I think you deserve it just as much as a chaffinch.'

*

Ostia's temple of the Bona Dea was surrounded by a high wall. Even standing on tiptoes, the Doctor wasn't tall enough to look over it. He walked alongside the wall until he found a gate, then gave a firm *rat-a-tat*. A few moments later, a girl of about ten years of age opened the gate, bowed her head and asked the Doctor his business.

'I'm the Doctor,' he announced. 'I have heard that the priestesses here are healers, and since I am feeling rather poorly – a bad dormouse or rotten lark's tongue at lunch, no doubt – I thought I'd pop in for a bit of healing.' He gave the girl one of his most charming grins.

She bowed her head again. 'I regret that men are not allowed within the temple, sir,' she said. 'But if you will wait here, I will fetch you herbs that should ease your pain.'

'Thank you,' he replied. 'Of course you can't let a man

in the temple, but perhaps I could walk in your grounds while I wait? I see you have a lot of fascinating snakes slithering about in there that I'd very much like to take a look at.'

The girl shook her head. 'I regret, you may not step inside our walls, even to examine the sacred snakes. Please wait here.'

The gate closed in his face.

The Doctor sighed. 'Maybe I should have tried a ribbon in my hair after all.'

Sarah awoke to the sounds of an argument. She still felt weak, but the crippling pains had gone. Thank goodness. She couldn't remember the last time she'd felt so ill.

'What do we do with her now?' she heard a voice say.

'The same as we did with all the others,' said another.

'But she has no knowledge that we need.'

'Maybe not, but her memory must be taken away.'

Sarah risked opening an eye. Two figures swam into focus: Marcia, the merchant's wife, and an elderly woman in the simple white robes of a priestess. They were standing in front of − and Sarah had to blink a few times to make sure this wasn't a fever dream − one of the most complicated pieces of machinery she'd ever seen. A machine that surely

shouldn't be anywhere within a few thousand years of
Ancient Rome. So what was it doing here? But, before she
could solve that mystery, Sarah's priority had to be getting
away. She glanced around for any escape routes, and spotted
two doors – one on either side of the room.

Sarah shut her eyes again and considered her options.
She was almost certainly physically stronger and faster than
her captors, so making a break for it before they realised she
was awake seemed the obvious course of action.

Sarah waited, watching the two women through nearly
closed eyes, until they both turned away from her. Then she
leapt up and dived for the nearest door. She was through it,
she was running –

But the goddess Fortuna was not on her side. Sarah
hadn't realised until she was up and moving how weak her
body still was from whatever it was that had struck her down.
Poison, she now suspected, slipped into her wine by Marcia.
She forced herself desperately forward, step by painful step,
but the walls had begun to swim around her and she seemed
to have forgotten how to breathe. She had thought she was
still running, but when Marcia and the other woman grabbed
her arms she realised she was actually on her knees on the
floor. She decided it was definitely time for Plan B; it was just
a shame she hadn't come up with one.

Well, her escape attempt might have been foiled, but there were still things she could do. The Doctor always said that nine out of ten times evil-doers were happy to explain their plans – not necessarily for grandstanding reasons, but because putting things into words acted as validation for them. Time for Sarah to put that theory to the test.

'I like your machine,' she said, as cheerfully as she could manage with burning needles of pain sticking into her stomach. 'Very impressive. Did you make it yourselves?'

'It was a gift from the gods,' Marcia said in the same condescending tone from earlier. Sarah thought she detected a hint of sarcasm there too.

'How very generous of them,' said Sarah. 'I hope the gods gave you an instruction manual. Perhaps you could explain what it does? Besides blinding people and wiping their memories, that is.'

'Do not mock our gods!' The priestess turned on Sarah – and Sarah saw her milky-white eyes.

'You're blind!' she exclaimed. 'This machine – whatever it does, it did it to you too.' She made her voice deliberately soft, sympathetic, persuasive. 'I'm sorry for mocking your gods. Tell me what happened to you. Please.'

'Do not indulge her, sister,' said Marcia imperiously. 'Let us get this task over with.'

But the other woman shook her head. 'No, it is fair to tell her what we know. After all, the gods granted me the gift of knowledge before they took my sight. I will pass on the favour.' She turned to Sarah. 'Child, know that I am Orbiana, servant of the Bona Dea. I will tell you of the gods' visit to us.

'The gods came to us in disguise, just as Jupiter and Mercury came to Baucis and Philemon. They told us that, to them, the female is the personification of knowledge, so their search for wisdom had led them here.'

'A pity the gods have never passed on this opinion to the men of our city,' commented Marcia, with a sniff. Despite the fact that Sarah was predisposed to dislike her – the poisoning and the imprisonment had rather coloured her feelings – she had to agree that Marcia had a point.

'They brought with them this device,' Orbiana continued. 'It is a way for the gods to know the affairs of our world. They share the eyes of mortals, taking all that they have seen and sealing it forever into a crystal for the gods to consult.'

'Deity TV,' murmured Sarah.

Orbiana went on. 'But, once the gods have seen through our eyes, it would be blasphemous for us to look through them again. So they took my sight away from me, but left me the gift of the memories of others.'

Sarah was working this out in her head as Orbiana
spoke. These visitors must have been aliens of some sort. A
female-dominant race, perhaps? That would explain why they
had targeted this temple, rather than the more obvious seats
of power, and had come to Orbiana, who was presumably in
charge.

*The machine must be some sort of memory-harvester*, Sarah
figured, her mind racing. *A device that reads minds in some way
and can record what it finds there – but for what? Exploration purposes?
Simple knowledge gathering? Military intelligence?* And it appeared
to have the side-effect of leaving its subjects sightless.
Damage to the optic nerve during the process, perhaps? But
what about 'the gift of the memories of others' that Orbiana
spoke of?

'What does that mean?' Sarah asked the priestess. 'Can
you access other recordings made by the machine? I mean,
can you see other visions that the gods have stored?'

Orbiana nodded, a rapturous expression spreading across
her face. 'That is so,' she said. 'Oh, the things I have seen!
The paths trodden by the gods! Truly, I have been blessed!'

'Hang on,' said Sarah suddenly. 'The women I've met,
the other ones who've gone blind, they didn't seem to have
been blessed. They didn't know anything about seeing the

paths trodden by the gods. In fact, they didn't seem to know what had happened to them at all.'

Orbiana's cheeks flushed, but it was Marcia who answered. 'They were not servants of the gods as my sister is,' she said defensively. 'Why should they share her blessing?'

'Oh, I don't think that's the whole story,' Sarah said. 'Would you like to explain to me how they got their memories wiped, but your sister here didn't?' Another question leapt into her head, one she kicked herself for not asking earlier. 'Actually, there's something else I want to know. Where are these aliens now?'

The two women looked puzzled.

Sarah sighed. 'The gods. Where are the gods now?'

Orbiana bent her head piously. 'The gods returned from whence they came.'

'Leaving their big, important machine behind, with all its big, important data?'

'They had a task for me to complete.'

'What task?'

'To gather more memories, to create a record of our time for them, which they would return to collect. A glorious task.' Her face shone. 'And such a boon to me, as I may so rarely leave our temple. To share the memories of others and see life as I have never seen it before! All of the temple can share in the life of the Empire, at last!'

Sarah saw Marcia's expression, and she understood. 'And by a strange coincidence, the first few memories you harvested were from the heads of merchants' wives, rooting out little nuggets of business information.' She looked at Marcia with disdain. 'The aliens didn't leave you with a task. Entrust their machine to primitives? I don't think so. They died – or did you kill them? – and you decided to turn it to your advantage.'

Orbiana was struggling to take all this in. Her head turned from side to side, seeking her sister. 'Marcia? What does she mean? You told me the gods had left us after entrusting me with their task.'

'I expect they died,' Sarah went on, still addressing Marcia. 'I don't know if even you would have the courage to murder a god. I suspect they usually erased their subjects' memories, but they died before they could do that to Orbiana. Did they tell you how the machine worked?'

Marcia snorted. She didn't seem ashamed or embarrassed, just irritated at the inconvenience of it all. 'I visited my sister and found her as you see her now, but sleeping. Those creatures were not gods – how *could* they be gods?! They were dying from a disease they had caught from one of the sick within these walls, a disease they said was unknown to them. As Orbiana slept, one of the creatures told me how their device worked, begged me to use it to take the knowledge of what they had done to my sister from her mind, then to destroy it.' She shrugged. 'Then the creature died.'

'And you didn't carry out its wishes? I don't blame you for that bit.' Sarah stared at Marcia, her face hard. 'I do blame you for what you did to those women, though. How could you?'

Marcia flung up her hands. '*You* ask me that? You, a woman, ask me that? I have intelligence, I have imagination, I have so many skills and gifts that my husband lacks, yet I can wield no power in this world of ours! I *dream* of a world such as those creatures came from, a world where the female is acknowledged as superior, yet in Rome the best I can hope for is to gain influence by persuading Pumidius to do this or do that. And he is a stupid man – *so* stupid! To be tied to him, to be told to run the household, to amuse myself with wine and honey cakes, while he fumbles his way through feeble business deals . . .'

'But how does sniffing out a few business tricks help you?'

'It will not give me power – not power of my own – but, if I can give Pumidius more wealth, more influence, elevate him to a higher place in society, then I will rise too, through him. Can you blame me for grabbing such a chance with both hands? A chance that not one in a thousand women has been granted?'

When she heard it put like that, Sarah could understand where Marcia was coming from – even though she couldn't excuse her actions. Inequalities certainly existed in modern-day England, where Sarah came from, but it wasn't a patch on Ancient Rome. And, given that women here had so few rights, what could they possibly do about it? Ancient Roman suffragettes throwing themselves under the Emperor's horse would probably find themselves and their families thrown to the lions instead.

'How do you feel about that?' Sarah turned to Orbiana. 'Knowing your sister here's been blinding women not for some heavenly purpose but so her husband can undercut others' trade deals, or steal their suppliers, or whatever? Not all that spiritual, you have to agree. This machine must be destroyed.'

Orbiana's indecision showed on her face, different emotions registering fleetingly, before settling on a determined expression. 'No. This device will not be destroyed. No one will take it away from me. I have already lost my eyes. You will not take the sights that the gods have given me in exchange.'

Sarah opened her mouth to argue, but before she could do so a young woman also in white robes hurried in. She curtseyed before Orbiana, then almost screeched, 'A man! A man in the temple!'

'A *man?*'

'A stranger. Strange in face, garments and manner.'

*Well, I think I can guess who that is,* Sarah thought.

'Has he been apprehended?' demanded Marcia.

'He has.'

'Then take him to the inner sanctum,' said Orbiana.

Sarah realised that the three women's attention was focused away from her. She had to make another attempt to escape. Praying that she had now recovered from the poison, she got up slowly and quietly, and slipped out of the room's second door. As she was closing it, Marcia spotted her and started to run towards her. To her delight, Sarah found a key in the lock on the other side of the door. *Thud!* She slammed the door and locked it in the nick of time.

Sarah pulled her white wool cloak over her hair. She was thankful that it was similar to what many of the women in the temple wore; unless someone looked closely, they wouldn't realise she didn't belong here.

With no idea where the inner sanctum was (or the exit, either, for that matter – but she wasn't about to desert the Doctor), she began to explore. A turn to the right, a turn to the left, up a stairway. In the distance she heard cries: the high voices of women, answered by a deep bass rumble. She couldn't make out any words, but she instantly knew that was where she must head.

As she got closer to the voices, she noticed other white-clad women going in the same direction, and she silently joined the back of a group of them. They soon entered a large chamber. On a raised platform in the centre of the room, the Doctor was tied to a wooden chair, priestesses flanking him with their daggers held high. Sarah was *pretty* sure they didn't practise human sacrifice in Ancient Rome – she hoped very much that she wasn't mistaken – but whatever was going on didn't look good for the Doctor.

Orbiana was being helped on to the platform by a young priestess. 'Stranger,' she said to the Doctor, 'you have defiled our temple. Do you plead ignorance of our law?'

The Doctor waved a hand, smiling ruefully. 'It's not so much a plea as a way of life.'

'He knows our law.' The young girl from the gate stepped forward. 'I informed him but a short time ago that no male was allowed inside, not even into the precincts.'

'Then he has no excuse,' said Orbiana. 'Fetch the vipers.'

As Sarah watched in horror, two priestesses moved on to the platform and each picked up a tall amphora. Out of the necks of the jars poked snakes' heads, some pale pink, some dark brown, all with massive yellow eyes and darting tongues. Sarah thrust her fist into her mouth to stop herself from gasping audibly.

'The goddess will judge you,' announced Orbiana. 'If she favours you, the bite of the snake will give you only pain. If you are condemned, the venom will be deadly. I have never known the goddess to favour any man. Release the vipers!'

'No!' Before Sarah realised what she was doing, she found herself striding towards the platform. 'Let him go,' she said to Orbiana. 'He is a good man. He only forced his way in here so he could find me.'

'A typical man,' sneered Marcia. 'He assumes no woman can cope without him.'

'Er, actually,' began the Doctor in his most deferential voice, 'I'm sorry to contradict you, being a man and so forth, but I have every faith in Sarah. It's the rest of you I'm not so sure of.'

'Child, he came here knowing that men are not permitted,' Orbiana said to Sarah. 'Our temple is contaminated, and only his punishment will cleanse it.'

'Please,' Sarah said, trying not to look at the writhing snakes' heads below her. The vipers were clearly desperate to be set loose. 'Please, let him go. If you free the Doctor –' she took a very deep breath – 'if you free him, I will give you my memories.'

Orbiana seemed surprised. 'But I do not need your memories. We have all those that the gods collected.'

'Oh, you won't have any like mine. You see, mine include the Doctor. And you have never met anyone like the Doctor.'

Orbiana appeared to consider this. 'You would do this?' she said. 'You would give your sight for his life?'

'If you could see my memories, you'd understand.'

The Doctor jumped to his feet, bringing the chair up with him. 'No one is giving up their sight for me!'

But Marcia had clearly had enough. 'Release the vipers!' she cried.

Yet this time, Orbiana turned on her sister, a stern expression on her face. 'You forget your place. You have no rights in this holy sanctum. Save your cares for the world outside.' She turned her unseeing eyes towards the crowd of priestesses. 'The ceremony is postponed. You may leave us now. I wish to see the memories of this young lady, and her so-called Doctor. Then I shall decide their fate.'

As the priestesses filed out, Sarah untied the Doctor's bonds, keeping a wary eye on the two abandoned amphorae. Frustrated hisses and slithery sounds came from within. She shuddered.

✳

As Orbiana and a fuming Marcia led Sarah and the Doctor to the room where the machine was kept, Sarah told the Doctor what she believed had happened. He nodded thoughtfully in reply.

As soon as they entered the room, the Doctor whipped out his sonic screwdriver and bolted straight for the great machine.

'What is you doing?' cried Marcia.

'Sorting out this mess!' replied the Doctor.

Tears suddenly welled up in Orbiana's white eyes, as she realised what the Doctor was about to do. 'Don't destroy it, I beg you. It has opened up the world to me!'

The Doctor opened a panel on the side of the machine and began to root around inside. 'I'm not destroying it. I'm fixing it. You're not blinding anyone again, ever.'

Within a few short seconds, the machine was emitting a new, ethereal humming noise.

'There. Done,' he said. 'Sarah?'

'Sarah what?' asked Sarah.

'Would you care to try it?'

'I'd be delighted,' she said breezily. (She *wasn't* delighted, and her breeziness was all part of the show. The Doctor wouldn't risk her losing her sight. He wouldn't . . . would he?)

He connected Sarah with the machine and she felt a sort of tickle in her mind, a rush of memories speeding past too quickly for her to take in: a kindly woman in a scientist's lab coat, a glimpse of a man with curly white hair, a brief 'Exterminate!', and, as the memories went on, a long scarf, a floppy hat and the biggest grin in the world weaving in and out of everything until her head was full of nothing but *DOCTOR DOCTOR DOCTOR* . . .

When the recording was complete, the Doctor turned to Orbiana and handed her the memory crystal.

'Now, here's a show for you.'

Sarah watched Orbiana's face as snatches of her memories played inside the priestess's head. Expressions sped across her face: excitement, apprehension, fear, relief, joy . . . Then tears came again to her blank eyes.

'Still want to kill the Doctor?' Sarah asked, as Orbiana put down the memory crystal at last. The priestess couldn't speak. She just shook her head.

'Sister, he is a man in your temple. He —' began Marcia.

'It is not my temple. It is the temple of the goddess, and I do not believe she would have him die in her name,' Orbiana snapped. She went on, speaking softly, 'He serves the gods – I have seen it in each and every one of his actions.'

'Well, I wouldn't claim in each and *every* action . . .' said the Doctor, glancing up at the ceiling. 'But think about who was with me throughout those adventures you watched. Think about who saved me time and again, just as she saved me today, willing to face her two greatest fears to ensure my freedom.'

He turned to look at Sarah, and she glowed.

Only, those weren't her two greatest fears. There was one above them, one which she would willingly give up her eyes for, that she would face every snake in the world in order to prevent. The thing she feared most was being without the Doctor. Oh, she could survive without him – she'd suffered losses already in her life, and she knew she was strong enough to survive more – but what could compare to the life they had together?

Orbiana, seemingly guided by a sixth sense, rested her milky gaze upon Sarah. 'Perhaps once again a god has walked among us in disguise,' she said.

Sarah opened her mouth to contradict the priestess, but the Doctor shook his head and put a finger to his mouth.

'Fear not,' continued Orbiana. 'I will not use this machine again.'

'Oh, I wouldn't go that far,' said the Doctor. 'No more industrial espionage, perhaps, but there's a lot more to it than that. Share the memories. Make more memories. See other people's points of view. Let women realise that the universe is a much bigger place than it might seem to them right here, right now. And, if they ever doubt a single woman can live her own life, by her own rules and not those of her husband or other men, that she can be brave and curious and confident and clever and hard-working and loyal . . . well, just show them Sarah, and they'll change their minds.'

'Well, that was another fine mess you got us out of,' said the Doctor, as he and Sarah walked back to the TARDIS.

'You made me blush,' said Sarah.

The Doctor waved a hand dismissively. 'Oh, I probably exaggerated.' But he gave her a grin that said otherwise.

'I hope Lucilla and the others will be all right,' Sarah mused. 'Being blind . . . ' But as she spoke, she realised she wasn't so terrified of the notion any more. Why should she be? If it ever happened – well, it would just be something to deal with. There were worse things. Losing her sight wouldn't make her a lesser person, it wouldn't make her someone to pity – just like being born female in Ancient Rome didn't make the women there lesser people either.

If she lost her sight, she would still, in every possible way, be Sarah Jane Smith, time-travelling with the Doctor. And so

Lucilla was still Lucilla, and the others were still themselves, and she would not patronise them by feeling pity towards them. She would merely wish them well.

As they reached the police box, Sarah wondered aloud, 'Was that a good idea, though? Leaving a huge piece of alien tech in Ancient Rome?'

'Oh, I don't know,' he replied airily. 'How much of what went on in the Bona Dea cult do we know about?'

'Well, practically nothing. We said that earlier . . . Oh. Right. Fair enough.'

'After all, if we can't trust a bunch of women with all the secrets of the universe, who can we trust?' said the Doctor.

Sarah smiled at him, and led the way into the TARDIS.

# ROSE AND THE
# SNOW WINDOW

· · · · ● ● · · ·

## BY JENNY T. COLGAN

R otating round the Earth is a giddying experience,
particularly when you have to go slowly enough to
see what you're looking for – but fast enough to avoid being
noticed by the International Space Station.

'It's all right,' said the Doctor, concentrating fiercely as
they swung by the station, causing its sensors to spin wildly.
'I'll send them another guitar.'

Rose crouched next to him over the monitor, trying to
see what he was staring at on the familiar blue-and-green
planet below. 'What are you looking for?'

'I'll know it when I see it.'

'Well, is it, like, a mountain? A panda? Spaghetti? What?'

'A puncture,' said the Doctor, as the TARDIS screen

zoomed in on the Himalayas, the monitor's picture sharp enough for them to spot the mountain climbers in their bright jackets.

'A puncture?'

'In time. A slow leak. It's small, but if you don't patch it up –'

'Your bike falls over,' said Rose, at the exact same moment as the Doctor said, 'The universe implodes.' He added one of those grins that seemed slightly larger than his mouth. She could never quite tell if he was joking when he grinned like that.

'Aha!' he pointed a finger at the north-eastern part of North America. 'There we are!'

The TARDIS dematerialised just as they were about to cross the path of the blinking ISS again. On board the station, a woman thought she'd seen a strange blue light out of the corner of her eye, but she dismissed it as wishful thinking, which it was.

'New York?' said Rose, excited. She'd never been there.

'Toronto!' said the Doctor. He looked at Rose's disappointed face. 'Don't be daft! It's just as good as New York. Go, Maple Leafs!'

Outside it was freezing. Entrancingly cold. The snow had
set hard against the pavements, and the cars moved almost
silently under the crystal-spotted sky. The high-rise buildings
downtown were incredibly dense and rose, glittering, into the
air. There were very few people on the streets; Toronto had
an entire underground city that made it possible to travel
across town without ever having to brave the ferociously cold
winter air.

'Ooh, it's nice,' said Rose.

'Course it's nice,' replied the Doctor. 'Everywhere is.
Come on. We'll be able to see everything from where we're
heading.'

The Doctor sniffed the air, then set off towards a huge,
brightly lit residential tower. They bundled into the lobby
behind a large man, then presented themselves to the
doorman.

The Doctor engaged that grin again. He had a tendency
to think it more charming than it actually was. 'Hello! We're
here to see . . . apartment 2714.'

The doorman smiled politely. 'Let me just call up –'

'No need!' said the Doctor, flicking out his psychic paper.
'We're –'

He looked up at the bland building, out of ideas for once.

'The birthday surprise,' said Rose quickly, noting how

kind the doorman looked. 'Please don't spoil it!'

'Oh, a birthday, eh?' he said, smiling. 'You know, I've got some left-over helium balloons from an office party through here in the back . . .' He bustled off behind his desk.

'Um. We do . . . we do a dance,' Rose called after him. 'He's the clown.'

'I see that!' the doorman replied, returning with several floating balloons, which Rose gratefully accepted. 'Do something funny!' He looked expectantly at the Doctor.

The Doctor glared at Rose.

'He's only funny when he's being paid,' said Rose, before running after the Doctor who had walked huffily into the lift and grumpily started pressing buttons at random.

'This TARDIS is rubbish,' he said. He pressed a few more buttons.

The elevator stopped on every floor. Each time the doors opened, the Doctor would stick his head out, sniff surreptitiously, then lean back inside again.

'What are you sniffing for?' said Rose.

'I'll know it when I sniff it,' replied the Doctor.

'What, time has a smell?'

'Of course time has a smell! Yours is of diesel and hair gel and satellite trails.'

Rose wrinkled her nose.

They hit the ninth floor, and the Doctor stuck his head out again.

'Come on, then!' he said.

As she stepped into the corridor, Rose took a deep sniff. Sure enough, there was a faint . . . something. Was she imagining it? It was like the faintest trace of candle smoke on the air. Not scented candles, but something rougher, greasier . . . Then it was gone again.

They carefully walked up and down the corridor, listening at each of the doors, until they found an empty corner apartment. The Doctor pulled out his sonic screwdriver and the door unlocked and swung open.

'Right,' said the Doctor. 'This will do.'

'Ooh,' said Rose, taking in their luxurious surroundings. 'Tell you what, the high-rises on my estate are *nothing* like this.'

She wandered through the open-plan sitting room. It was sumptuous, but it was fitted out rather like a hotel, in shades of beige. There was no sign of personal photographs or knick-knacks. Rose wondered if it was a rental apartment, or perhaps someone had simply bought it as a glass box to store their money in? It didn't feel like a place to love or call home; it felt more like something to have. The thought saddened her.

One corner of the sitting room was just two walls of glass, and snow flurried past the windows. The views were indeed astonishing. Skyscraper after skyscraper glistened all around, great towers of steel and glass. It was dizzying at this height, like being in a city of lights in the sky, with the honking of the cars wafting up from far below.

'Don't touch anything,' the Doctor said from behind her. 'It's not ours.'

'You just broke in!'

'Yes, to save the universe.'

'Would the universe really mind if I made myself a cup of tea?'

The Doctor pursed his lips.

'Glass of water, then?' said Rose.

The Doctor seemed to consider this, then nodded, before returning to setting up the telescope he'd brought with him.

'Would you look at that,' he said, when Rose returned with water for each of them. He gestured out of the enormous windows.

Rose stared out in wonder. From where she stood, she could see into hundreds of other people's apartments, right into their lives. Some people were getting changed, some were eating, and in other rooms the blue lights of televisions flickered. It was captivating.

'Life unfolding,' the Doctor said. 'In the dawn of the twenty-first century, everyone blissfully unaware of what . . .

Well, never mind about that right now.'

'You sound like David Attenborough,' Rose said. 'Is that what you do? Look on us as just another species?'

The Doctor blinked, which, since it was something she never thought he did quite often enough, Rose noticed whenever it happened. 'But you are,' he said.

'Just animals in the wild?'

He shrugged. 'We're all animals in the wild, Rose.'

Rose pressed her nose to the glass, catching sight of her own reflection. She grimaced. It was harder than you'd think to get your roots done while travelling through the whole of time and space. 'So, what are we looking for?'

'Not sure.' The Doctor came and stood close to her. They gazed out across the frosted city. 'It's not in this building, but it isn't far, and from here we can see just about everything. A panopticon.'

'A panopti-what?' said Rose. 'Never mind. Here's a question: what are we looking for that's nine storeys off the ground?'

The Doctor glanced at her and she prepared, as usual, to feel stupid.

'That,' he said, 'is an excellent question. Either something from a period where the geology of the region was different –'

'What, like a caveman or something?' said Rose.

'Could be. Or the thing itself could be geographically off.' He frowned. 'Then we're really in trouble.'

'Worse than the universe imploding?'

The Doctor thought for a moment. 'Faster.'

Night came and the city settled into a quiet hum, as the lights in the apartments all over steadily turned themselves off. The Doctor didn't move from his position in front of the telescope. Eventually, Rose lay down on the immaculate and very comfortable sofa, pulled a cashmere blanket over herself, and fell asleep.

When she woke to a chilly, perfectly pink-and-white dawn, the Doctor still knelt, unmoving, in front of the telescope. He looked like a sniper at his post – so much so that Rose felt an uncharacteristic stab of fear looking at the black-clad figure.

'Do you want me to take over for a while so you can rest?' Rose said.

The Doctor looked at her as if he hadn't understood the question, because he hadn't.

But they took turns at the telescope regardless, the windows all around them waking up to the new day. Rose

wondered about the people getting ready in the rooms she
saw: the young woman who ate half a grapefruit and did
sit-ups before getting dressed; the old man who got dressed in
a full suit and tie, then sat down by the window (Rose thought
he was looking back at her, but he wasn't – he was staring at
nothing); the two young men, clearly in love, making breakfast
together.

'I have to eat,' Rose said eventually. 'I'm going to go out
and find something. Do you think they'll take pounds?'

'Give me your bank card,' said the Doctor, sonicking it.

'What, so breaking and entering isn't a crime, and
stealing from banks isn't a crime, but taking a teabag is?'

'Trust me,' said the Doctor. 'You'll pay the banks back.'

Rose blinked and turned to go.

'Also, get me a blueberry muffin!' shouted the Doctor.

Inside the coffee shop at the bottom of the building Rose
stared at the incredible choice. The array of coffees,
doughnuts, pastries and buns available was stunning. She
could, she thought, learn to like Toronto. Although, she could
also do with a scarf and a hat . . .

As she reached out to collect her takeaway coffee, she
suddenly caught it again, just for an instant, lingering above

the smell of fresh bread that filled the coffee shop: candle wax, but greasier, somehow more insistent than a normal candle. She glanced around but it seemed no one else could smell it; everyone else was busy with their papers and their coffees.

She rushed out of the café, and found the scent was stronger outside. She looked around, then bent her head back to gaze up at the huge skyscraper directly opposite.

❋

'It's across there!' Rose yelled, tumbling through the apartment door, coffee slopping over the side of her paper cup.

The Doctor glanced up from the telescope.

'That building! Just across the road! Look at it! Look in there! Let me do it!'

She shoved the Doctor aside and positioned herself in front of the telescope.

'This isn't blueberry,' he said, rustling around in the bag she had thrust at him.

Rose didn't answer. She was scanning the apartments opposite one by one through the telescope. Some had the blinds or curtains drawn, but most didn't. Empty . . . Empty . . . A mother with a child clambering around the sitting room. A woman working on a computer, fingers dancing over the keyboard. A man doing weights – Rose swung the telescope quickly back to that one. *Nice.*

Then she carried on. She panned down. She panned back up. *Ooh, bit fancy, that one.*

'How do you tune this in?' She fidgeted desperately with the dials on the telescope.

'You don't tune it in. You focus it,' said the Doctor, effortlessly twisting a knob on the side.

Instantly the fancy place that had caught Rose's eye jumped towards her through the viewfinder, and she flapped her arms furiously.

'Doctor! That room, there!'

He rushed to the window and put his hands around his eyes to see what he'd missed.

Toronto seemed to be a clean, orderly place. The apartments were tidy, up to date and fashionable. But the fancy apartment opposite, it was different. The room looked oddly as though it was far too large for its big wooden-framed window. It wasn't a neat room, either – unlike the room they were currently standing in and all the others in the modern glass buildings. What she was looking at was a vast salon. Its red-painted walls were lined with wooden-panelled doors that led who only knew where. A fire burned in the grate, although Rose hadn't seen any sign of chimneys on the outside of the apartment building. A long dining table with flickering candles and silver plates up its length showed a recently abandoned dinner. What's more, it didn't seem to be morning in the room, but rather evening; the windows to the side of the room (which, now Rose thought of it, shouldn't have been there at all) looked out on to darkness. Grand oil paintings hung from the walls, and a sideboard on the back wall was covered in papers and seemed to be in some disarray.

It was as though this apartment existed outside of the Toronto that surrounded it; almost as though it existed outside of time altogether.

As she gazed into the room, a solitary figure emerged through one of the doors.

Rose pulled away from the telescope and blinked, suddenly chilled. Then she steeled herself and lowered her eye to the telescope again.

The figure who had entered the room was male. His hair was long on top, short at the sides and pale, as was his skin. He had very high cheekbones, and his eyes were bright blue and hooded, his expression distracted. He pored over something on the sideboard, reading it very intently. Then, he straightened up and glanced at the door he had come through – had someone knocked? – and strode across to it. He was wearing an embroidered topcoat over a waistcoat and what looked to Rose like jodhpurs and riding boots. He pulled open the door and, just as Rose caught a tantalising glimpse of a candlelit hallway beyond, vanished from sight.

'Did you see? Did you see?' said Rose, jumping up. She had witnessed many things with the Doctor, but peering into the past from the present – this was something new.

The Doctor looked through the telescope himself then, arms folded. 'Russian. Early nineteenth century. If he's this high above sea level I'd say –' he snapped his fingers – 'the Orekhovaya hill. Saint Petersburg. Epaulettes, but soft hands. He hasn't served. Yet.'

Rose was already pulling on her coat. 'Right,' she said. 'Come on, then. Are we going?'

The Doctor frowned. 'It might not be that simple. Don't just go stomping in like you usually do.'

'You can talk!'

Outside on the street, the Doctor and Rose ran across the road to the apartment building opposite. The road was now busy with long lanes of cabs and honking cars, the winter sun glinting off the windscreens.

Inside the lobby, they were again greeted by a doorman. The Doctor cheerfully held out his psychic paper, and the doorman nodded and ushered them towards the elevators without further ado. As they entered the elevator, Rose sniffed so loudly that the people already in it looked strangely at her, but she could no longer detect the scent of candle wax. Someone asked Rose what button she wanted pressed, and she realised she hadn't thought to count how high up the salon had been.

'He knows,' she said, pointing to the Doctor, who was leaning against the back of the elevator with his arms folded.

'Eight,' he said smugly.

The eighth-floor corridor was long and silent when they stepped out into it. The Doctor counted the doors as they walked, until they reached the right one. He glanced at Rose. She could smell it again, and it was much stronger: an earthy, guttering flame.

The Doctor knocked. 'Hello? *Zdravstvuyte? Bonjour?*'

There was no answer. With Rose right behind him, he sonicked the door and threw it open to reveal . . . nothing. There was nothing there at all; or rather, it was just a normal apartment, quite small. It looked like a young woman lived there, Rose thought. Fairy lights festooned the walls, and there was a fluffy throw on the couch. It was very much the kind of place she might live in herself. She ran to the large window and gazed back at the building they'd come from.

She could even see the telescope glinting in the sunlight.

'Sure you have the right room?' she said.

'I don't know,' said the Doctor crossly. 'Why don't you check it against your own calculations?'

'But where's the man we saw?'

The Doctor quickly scanned every inch of the small apartment with his sonic screwdriver, looking concerned. 'Nope,' he said. 'Wherever the puncture is, we can't access it from here.'

'Well, can we get the TARDIS to take us back in time to it?'

'No, because then we'd be *there*, and *there*'s not where the problem is.'

Rose frowned. Then she rummaged in her pockets, and took out a lipstick.

'What are you doing?'

She wrote on the window in big, bright red letters: LOOK. Then she wrote it again in Russian.

'Ooh,' she said. 'I will *never* get tired of that TARDIS translation circuit.'

'You're going to really freak out some twenty-two-year-old marketing graduate with that, you know,' said the Doctor.

'Not as much as the universe imploding would,' said Rose, adding a lipstick arrow in the direction of their building for good measure.

Back in front of the telescope, freshly armed with paper and pens, Rose squinted across the street.

'Why?' mused the Doctor, pacing up and down the immaculate rug. 'Why can we see it here and not there? That's not how it should work. Holes have two sides.' He thought for a moment. 'Mind you, I have more or less given up on knowing how anything *should* work . . .'

Rose looked at him askance. 'What, you? Universe's biggest know-it-all?'

'What do you call a know-it-all who's wrong about everything?'

'He doesn't appear to have a name,' said Rose, smiling.

She continued to watch the room across the street. It was still evening there; although, thankfully, the heavy red-velvet curtains were not yet drawn.

As she watched, one of the wooden doors flew open, and the pale young man from earlier stormed back in. He sat down at the table and dropped his head in his hands. If he wasn't weeping, he was certainly deeply distressed.

'There you are!' said Rose.

She scribbled 'HERE' on a piece of paper and held it up, waving frantically. Some of the other inhabitants in the other apartments opposite caught sight of her and waved back enthusiastically.

'Not you!' she shouted. 'Not you! *You!* Come *on*! You!'

At long last the man looked up, his face white and drawn. He poured himself a glass of wine from a jug in front of him on the table, gulped it down, then sighed.

'Hey! Hey! Hey!' shouted Rose, jumping up and down even more fiercely.

'You're attracting attention,' observed the Doctor.

'Good!' said Rose. 'HEY!' She leapt even more furiously up and down.

Slowly, the young man lifted his head once more. His eyes were red-rimmed. He stared straight ahead, unseeing, into their world.

'Hey! HEY!'

At last, his eyes caught hers.

'Hello,' she mouthed.

The Doctor started and moved closer. 'It's leaking. The puncture.' He shook his head. 'This is going to get worse before it gets better.'

But Rose wasn't listening. She placed the palm of her hand against the window-pane, stretching her fingers up in greeting. She barely dared to blink or breathe, desperate not to break the young man's gaze. From across time and space, he squinted back at her, looking incredibly puzzled.

'Paper!' she hissed out of the side of her mouth at the
Doctor.

The Doctor rolled his eyes, already in the process
of handing her a piece of paper on which he'd already
written 'Hello' in English, Russian and French. Rose didn't
even glance down, didn't notice the unusual beauty of the
handwriting.

Across the road, the young man very gradually lifted one
hand to his window in response. Rose could see the details
of his palm through the glass, even across the centuries. She
smiled tentatively.

'More paper!'

'What do you want it to say?'

'Um. "Hello" again. And "Where are you?"'

'He knows where he is. Just like you know where you are.
You just shouldn't be able to see each other, that's all.'

'How about asking if he can smell something weird. If
he's out of time?'

'All of this is going to be a bit much for him. As far as he
can tell, you're just an oddly dressed child across the street.'

'I'm not a child!'

The Doctor glanced over. 'Everyone's a child to me.'

Rose shot him a look. 'Just write my name, then.'

The young man across the way read the new sign as she held it up, then turned round. Holding up a finger telling her to wait, he turned to the sideboard against the wall.

'Oh, look! He's got an ink pot!' said Rose. 'And a quill!'

'Yes, there were very few pre-revolutionary Russian biros,' said the Doctor.

Rose gave him a look.

'And well done,' he said grudgingly. 'Keep at it.'

The strange Cyrillic letters on the piece of paper the young man held up to his window seemed to swim and reorganise themselves in front of Rose's eyes. 'Count Nikolai Artem Livosich,' she read aloud. 'Wow. I should probably have put more than just "Rose".'

Rose noticed how the young man's long eyelashes cast shadows along his high, pale cheekbones. The count lifted his glass of wine from the table and held it up to her in a toast. She giggled and, casting about, grabbed one of the helium balloons from the doorman and shook it.

The effect on the count was almost comical. His eyes widened and he appeared completely astonished. Quickly he scratched out 'Montgolfier?' on a scrap of paper.

'What does he mean?' said Rose.

'*Montgolfier*. It's what they call hot-air balloons,' the Doctor explained. 'Quite the rage back then. And brand new. Not normally something you'd find in a house. He's astonished by you. You look like you're holding up a car.'

Rose found herself grinning, even as the count was shaking his head in disbelief. Then he laughed too. On his piece of paper, the Russian now being translated into English by the TARDIS, he wrote 'Show me?' and made a beckoning motion.

Rose turned round. 'Shall I go?'

The Doctor rubbed his short hair. 'I can't think of a worse idea. Or,' he added gloomily, 'a better one. But he can't have made a hole in time. They don't even have clocks that work properly.'

'When is he?'

The Doctor squinted through the telescope at the newspaper on the count's table. '1812.' He blinked and straightened up. 'The Corsican Crocodile is already on his way. Napoleon,' he said to Rose's querying face. 'Not a chap I like.'

But Rose was transfixed watching the count again. Bent over, she saw one of the doors behind him open. Beyond the salon, young men and women were flooding along the candlelit corridor, dressed in the highest finery. Rose turned to the Doctor, eyes shining. 'It's a ball!'

'Or a wake,' said the Doctor, with feeling.

In the TARDIS, the Doctor was still pondering the time-puncture problem when Rose emerged from the wardrobe.

'How?' she exclaimed, twirling round, her heavy skirts rustling. '*How* did women manage being dressed like this? All this *stuff?*'

'It was a very ornate period,' said the Doctor, without looking up. 'If you were rich, ostentation was the name of the game. Of course, if you weren't, you were lying frozen in a field without a headstone.'

'This is my night out at a Russian ball,' said Rose. 'Can we save the downers for later?'

She smoothed out the long silk gloves she was wearing. Her dress left her shoulders bare, with wide satin straps across her upper arms; the weighty silk was cinched in at the waist over a corset, and the skirt was deep red and inlaid with brocade. It was incredibly heavy, made her stand up very straight, and Rose had no idea how she was going to go to the toilet in it.

*She loved it.*

'Well, what do you think?' she said, displaying neat little boots with ankle buttons.

'In human terms, breathtaking, I'm sure,' he said, looking

at her at last, and she grinned. He squinted at her. 'Put your hair up.'

'What?'

'Women of the era wore their hair up.'

'Oh, did they?' said Rose, pleased he'd referred to her as a woman rather than a child.

Firmly, the Doctor took hold of her blonde ponytail, quickly braided it round the back of her neck, then deftly did something with his sonic screwdriver so that it all stayed up on top of her head.

'What did you just do?' said Rose. She tried to see her reflection in the TARDIS console. 'Are you actually an intergalactic hairdresser? Is that why you never mention your job?'

'Here, take this.' He handed her one end of a long red ribbon. Then he took the ends of it, sonicked them together, then broke them apart again.

'What did you do that for?'

'I got the TARDIS to give you a sonic time loop. Tug on the ribbon and you'll get back to this time – back to this apartment. Back to safety. Even if I can't see you. Even if I'm hundreds of years away. Pre-revolutionary Russia is not a place I'd want you stranded.' He paused. 'There isn't *any* place I'd want you stranded.'

Rose tied the ribbon carefully to the top of her dress. 'Okay,' she announced brightly. 'I'm ready.'

'And you have to get home before midnight.'

'Seriously?'

'No,' said the Doctor. 'Time is an imaginary construct. Midnight doubly so.'

Rose gave him a look.

'Don't be nervous,' said the Doctor. 'Talk to the count. Find out what he knows, if anything strange has been happening recently. I'll scout around, see if the puncture really is on their side. I'll be inconspicuous.'

'Dressed like that?'

'I'll be the stable boy. You can be Cinderella.'

The Doctor and Rose were both quiet as the TARDIS heaved to a landing. When they stepped outside once more, all the lights of the big city were gone. Saint Petersburg was lit by oil lamps and candles at the windows, and shadows flickered on the snow. It was magical. It was also shockingly cold, even colder than Toronto.

Rose turned to see that the TARDIS's lamp had altered its usual steady beam and now flickered too.

People passed here and there on sleighs, covered in

thick furs, and the bells tinkled as they came and went, their laughter frosting the air. Rose noticed others, less fortunate, not dressed for the weather, skulking in side alleys. She sighed. She hadn't yet been anywhere in time or space where there weren't people suffering. She wondered what it was like where the Doctor came from. Maybe there was nobody like that. Maybe that's why he felt such an urge to fix things for everyone else.

They came to the main door of the palace, and the Doctor shot off round the side of the building searching for the hole. Rose took a deep breath. Normally, she went to parties with Mickey and Shareen, and they'd grab some cheap cider, then turn up *en masse* and know everyone. Rose would no more go to a party by herself than she'd . . . well, than she'd speak to the reanimated spirit of a dead Welsh person or meet Charles Dickens, and she'd done both of those things. She had, she realised, changed quite a lot.

She presented the Doctor's psychic paper to the guard on the door. The guard immediately bowed so deeply she wondered who, exactly, the paper had claimed she was. Then she stepped through the door into a courtyard lit with great braziers. Glowing windows on all sides exuded laughter and chattering, and she could hear the strains of violins. On the other side of the courtyard, great French doors had been flung wide open on to the freezing cold of the Russian night. The clicking of soldiers' boot heels resounded from the floor of the ballroom beyond, and the air was heavy with the scent of candle wax and cigars.

Rose climbed the staircase to the glittering doors, then turned and stood for a moment, looking back over the courtyard. She took one more deep breath, then entered the ball.

Heads turned to stare at Rose, and she swallowed and tried to remember to stand up straight as she walked into the ballroom. The music launched into a dreamy waltz, and she felt her face flush as she suddenly caught his eye. Because there he was in front of her: the count. Nikolai.

He was one of the taller men in the room. There were still purple shadows smudged beneath his eyes, but the second he saw her his face broke into a broad smile that he immediately attempted to hide. A footman in a wig presented Rose with a glass of champagne, but she waved it away.

Carefully, in case she tripped, she walked towards the young count, and he was beside her in a second, lending her his arm.

'You changed into a gown,' he said, as she took his hand gratefully. 'I liked your casual attire.'

Rose's face fell.

'A joke: excuse me,' he said. 'You look beautiful, *mademoiselle*. You have a dance card?' he said.

Rose was suddenly aware of an older man watching them both like a hawk. He scowled at them. 'Who's that, then?' she asked.

'My father,' said the count.

'Bit over-protective?'

The older man started to make his way over to them.

'Let's dance! Quickly,' said the count with a smile, putting his hand on her waist and whirling her across the huge, sparkling ballroom floor, out of his father's way.

The music was beautiful and Rose was acutely conscious of how close she was to the count. She soon found that, if she simply followed his lead, she was able to lose herself in the dance. Until she stumbled over another lady's long train, that is.

The woman turned and began to say, in a rather shocked tone of voice, 'Nikolai Artem, shouldn't you —'

'Come on!' he said, and waltzed Rose right on out of one of the ballroom's side doors.

In the corridor beyond, which ran the length of the ballroom, Rose collapsed, exhausted and giggling, beside Nikolai on a low chaise longue. Male servants wearing wigs rushed past with glasses, large plates of food, and huge bowls of flowers. Rose watched them.

The count was looking at her. 'Tell me, where are you from?' he said. 'I looked out in the village square, but that strange space of yours was suddenly there . . . and I thought I knew everyone in Saint Petersburg.'

Rose shook her head. 'I'm from London.'

'London! How goes your war against that demon?'

Rose wished she'd studied harder at school. 'Um . . . up and down.'

The count nodded. 'Ah,' he said.

'Anyway.' Rose sat up straighter, reminding herself why she was there. 'What have things been like around Saint Petersburg? Have you noticed anything new around town? Anything, you know, out of the ordinary?'

'Apart from you?' replied the count. 'Oh, and that place you live. Is it a greenhouse?'

'Something like that . . .'

'It seems very strange to me.'

'Um, yeah. But anything else?'

'I like both the colours of your hair,' said the count, then put his hand to his mouth, flushing slightly, as though he'd said too much.

'Oh, thank you,' said Rose. 'That wasn't quite what I meant, but . . .'

They looked at each other for an instant, and Rose smiled awkwardly, feeling her cheeks warm and her heart beat fractionally faster.

Then the count sighed. 'Oh. I wish . . . I wish I had . . .'

'What?' Rose said softly. 'What is it?'

At that moment, the side door they had escaped through burst open.

'Nikolai Artem!' It was the count's father. 'The lady is arriving. It is time!'

Nikolai's pale face blushed bright red, and Rose recalled seeing him in the room, the despairing expression he'd had on his face.

'Ah,' he said.

'Ah?' said his father, moving forward, ignoring Rose completely. 'You understand how important this is. You know how much I have borrowed to put this on for you tonight. This is our last hope.'

'But, Father –'

'No,' said his father firmly. 'I don't *care* what your feelings are. This family is close to ruin. It is on the edge, Nikolai. Either you make this marriage or –'

Suddenly there was a blast of trumpets. The noise made

Rose jump.

'And she is here,' said the older man. 'The priest is arriving, the whole of Saint Petersburg is here. Nikolai Artem, it is time!'

Meanwhile, the Doctor was still outside, carefully examining the salon window that he and Rose had spied through the telescope. He jerked his head up as a woman, with two men in huge fur hats following closely behind like bodyguards, glided up the gravel path past where he stood. The palace butlers and footmen rushed out to greet her.

She was very beautiful. She wore a flouncing white dress and clutched a bouquet of lilies that were wilting in the frosted air. Her skin was pale as milk, almost wax-like in the moonlight.

The Doctor lifted his nose and sniffed. Then he immediately turned and charged back round to the main door of the palace to get Rose.

Among the throng in the ballroom, the Doctor couldn't see Rose. He kept tripping over the ladies' huge dresses and bumping into the people about him, who were taking their places for what looked very much like a wedding.

'Rose!' he shouted, but his voice was inaudible above
the orchestra playing sweeping, romantic tunes as the guests
found their places. 'Rose!'

Suddenly he felt a strong, heavy hand grab the back of
his collar.

'Oi!'

Nikolai's father sternly marched off, and Rose glanced up at
Nikolai, whose face betrayed the truth.

'You're getting *married*?' she asked. 'Like, *now*? I have to
tell you: this was a really terrible time to invite me over . . .'

Nikolai swallowed. 'I was going to tell you. She is . . . she
is rich. My family is on the edge of ruin, but my bloodline is
good . . . she chose me.'

'Can't you just say no?'

Nikolai went even paler than he already was. 'If I do,
then I must join the army. It is the only way open to me.
And, Rose, Bonaparte's men are already nearing the gates of
Moscow. They say the people are blocking up their windows
with the bodies of the dead just to keep warm.'

Rose grimaced. 'I see. Who is she?'

'She is new to Saint Petersburg, just like you are. She has

money.' A thought appeared to occur to him. '*You* don't have any money, do you?'

'Not a rouble,' said Rose. 'Sorry, mate. I work in a shop.'

Nikolai looked surprised at this. 'Oh well, no matter.' He turned to go. 'I have given my word as a gentleman, after all. It is not just me who needs saving – I have five sisters and . . . so on.'

As he stood and attempted to put on a brave face, a strange man wearing a large fur hat that almost obscured his waxen face entered the room.

'And here is one of her footmen, to bear me to my fate!' Nikolai said, trying to sound jovial.

The man ignored the young man, however, and headed directly towards Rose. 'Anomaly,' he said in a low voice that was almost a growl.

Rose blinked and jumped up. This was interesting. 'Uh, it's Rose actually.'

'Anomaly detected.'

'Ooh. I'm not sure people say that in whenever we are,' said Rose.

The count looked confused.

Rose leaned forward to peer more closely at the approaching man's very white face. 'So what are *you*?' she mused.

The man didn't answer. Instead, he said again, 'Anomaly detected', and drew from his coat a large weapon shaped like a mace that blinked with a small red light. It didn't belong in the nineteenth century any more than Rose herself did.

'Aha!' said Rose. 'I've found it! Doctor!'

'You need a physician?' said the count, his brow crinkling, before the man harshly shoved him out of the way to get to Rose.

✸

'Get your hands off me!' said the Doctor.

He had noticed straight away that the two men following the lady were either identical twins – or they were wearing the exact same version of a face. This one had extraordinary strength. He manhandled the Doctor through the crowd and eventually deposited him in the salon he and Rose had first seen through the telescope. From far away, down the end of the corridor, the Doctor could hear Rose shouting for him.

'Sorry,' he said to the large man, twisting neatly out of his jacket and bounding aside. 'I really have to go.'

'Anomaly detected,' said the man.

The Doctor grinned. 'Oh, and how!'

He was almost at the door when he found himself face-to-face with a large mace.

The man rushed at Rose. He gave off a clammy, damp smell, like something wet around the edges. She wrinkled her nose. It wasn't a smell she recognised. He put out a moist hand. 'You are an anomaly.'

Rose kicked him in the shin. It was like kicking a block of wood, and she recoiled, hopping about in agony. 'Oww! Oww!'

'Unhand her!' Nikolai had drawn his sword.

The man gazed at the count with contempt, not letting his tight grip of Rose drop. The count slashed at his arm. Without flinching, the man grabbed the count's sword in his free hand and, showing no sign of pain, tore it from the young man's grasp and whirled it across the room.

Startled, Rose twisted to see it, forgetting her voluminous skirts and knocking a nearby candelabra over as she did so. The candles instantly fell on to the papers beneath, which whooshed up in flames.

The man backed away a little. Apparently, he wasn't comfortable with fire.

Rose seized her opportunity and grabbed the candelabra, brandishing it at him. 'Stay back!'

But the man, sweat dripping from his forehead, pushed

aside his fear and lunged at her – just as Nikolai retrieved his sword and launched himself at the both of them. The three of them overbalanced, and the man caught hold of the long red ribbon tucked into Rose's dress. He pulled hard and, as he did so, the room seemed to shimmy around them. The candles wavered and vanished, the walls contracted and squeezed, and Rose found herself standing next to a window, alongside Nikolai. The man in the fur hat had vanished; all that remained was the long length of red ribbon, torn at the end.

To her horror, Rose spotted the telescope and realised where they were: back in 2005, in the bright daylight of modern Toronto. Together, she and the count looked out of the window and down. Nine storeys below, embedded in the snow, lay a brown, horribly twisted shape.

Instinctively, Rose did the first thing that crossed her mind: she pulled the blinds shut, blocking out the great shining view of the city beyond.

'What happened to him?' Nikolai asked.

'We . . .' Rose flapped her hands. 'We moved. To a different space. But he must have been on the other side of the window. Whatever he was, he's gone.' She covered her mouth with her hand. 'He would –' She forced herself to slow her breathing. 'He would have killed us. He was trying to kill *me*.'

But by now Nikolai was looking about the apartment, utterly astonished. He had grabbed a television remote, and stared at it blankly, then felt the shape of it almost reverently.

*He can't have ever seen plastic before*, Rose realised. And that, it occurred to her, was only the start of it.

'What? What is this? Am I —' He clutched his head.

Rose desperately wished that the Doctor was there; partly to help, but mostly to do the explaining bit that he was so good at.

'Um, maybe you're . . .' She wanted to lie and say 'concussed', but instead she blurted out, 'I'm sorry. We've moved forward in time.'

Nikolai shook his head, his face contorted.

'Um, you know, time travel?' Rose tried.

'I never . . . What could that be?'

'Well, you know "today"?' Rose started, feeling this was only going from bad to worse.

Nikolai looked at her.

'It is no longer the same . . . ?' He sniffed suddenly. 'What *is* that smell?'

'Not sure,' said Rose, sniffing too. 'Coffee? Diesel?'

Nikolai sniffed again. Then he twisted round. 'Oh my,'

he exclaimed, his face incredulous. 'It's me!'

Rose couldn't help it: she smiled.

*

Rose sat next to the telescope, amused by the sounds of extraordinary happiness emanating from the bathroom, even as she was conscious that she'd left her phone in the TARDIS and didn't know how on earth she was going to contact the Doctor.

'Oh my . . . oh. This is the best . . . this is . . .'

'It's just a shower,' she called. 'Okay, a power shower, but still!'

Nikolai could barely find the words for his joy. 'It is . . . oh. I have never known such . . .'

'You'll have to get out.'

'Never!'

'You will! I've put your towel on the radiator.'

'What's a radiator?'

Covering her eyes, Rose edged the bathroom door open just a touch, then thrust her arm through the small gap to hand him the warm, fluffy towel.

'Ooooh!'

*

The Doctor felt something twinge. He looked down. The red ribbon he had been carrying had glowed briefly, and now the colour had all gone out of it. Rose had gone. *Thank goodness.* She was safe.

He, on the other hand, was still staring at the big man's large, curved mace.

'Now,' the Doctor said quickly, 'I'm sure you don't *mean* to be trying to blow a hole in the fabric of space and time, so why don't we sit down and talk things through.'

'I must kill the anomaly.'

'I like that name,' said the Doctor. 'The Anomaly. That could work – if only anyone could spell it.'

The man raised his weapon above his head and prepared to strike.

Nikolai came out into the sitting room, blinking. He turned the lights on and off over and over again, marvelling anew each time.

'I'm definitely not showing you the internet,' said Rose.

Nikolai looked across the room, frowning slightly. 'Where is the rest of this palace? Where are all the servants and footmen?'

'Ah,' said Rose. 'Don't worry about that for now.'

There was one muffin left from that morning. She

handed it to Nikolai, just to see his face as he ate it, and laughed when she did, vowing that the first modern item she would buy him was a toothbrush.

The Doctor frantically scanned the room, looking for something to use in self-defence, but there wasn't much beyond sealing wax and parchment. *Aha!* He spied a large pewter jug on the table, and quickly pulled out his sonic screwdriver and increased its magnetism. Instantly the mace curved over the man's shoulders like a fat scimitar, then plunged into the jug.

The Doctor had bought himself several seconds. He had to get to that window. *Now.*

'Rose,' he breathed, as he peered out of it. 'Can you see me?'

He centred himself, using his intense powers of focus to tune out everything that was in the foreground and bring up what was lurking just below the surface. The pedlars, the flower sellers, the shivering footmen stamping their feet as they stood by their horses, the steam rising from the beasts' noses: he tuned it all out.

And then he saw it. Just a glimpse, a mere blip, but clearer now than ever. The hole. *It must be growing larger.* He could see the apartment window quite entirely now, the skyscraper outlined behind.

'Rose!' he mouthed, even as he heard the figure behind him grunt and pull the mace out of the pewter jug. 'ROSE!'

✳

Rose was once more at the telescope, even as Nikolai had exclaimed his way around the contemporary apartment. She spotted the Doctor straight away. The window in Russia, its sill covered with a thick layer of snow, flickered softly; it was dark there, where everywhere else was light. She could see the Doctor was calling her name, and behind him a huge man was bearing down on him . . .

'Oh no! We have to go back!' She jumped up. 'Come on!'

Nikolai didn't move. 'I don't want to.' He was dressed, his blond hair wet and flopping in his eyes. He had his back against the radiator. 'Can't I stay?'

Rose was so tempted. She looked at him sitting there, clean and content. She could leave Nikolai there while she went back to the Doctor, then they could come back for him . . . But what if they didn't?

She glanced out of the window again. Amidst the honking traffic below, suddenly a sleigh careered, driven by a

very, very confused-looking man and pulled by four terrified
horses, with a screaming woman in a ball gown seated inside.
The sleigh sluiced across eight lanes of traffic, before finally
coming to a halt at High Park.

'No,' Rose said firmly, tugging Nikolai roughly up from
where he rested. 'We have to go. *Now.* This isn't good, and it's
getting worse and . . . you being here. I think that might be
part of it.'

❋

Rose was in such a desperate hurry to get back to the Doctor
that she couldn't think of a story to tell the doorman in
the lobby of the apartment building across the road. The
doorman looked at her and Nikolai – and, in particular, at
Nikolai's sword – askance as they rushed past him.

'We don't mean any harm!' Rose shouted over her
shoulder, but it was already too late. The doorman had
pressed the panic button, and the elevators, Rose instantly
saw, had all frozen in place. She cursed under her breath and
banged through the fire-escape door into the stairwell.

Climbing eight flights of stairs is the kind of thing
that would be a challenge when you've warmed up and
are wearing sweatpants and trainers, let alone when you're
wearing a tightly laced corset and have a very confused

Russian count in tow. Rose's lungs were bursting by the time they reached the eighth floor, and the sirens were blaring in their ears. Nikolai was having no trouble keeping up, but the look on his face indicated just how very, very difficult he was finding it all.

Rose dragged him along the corridor to the correct door and, gathering the last of her strength, she kicked it open. But it opened on the wrong room. There it was: the small sofa, the furry throw, the fairy lights. This time, though, a young woman was sitting on the sofa with her laptop. She rose up, terrified.

'Oh my gawwwwwd! Was it you who put the lipstick on my window?'

'Sorry. Sorry! Sorry!' said Rose, retreating in a panic and closing the door behind her.

*Oh god. What now?* The Doctor needed her.

Then she smelled it again. It was wafting off Nikolai, even after a shower: that whiff of tallow wax and parchment. The whiff of time.

She thought about it. Then turned towards him.

'*You* open the door,' she said.

'Will it take me back?'

'I think so.'

'Will you come with me?'

'Yes,' said Rose.

She could tell he didn't want to do it, but he did it anyway. This time, when the door swung open, Rose was not surprised to see the salon there. The Doctor, looking exhausted, had shinned up one of the heavy velvet curtains, while below him a large man feinted and swiped at him with the point of a huge mace.

'Help us!' shouted Rose, charging in.

'Which one?!' said Nikolai.

'The one with the nose!'

'Oi!' The Doctor's relieved but nonetheless offended voice called from the curtain.

Wielding his sword, Nikolai leapt on to the back of the man with the mace, even as Rose had gone for his ankles to try and knock him off balance. The man reared up with a roar that sounded distinctly unhuman, dropped his mace, and Nikolai tore half the shirt off his back, exposing blue, nobbled reptilian flesh under a white carapace of what looked like wax.

'Ooh,' said Rose, grabbing the rest of it.

The Doctor jumped lightly to the floor. 'Causubus!' he cried, as Rose kicked out at the creature's knees before it could swing its mace back round, bringing it crashing to the floor. Nikolai held the point of his sword at the creature's neck, and the Doctor came over to them. The fake skin the monster was wearing – the wax-like carapace – was peeling off.

'Causubus origina. Oh, how you little souls cling on.'

'What foul thing is this?' said Nikolai.

'Something you should definitely keep pointing your sword at for now,' said the Doctor, grabbing the creature's mace from where it had clattered to the floor nearby and holding it alongside the count's sword. 'This too, for good measure. It's a parasite,' the Doctor continued. 'Steals little bits of time energy from all over the universe to use as fuel by binding itself with a host. I have no idea how he's ended up here.'

Rose looked at the creature, then back at Nikolai, as an idea dawned.

'Um, when you say "bind",' she asked, 'could that also mean "marry"?'

The Doctor turned to her.

'It could do. Why?'

Meanwhile, the creature's face was melting off, pieces of wax falling to the floor. It groaned.

'Shall I kill it?' asked Nikolai, still standing there. There was a tremor in his voice and, Rose noticed, he was shaking.

'Are you built for killing, do you think?' the Doctor asked the young man.

'No,' said the count, his face turning pink. 'I have no stomach for it.'

'Good,' said the Doctor. 'Quite right too.'

'But of little consequence,' said a voice behind them. In the doorway stood the beautiful woman in a white dress, clutching a small bouquet of wilted lilies.

'You,' the Doctor said, before turning back to the creature on the floor. 'Of course. This is just one of your goons.'

Rose looked closely at the woman's beautiful, perfect skin, at her waxy complexion.

'My love.' The woman turned to Nikolai. 'It is time for us to be wed. Ignore my pet.'

Rose laughed. 'I don't think he's up for it, mate.'

The woman ignored Rose. 'Your family,' she cooed to Nikolai, 'has lived here for hundreds and hundreds of years. Land and titles and fealties passed down. You are rooted in time. You are delicious, a fertile well . . . You shall have money. Your family will be safe and cared for. There will be no offspring. No harm.'

Nikolai blinked.

'Look. He just doesn't fancy yours much,' said Rose. 'Really. Aren't you all blue and scaly under there too?'

The woman made to move away, but she kept her eyes on the young count, her beautiful face outlined in the firelight. 'No, I am not,' she said to him. 'Come now, Nikolai. Everyone you know is out there, waiting for you. But you and your family may starve, if you prefer, or die on the slaughter fields of Russian winter.'

The Doctor's eyes blazed. 'You, Causubus. Parasite. I know what you are. I'm here to stop you.'

The woman smirked. 'But this is a wedding! You cannot stop a binding when both parties are willing. And we *shall* be bound.'

She opened a purse she carried on her belt. Inside, it glistened with gold and jewels.

Nikolai's eyes widened.

'All yours, my love,' she said. 'The instant we are bound.'

'Money,' the Doctor muttered to himself. 'Why money gets people to do such extraordinarily stupid things will always remain a mystery to me.'

The woman still had her eyes fixed on Nikolai.

'Come, my love.'

And she disappeared through the door and glided back into the ballroom.

The Doctor, Rose and Nikolai glanced at one another, then charged after her.

As the three of them clattered into the ballroom, the music stopped. Everyone turned to stare at them, and also at a very old man dressed in black, with a long beard and a curved crucifix hanging heavy round his neck, who had walked into the ballroom at that same moment. As he shuffled by, the assembled guests sank to their knees.

'The priest!' said Nikolai, looking panicked.

The woman in white was already in front of the assembled guests, kneeling as she waited for the priest to reach her. Rose hung back and grabbed the count.

'Run!' said Rose.

'Where?' said Nikolai.

Outside, a freezing gale blew off the lake and rattled every door and every shutter.

Rose looked imploringly at the Doctor. 'Can't he come with us?'

Nikolai's face lit up. 'I would like that very much. To come where the lights glow and the water falls and where there are tumbling, sweet fountains of steam. Yes, I would like that very much.'

The Doctor's face was absolute granite. He refused to make eye contact with either Rose or Nikolai.

Then, from far away, there came the sound of a police siren. Rose didn't notice the anachronism at first, until Nikolai stiffened. He had no idea what the siren was.

'It's getting worse,' Rose said to the Doctor in a low voice.

'Yes, it's getting worse every second, and we're all part of the problem. We need to seal both ends. With everyone in their right end.'

Rose blinked. Her mouth moved, but barely any sound came out.

The Doctor folded his arms and bent down to listen to her.

'To send him to war . . .' she was saying.

'Sometimes, people go to war.'

'You could stay here, for me,' Nikolai beseeched Rose. 'We could be happy.'

'There is,' said the Doctor, speaking so quietly only Rose could hear, 'something of a time limit on happy Russian aristocrats.'

Rose remained as frozen as the statues outside in the winter garden, and avoided meeting Nikolai's pleading eyes. Looking forlorn, he turned his attention to the assembled guests, and in particular to the front row. There they were, anxiously gazing back at him: his father, his mother, looking fretful, and what were obviously his five sisters. He glanced once more at Rose, who still did not move.

There was no way out.

The candlelight gleamed on the beautiful woman in

white's hair, flickered over the purse hanging from her waist, and Nikolai found himself moving forward like a man in a trance. He knelt obediently opposite the woman.

Rose lifted her head and sniffed. There was that soggy scent in the air again. What *was* it?

'Mud. Mud, decay and earth,' the Doctor whispered to her. 'It's all they have.'

The priest withdrew a long piece of material to bind the count and the woman's hands together. It was a long strip of red ribbon. As he wound it round and round the couple's wrists, he intoned the ancient words of the marriage ritual over their bowed heads.

Rose couldn't bear to watch. Instead, as if hypnotised, she watched a long drip of molten wax run slowly down the back of the woman's white neck. The woman flinched, but did not look up.

'Repeat after me,' the priest commanded her. 'I take you as my husband, to be with you always, in wealth and in poverty, in disease and in health, in happiness and in grief, from this day until death separates us.'

The woman parroted the vows.

'And now you.' The priest turned to Nikolai, who repeated them.

'And now,' said the priest, 'if anyone here knows any

reason why these two people should not be joined in holy matrimony . . . '

'I do!' shouted Rose, bounding up. 'Don't! Don't you dare!'

There was a gasp from the crowd as Rose tried to pull the woman away, but she simply smiled her beautiful smile and turned to the assembled company.

'Ah,' the woman said. 'An uninvited guest. A jealous one. And who can be surprised? Guards!'

Several men with large lances stepped forward. Two of them picked up Rose, still wriggling and shouting, and started to bear her away.

Nikolai glanced up at Rose from where he knelt. Then he looked back at the woman in white. He looked at his family. Then he took a very deep breath, and he lifted his sword and sliced through the red ribbon that bound their hands together. Then he jumped to his feet to run after Rose.

The woman let out a loud screech, an unholy noise, and the Doctor leapt towards her, in his hands a torch. The deep, dark, muddy smell of decay hung all about her, and there was death in her eyes.

'Nikolai, my darling,' she attempted, but the count's face was a mask of horror as the Doctor waved the torch closer. Her mouth opened – and then kept on opening, until

the skin around her mouth began to crack like wax, all over
her perfect white face. Her mouth opened still wider, into a
horrifying stretch. Bits of skin started to flake off, revealing
blue scales beneath.

There were terrified gasps from the throng. The soldiers
holding Rose froze in terror and let her go.

'If I cannot *have* it, I can still *take* it!' the woman
screamed. 'Give me your hand! Give it to me!'

She had by now morphed completely into a hideous,
flaking, ancient monster, its mouth a gaping hole in a white-
and-blue face. The creature turned its attention on the
painted throng. 'YOU HAVE NO FUTURES!' it hissed
at them. 'You. You. You. You. You will *all* die. This will *all*
crumble into dust. We know this.' The creature's voice was a
cracked husk, a rasp in the ballroom.

'Go,' said the Doctor. 'Or the humans will rip you to
shreds, and you know it.'

'Yeah!' shouted Rose, grabbing a sword from the nearest,
rather confused-looking chap.

The creature looked around, as the crowd shrank back.
But already the guards were recovering from their initial
shock and drawing their swords, and those guests in military
uniform were edging closer. The creature looked back at the
Doctor, who simply sighed.

'I'll take you in the TAR–' he began, as a phalanx of guards moved to block the ballroom door. Not all of them, the Doctor realised to his alarm, were Russian, nor even men. There was now also a group of extremely confused-looking Canadian Mounted Police just beyond the doors, their horses kicking up the snow in the garden, and the wind was blowing stronger and stronger

There was no time left. No time at all. The two worlds were about to collide and pull everything else along with them, like soap suds down a plughole . . .

The Doctor's eyes travelled to the red ribbon, still half-tied round the creature's wrist. 'Is that what I think it is?' he asked.

'You will bind to me?' hissed the creature.

'Well, don't go getting any ideas . . . '

There was a sudden commotion beyond the doors. The soldiers inside were moving closer, and the Mounties and the guards at the door were trying to communicate with each other. The Doctor had to hurry.

'I can give you enough energy to get you home,' he said. 'Not enough for you to move again. Not an ounce more.'

The creature looked at him. 'Do you have enough?'

'Far too much,' said the Doctor curtly. He grabbed the remnants of the red ribbon from the startled priest and, with a swift motion, bound his wrist to the monster's.

In an instant, they both vanished from the ballroom.

◉

Rose took the opportunity of the commotion at the doors to dash back outside. She headed straight for the TARDIS. As she stepped out the main door at the front of the palace, she skidded to a halt. Nikolai was standing at the bottom of the stairs in front of her, head bowed, but he was not alone. He was surrounded by his family. His father was shouting at him. His mother was crying. His five sisters looked forlorn. Nikolai glanced up and caught Rose's eye. She slowly raised one hand.

A look of determination crossed his face, and he strode over to her. Behind them, the crowd of ball guests had begun charging out of the palace and down the front steps.

'I can't take you with me,' Rose said, feeling her resolve wobble and thinking, *But he's just one man.* It wouldn't really matter, would it? The Doctor would be able to fix it, wouldn't he?

But Nikolai was nodding his head. 'I understand. I realise I cannot go with you,' he said. 'You have shown me what I have to do. You have shown me what I need to fight for: a happier world. The world you come from.'

'Oh, I wouldn't say that my world is ha–' Rose began,

but Nikolai had bent down quickly and taken her hand.
He kissed it gently and firmly, and his lips lingered. Then
he straightened up and, with one last look into her eyes, he
marched away from her, out alone into the cold, cold night,
the crowd parting to let him through.

●

The Doctor was already back in the TARDIS by the time
Rose got there, returned from the sudden journey to the
Causubus ship, and possibly the shortest marriage in his
history. He was preparing what he called a 'puncture repair
kit'. Rose was too tired to ask him what it really was. He
seemed tired. He looked older. Rose asked him what he had
had to give; but he did not answer, and there was silence as he
busied himself tidying up the edges of Saint Petersburg.

She sat in silence as they travelled back to 2005, and
the Doctor did the same thing there – carefully repairing the
puncture in time while she listlessly packed up the telescope
and tidied the apartment. Finally, Rose changed back into
her jeans, which felt strange to her now. She picked out the
biggest, warmest coat in the TARDIS wardrobe, then made
one request of the Doctor.

●

Before long, the Doctor and Rose were standing together
in front of the Alexander Column, which stands in Palace
Square in Saint Petersburg and was raised to commemorate
Russia's victory over France in the Napoleonic wars. From
there, they then went to visit the archives of the war dead.

When they returned to the TARDIS, Rose disappeared
inside before emerging once more into the frosted air. She
was holding a helium balloon. She let go of the ribbon and let
the balloon float off up into the air.

Silently, she and the Doctor watched it until it vanished
into the sky far, far above.

# CLARA AND THE
# MAZE OF CUI PALTA

· · · · ● ● ● · ·

## BY SUSAN CALMAN

The Doctor stood at the door of the living room, his head cocked to one side like a curious sparrow.

Clara sighed heavily, turned to face him, placed her hands very deliberately on her hips and spoke in a tone that warned of impending annoyance. 'What? Why do you keep staring at me? Have I grown a horn from the middle of my forehead?'

As Clara glowered at him, the Doctor tried in vain to diffuse the tension by saying all the words in his head at once. 'No, no! Of course you haven't. And, even if you *did* have a horn in the middle of your head, you wouldn't need *me* to tell you about it. For a start, the force of keeping your head in an upright position would put extra strain on your neck, meaning that you would have already realised you were staring at the floor a lot, what with the big, heavy horn in the middle of your face.'

Clara narrowed her eyes as the Doctor babbled on.

'On the other hand, if you did have a horn on your head, imagine how useful that would be! You could store bits of paper on it, eat sushi with it – I know you like sushi. It's healthy *and* tasty at the same time, and so very tiny and perfect. In fact, I often think how good it would be if I could eat it on the go, you know. Perhaps if I had a horn growing from the middle of my forehead to keep it on . . .'

His stream of consciousness slowly ground to a halt as Clara started tapping her foot. The Doctor knew that hands on hips and a tapping foot were signs of a dangerous level of annoyance for Clara.

'Well? What is it then?' she said. 'What's so fascinating about my face?'

The Doctor gulped, carefully choosing his words. 'Well, it's not so much your face as your hair, actually. You just appear to have something in it. It's all sort of . . . lumpy.'

Clara put her hands to her head and ran them through her hair. As she did so, a shower of popcorn cascaded to the floor. One little bit remained fixed in place though, and stood proudly on the top of her head, making her look like a cupcake with a cherry on top.

'Great! Now I have to clean this up as well!'

Clara flopped down on to the sofa and sighed. The Doctor quickly sat down next to her, taking the bit of popcorn from her head and eating it before she realised it was there.

'I love Artie and Angie, but sometimes I feel like all I do is clean up after them!'

The Doctor nodded, because he knew that's what he was supposed to do. Meanwhile, he was quietly and slowly chewing what was turning out to be a very stale piece of toffee popcorn that refused to be eaten no matter how hard he tried.

'I got excited the other day trying out a new fabric softener. Can you imagine? A new fabric softener! Life on Earth can be pretty dull sometimes . . .'

The Doctor nodded again. Somehow the toffee had made a bond between his teeth – his jaws felt like they were being superglued together. He grinned manically, trying desperately to prise his molars apart.

Clara appeared to take this as an encouraging sign. 'But the solution is right here, isn't it? Well, not right here but right outside. The TARDIS. We should go somewhere new! Mix things up a bit.'

The Doctor's teeth remained firmly stuck together. He had no choice but to continue to nod. The more he did so, the more excited Clara got.

'Yes!' she enthused. 'Somewhere beautiful, somewhere magnificent! As far away from fabric softener as you can get.' She jumped up, put on her jacket and went to the front door. 'Come on then! We've got an adventure to go on! And you can stop nodding now. You're excited – I get it.'

Clara disappeared through the front door, and walked purposefully towards the TARDIS.

At last, with an aggressive and somewhat uncomfortable wrench, the Doctor managed to disconnect his mandibles from the sticky treat. He let out a huge gasp of relief, and rubbed his jaw.

'Looks like we're going on a trip then,' he muttered.

On his way to the front door, he stopped, turned suddenly and eyed the pile of popcorn on the floor. He bent down quickly and stuffed a handful in his pocket.

'Just in case I need a snack. We are going on an adventure, after all . . .'

Inside the TARDIS, Clara clapped her hands gleefully. This was her favourite bit of any adventure: the not knowing exactly what was about to happen.

She watched as the Doctor flicked switches and knobs on the console, moving from one to the other in a seemingly random order. It was like he was dancing to an ethereal tune only he could hear.

'Beautiful and magnificent, you say?' he said. 'Away from everyday life, I hear you ask? I think I have just the place!'

Clara gripped the railing as the TARDIS tumbled and turned its way through space and time. She was sure that the Doctor was making the ship fly with even more speed and vigour than usual just to cheer her up.

'So where are we going?' she asked.

The Doctor threw another piece of popcorn into his mouth and started chewing. Fortunately for him, this piece wasn't as stale – or as sticky – as its predecessor, and he happily chewed and swallowed it before taking another piece and popping it in his mouth. 'That's more like it!' he said to himself, and Clara glanced at him quizzically.

He spun the TARDIS monitor round, revealing a message on the screen: IT'S A SURPRISE!

They bumped to a halt and Clara whooped, punching the air with delight. This was what she loved – time away from babysitting and laundry and all the boring bits of everyday life. Laughing, she ran across the control room, ready for the TARDIS door to swing open. When it did, though, she had to turn away suddenly, covering her eyes. The interior of the ship had been flooded with the brightest sunlight she'd ever seen.

'Use these, Miss Oswald.' The Doctor threw her a pair of sunglasses, which she put on. Her eyes quickly adjusted to the sunlight, and the Doctor joined her at the door, wearing a matching pair.

'Sunglasses are cool,' said the Doctor, as he stepped out into the sunshine.

✷

Clara could barely conceal her joy as she took in their surroundings. Everything sparkled and shimmered, and vibrant colours sprang from every nook and cranny of the bright white buildings that littered the landscape. Houses and shops rose out of the terracotta earth, and it was as though a giant had looked down on the planet and dropped the buildings in a pretty arrangement. A vast, glowing city spread out in front of them like ripples from the waves.

The Doctor stood in the middle of the street and opened his arms wide. 'Welcome to Cui Palta! Voted Most Beautiful City in the Galaxy three years in a row by readers of *Space Health Monthly*.'

'You made that up, Doctor.'

'I did not! How do you think I keep in such exceptional shape? I particularly enjoy *Space Health*'s pull-out sections on exercise while in zero gravity. Amazing what you can do with a bag of rice and some rope!'

Clara hugged the Doctor quickly and started to walk down the street. Together, they wandered slowly through the city, peering into doorways, standing at the top of winding stairways, breathing in the fresh air deeply. There were signs everywhere for treatments and spas, deckchair rentals and sweet treats. But, as they explored, Clara grew increasingly uneasy. Something very important was very obviously missing from this beautiful place.

After a while they came to a small, shady square. As the Doctor moved forward, Clara grabbed his arm.

'Doctor, don't you think there's something strange about this place?'

The Doctor shrugged, apparently unconcerned. 'It seems perfectly lovely to me. Maybe a little warm for my liking, but I'll get used to it.'

Clara shook her head. 'No, not the weather. There's no one else here! Not a single soul. We've been past all these spas and things, so why isn't there anyone in them? Customers, staff – anyone?'

The Doctor seemed to reconsider. He narrowed his eyes and slowly swept the horizon with them. 'Hmmm . . . I suppose it *is* a little odd. It was a lot busier the last time I was here. The queue for the hot tubs went right round the block. Maybe it's a bank-holiday weekend?'

Clara smiled. The idea of an alien planet having a bank holiday seemed ridiculous. She was still uneasy, though. It was so *very* quiet. More than that – it was completely deserted.

Seeing her frown, the Doctor tried to lighten her mood. 'Sometimes people just move on. Maybe they found the constant sunshine a bit too much. I may even have to take my jacket off soon, which as you know is a *very* occasional event. Now, let me show you the bluest water you'll ever see!'

He held out his hand and Clara took it. They trotted down some steps carved from stone. On either side was a stream that gurgled and stuttered its way to a pool so blue it looked like it had been painted by an artist.

*Nothing should be that perfect a shade of blue,* Clara thought, but she kept it to herself. The Doctor didn't seem worried. She was probably being too cautious.

They carried on, and eventually reached the crest of a hill. From where they stood, the Doctor pointed out the various temples below, each ornate and intricate in its design. Here and there between the white buildings of the city were forests of tall bushes laden with yellow flowers. Some stood as high as the buildings themselves, and they waved as one with the gentle breeze, like reeds in the water.

The Doctor took a deep breath and exhaled noisily. Clara did the same, taking in a huge lungful of air. She immediately sneezed – a violent, noisy sneeze that reverberated around the streets like a small explosion.

'Oh dear! That was a loud one. Take this.' The Doctor pulled his handkerchief from his top pocket and passed it to Clara. 'You seem to need it more than I do.'

Clara dabbed her nose with the hankie, then put it in her jacket pocket.

The Doctor scrunched up his face, looking out over the bright, sunlit city. Putting one hand on his hip, he placed a foot upon a convenient rock and gestured with his free hand at the great outdoors.

'Sometimes, Clara,' he said grandly, 'it's important to stop and smell the flowers. To get away from all the rush and bother. To take a deep breath and enjoy the beauty. Lovely, isn't it, Clara? Clara!'

She had disappeared from the Doctor's side. He spotted a shady alleyway behind him – the only place Clara could've gone – and walked quickly down it, calling her name. The alleyway soon broadened out and he spotted her, sunglasses in her hand, squinting at a wooden sign. It was weatherworn and obviously very old, with faded writing that was only just legible.

'The Maze of Cui Palta,' Clara read aloud. 'How exciting! A puzzle to solve!' Clara grinned at the Doctor, who had come to stand beside her. 'This place is gorgeous, but there's not much else to do, is there? Let's go in!'

The Doctor groaned.

'Oh, come on, Doctor! Mazes are fun!'

'Fun!' he scoffed. 'Hardly! Not much of a challenge, are they? Mazes are a simple matter of mathematics. I could solve any maze in the galaxy quicker than you could say "Daleks smell". Mazes are *rubbish*. Let's look in the temples instead. Lots of lovely temples around here.'

The Doctor turned to walk on, but Clara stopped him in his tracks with one sentence.

'Are you worried you won't be able to solve it, Doctor? Is that it?' She gasped theatrically. 'What if this is the ONE maze that defeats the Doctor? I mean, if you don't want to take it on, that's fine. It's a pretty big-looking maze. I suppose someone else will come along and solve it eventually . . .'

The Doctor turned round slowly, narrowing his eyes at

Clara. Then, without a word, he took her hand and dragged her into the maze, his face splitting into a big grin as they ran. The sound of Clara's laughter echoed off the empty city's walls.

✦

Clara and the Doctor only stopped running when they found themselves suddenly faced with a wall. Tall by any measurements, it was dwarfed by the gigantic yellow flowers that created an archway just in front of it. They could choose one of two options: go left or go right.

'Well, Doctor,' Clara said, 'show me how easy this maze-solving is, then!'

Smirking, the Doctor walked confidently along the left-hand passage, gesturing for Clara to follow.

They wandered for a while in companionable silence. It was pleasantly cool, far nicer than being in the blazing sunshine, and Clara felt herself relaxing; even the fact that Cui Palta was so quiet stopped bothering her. This was fun!

At the Doctor's instruction, they took every left-hand turn available. The Doctor seemed pretty confident with his strategy, even waggling his eyebrows at Clara occasionally as if to remind her of his genius. But Clara soon started to have her doubts. When they passed a rock that looked like a grumpy frog for what she felt sure was the third time since they had entered the maze, she stopped. The Doctor was a few paces up ahead of her; without him noticing, she bent down and gently turned the stone so that the 'frog' was facing the wall. Then she stood up again and hurried after the Doctor.

Just a few minutes later, they rounded another corner – and there it was! The little frog with its face turned to the wall, looking as though it had been banished to the corner for misbehaving.

'Doctor! Stop!'

'What? We're nearly there!'

'No, we're not! We've been this way already. Look at the frog!'

The Doctor moved towards Clara, a concerned look on his face. 'Have you had too much sun? I knew I should have brought the fez . . . Or are you hungry? I have lots of popcorn.'

He reached into his pocket and pulled out a handful of toffee popcorn, sticky and oozing in the heat, bits of pocket fluff all over it.

'I'm not hungry, and I don't have heatstroke! I've seen this rock before,' Clara insisted, pointing at the rock. 'The last time we passed it, I turned it to face the wall so I could be absolutely sure that we are *definitely* going round in circles!'

The Doctor made a noise that sounded rather like *Pshaw!* He shook his head. 'Of course we aren't lost! This is a tiny little maze in a tiny part of the city. Look!' He pointed to the top of the wall next to them. 'We can still see the big yellow flowers and the tops of the temples! This maze can't be more than half a mile long at best. We just need to find the right formula and we'll be out in a jiffy, okay?'

They set off again, this time taking every right-hand path, turning and turning and turning, and with every passing moment Clara became ever more uneasy. Before long, they turned another corner . . . and found themselves staring at the frog again.

Clara couldn't help it now: she was starting to panic. Her worst fear as a child had been of getting lost, and here they were on an alien planet, in a maze, with no exit to be found.

'Can't you just use the screwdriver to locate the TARDIS and find a way out?' she said.

'What, already?' the Doctor replied. 'You're such a maze killjoy! We've hardly even started enjoying ourselves.'

'I think I'd like to get back to the TARDIS now. We must have been in here for at least an hour . . .'

'All right,' the Doctor said petulantly. 'But only if you acknowledge that I *definitely* could have solved this maze *very* easily, but you were the one who wanted to give up.'

'Fine.' Clara folded her arms. 'You know exactly what
you're doing. I believe you.'

'And . . . ?'

'And what?'

The Doctor raised his eyebrows.

'You are the king of the maze! Are you happy now? Can
we please go?'

The Doctor grinned and nodded vigorously. 'Since you
have admitted I am the maze-solver supreme, we can leave.
Let's go and have a good laugh about this over a nice, cooling
lemonade.'

He pulled the sonic screwdriver from his pocket and
held it above his head triumphantly. A persistent beeping
emanated from it, but the tone of the beeps didn't change
as the Doctor walked slowly along the path. There was no
sign at all to indicate whether they were getting closer to
the TARDIS or not. It was as if the world outside the maze
simply didn't exist.

'Hmm. Something seems to be broken,' the Doctor said,
holding the sonic in front of him and peering closely at it. 'It
isn't connecting with the TARDIS.' He hit the screwdriver
a few times with his hand, then held it aloft once more, and
walked onwards . . . but still the tone of the beeps didn't

change. The Doctor switched the sonic off and on again. 'Sometimes the simplest solutions are the best!'

But the sonic still wasn't behaving as it should.

They walked for another twenty minutes, with the sonic's constant, unchanging beeping accompanying every step, and yet the TARDIS seemed to stay out of reach.

Clara leaned against a wall, defeated and tired.

The Doctor tried to lift her spirits. He crouched down beside her and smiled. 'Sometimes even Time Lord technology can be temperamental. Don't despair! You forget, I have at my disposal the most powerful weapon in the universe.' With a flourish, he pulled from his pocket a small piece of white chalk. 'Let's do things the old-fashioned way, shall we?'

The Doctor scrawled on the wall: THE DOCTOR WOZ HERE. He then drew an arrow pointing left, along the passage they then took.

As they rounded each corner, the Doctor marked their progress with a different message – things like TARDIS 4EVA, and DALEKS SUCK – every time throwing a big smile in Clara's direction. She couldn't help but be comforted by his apparent nonchalance, drawn into his irresistible orbit. But when they rounded a corner to find their original message – THE DOCTOR WOZ HERE – waiting for them,

Clara started to feel very uneasy again.

'That's fine. It just means we have to go the other way. To the right!' cried the Doctor, and they ran on.

By this time, the sun had started to set, casting long shadows around them; dark corners loomed towards them, and their pace quickened. They turned yet another corner and read: TARDIS 4EVA. Then, round the next: CYBERMEN JUST WANT TO HAVE FUN.

There was no denying it now. This was no ordinary maze. They were trapped, walking round and round in endless circles.

The Doctor had stopped smiling now, and his face looked uncharacteristically grim. A heavy silence descended between the two of them and, without uttering a word, they stumbled on through the shadows until they found themselves facing a wall twice as high as any they had seen so far. Clara gasped when she saw what was drawn on it: arrows. Hundreds and hundreds of arrows, of all sizes, pointing in every direction.

'Clara?'

'Yes, Doctor?'

'I think this maze might not be as simple as I first thought.'

'You *think*?'

'What we need to do is keep going. Perhaps just a little bit more quickly than before.'

The Doctor held out his hand, and Clara took it. In his other hand, he held the sonic screwdriver. He lifted it up, and a beam of light lit the now-darkened path ahead of them. Together, they ran onwards. Gradually, the maze started to change. Small yellow flowers – miniatures of those that surrounded the city – appeared on the walls, in the gaps between stones, and in the crevices of the ground.

Suddenly Clara stopped and let out a cry. 'Doctor, look!'

She pointed to the end of the long passageway in front of them, where a figure was sitting on the ground, one arm outstretched as if warning strangers to stay away.

The Doctor held his sonic screwdriver higher, throwing light over the figure. 'Hello there!' he called, but the figure remained motionless.

'Why aren't they moving?' Clara whispered.

'Maybe they're just a bit tired,' the Doctor replied, but he didn't sound very convincing. They inched towards the figure and the Doctor called out another cheerful greeting, but there was still no reply. In fact, it was so quiet that Clara was sure she could hear her heart beating through her chest, louder than a drum.

'Are they . . . dead?' she whispered fearfully, as they

neared the motionless figure.

The Doctor reached out with the sonic to illuminate the shape slumped against the wall . . . only to discover it wasn't a person at all. It was a skeleton.

The tatters of clothes hung off the bones. One knee was propped up, supporting an arm, which was perpetually stretched out as if to indicate to passersby an escape route from the maze that the skeleton would never find.

The Doctor gulped. 'If he's not dead, then he's very much in need of a good dinner.'

Clara reached forward and gently touched the middle finger of the bony hand. The entire finger wobbled, then fell and hit the ground with a thud.

'Doctor, I don't think this is a good sign.'

There was a small crunching noise, and the Doctor and Clara watched in horror as the skeleton's skull shuddered, as though nodding in agreement, then dropped from the body and slowly rolled away into the darkness.

'Not everyone is cut out for puzzles, Clara. This fellow just didn't keep his head.'

Clara stared at the Doctor. Not even his terrible jokes could stop her from being frightened now.

Seeing the look on her face, his weak smile faded. 'Come on. Let's keep moving.'

They ran in step with each other, checking over their shoulders every few seconds, as though to make sure an invisible enemy wasn't on their heels. Everywhere Clara looked, she saw evidence of others who had also become trapped in the maze: a discarded shoe, a notebook, lines that looked horribly like fingernail marks on the walls . . .

Darker and darker and darker it got; deeper and deeper and deeper they ran.

At the entrance to a familiar-looking passage, the Doctor stopped. 'This is new,' he remarked, breathing heavily. 'We've definitely been here before, but this wall wasn't here last time.'

He approached the new obstacle: a wall lower than the others within the maze, which only came up to his shoulder, but which cut directly across their path. He peeked over the top to check what was on the other side, then turned to Clara and shrugged.

'Well, this is interesting. On the other side, the path simply carries on. The wall is definitely new, though.'

'Should we go over it?'

'Of course! When a wall like this appears in a devious, tricksy maze, its purpose *must* be to prevent people from getting to the exit.'

The Doctor pulled himself to the top of the wall, scrabbling and groaning as he heaved himself aloft.

'See – king of the maze!' he exclaimed, throwing his arms up, then quickly regretting the move when he started to wobble.

'Doctor! This is not the time for messing about!'

'Sorry! The time for messing about is first thing in the morning, as everyone knows. Right, give me your hand and I'll help you over the top.'

Clara stood so the toes of her shoes were brushing the wall. She stretched her arms up as the Doctor leaned down, but just as their hands touched there was a noise. A rumble. It started quietly, then grew and grew until the vibrations were shaking Clara's teeth.

'What's happening?' she shouted.

'I have no idea!' the Doctor yelled in return.

'Maybe you should come down from that wall!'

'What? I can't hear you!'

'I said maybe you should come down from that wall!'

'I'll need to come down from this wall! I can't hear a thing!'

The Doctor moved to jump back down, when he was suddenly thrown into the air. Initially, he felt as though he was floating, like he had somehow been catapulted into the atmosphere, but after only a split second he realised that the wall itself was rising. With incredible speed, it shot higher and higher into the sky. He hugged the bricks tightly, his cheeks wobbling as the air rushed past him, the temperature dropping as he watched the city fall away below him.

'Claraaaaaaaaaaaa!' he yelled as far, far below him she became a dot barely bigger than a speck of dust.

On the ground, Clara watched the Doctor fly up and away from her.

'Come back! Don't you *dare* leave me here!'

She stretched an arm out towards him, but snatched it back when she realised that she was echoing the skeleton, that poor person who had ended up trapped in the maze forever.

'DOCTOR!'

The Doctor couldn't hear Clara's cry. He was still ascending, faster and faster. Then, as suddenly as he had started climbing, he stopped.

Carefully, he raised his head, looking around nervously in case the wall started to move again. It didn't, so he risked looking down to see where he was, shaking his head to clear it. Everything was topsy-turvy and his senses were dulled. As he focused his eyes, he saw that, despite feeling as though he should be in the clouds, he wasn't actually that high above the city at all. He searched for landmarks, for anything he had seen before – temples or markets – but there was nothing familiar. Instead, stretching from horizon to horizon was the maze, twisting and turning and flowing seemingly without end. It was as if the whole planet was a maze . . . but how could that be? When they'd landed here, the maze hadn't even been visible – not even from the hilltops in the city.

Though reluctant to admit he'd been defeated by the maze, the Doctor decided it was probably time to put his secret 'Plan B' in motion: to call the TARDIS into the maze, using the key in his pocket, and get off this planet as soon as possible. Things were getting a bit *too* dangerous, even by his standards.

The Doctor was so wrapped up in his thoughts that he didn't notice the wall begin to slowly descend again. Only when he heard Clara shouting did he realise that he was moving gradually downwards, a gentle breeze ruffling his hair. At last, the wall came to a halt back in its original position.

Clara was eager for information. 'What could you see from up there? Could you see the way out?'

She was clearly still frightened, so the Doctor made a

decision – one of the decisions he often had to make when he needed to protect the people he loved. 'Yes. I could,' he replied confidently. 'It's not far away, but I think we should take a shortcut and call the TARDIS for a lift.'

Clara clasped her hands together in relief. 'You've got the key in your pocket! Why didn't you say so?'

'Well, since I am the maze-master extraordinaire, I don't like to take the easy way out. But it *is* rather dark in here now, and I *could* do with a cup of tea . . . and this doesn't appear to be your usual sort of maze.'

Clara sighed in exasperation. 'You don't say!'

The Doctor ignored her. 'First thing, though, let's get over this wall in case it decides to move again.'

The Doctor held out his hand, but this time Clara hesitated.

'Trust me,' the Doctor said.

She took hold of his hand and he hoisted her up. The two of them tumbled over the wall, ending up in a heap on the ground. Clara laughed, and it was a good feeling – a nice change from the fear the maze had churned up inside her.

The Doctor smiled. 'Right then. TARDIS?'

'Yes please.'

The Doctor put his hand in his pocket . . . but, to his horror, the key wasn't there. Perhaps he had put it in the other pocket, or in the inside pocket for safekeeping? He searched, keeping the smile on his face. But, as his scrabbling became more and more desperate, Clara realised something was wrong.

'Don't tell me you've lost it!'

The Doctor dropped to the ground and started to search around in the dirt. 'Must have dropped out of my pocket when the wall moved. Has to be here somewhere!'

Clara looked around desperately, hoping to spot a glint of metal in the dirt. 'Maybe it's on the other side of the wall?' she said hopefully.

The Doctor threw his hands up. 'Of course it is!'

He walked towards the wall, but as he did it moved once more, shooting into the air and blocking any chance of getting to the other side. The Doctor turned slowly back to Clara. Even he was going to struggle to put a positive spin on the latest developments.

'Clara. I think we may have to consider that we might be just a little bit lost.'

Clara sighed and shook her head, wiping the dirt from her hands.

'Come on, Oswald. Chin up. A maze is simply a puzzle, and this just happens to be a very, very good one. This is absolutely not the time to panic. We need to find the way out.'

Clara looked exhausted, but the Doctor persisted.

'Come on! We've been in worse scrapes than this! A brick wall can't be more frightening than a Dalek, can it?'

Clara raised her eyebrows.

The Doctor simply pointed down the passageway ahead of them. 'Onwards!'

They set off in silence, Clara's face set in a steely expression of grim determination. As they walked, she felt sweat trickling down her brow. The air seemed to be closing in around them, and even though the maze remained shrouded in darkness it felt as though it was getting warmer. The walls, all partially covered with great blossoms of the ever-present yellow flowers, seemed nearer and tighter than before, the turns more frequent and extreme. Clara started to feel lightheaded and sick; it was as if the maze was whirling around her. Then she saw something move a little way up ahead.

'Doctor, stop,' she whispered, grabbing him.

'What is it? Why are we whispering?'

'I don't think we're alone,' she said, pointing to where she'd seen the movement. 'I saw something up there. Maybe it's someone else trapped in here? We could ask them for help finding the way out.'

She suddenly sneezed again, trying to stifle the noise with the Doctor's hankie as best as she could. *Now was really not the time to be making sudden loud noises!*

The Doctor shook his head. 'No! If they're trapped in here, they won't know where the exit is, will they?'

Clara was determined. She spoke quietly and firmly. 'I'm going over. You can wait and see what happens. If I need rescuing, you can jump in.'

Before the Doctor could argue, Clara started to edge slowly towards where she had seen the movement.

'Hello?' she said, trying to keep her voice light and cheerful. 'Hello? Is there someone there?'

As she moved closer, she was sure she could discern a figure shrouded behind the yellow flowers covering the wall. With every step, the figure seemed to move closer and became more clearly human in form.

'Are you trapped here as well? We don't want to hurt you. We just need some help.' Clara hesitated. 'Say something? Please?'

The Doctor, who had crept along behind Clara, was ready to pounce at the slightest whiff of danger.

Clara was now within touching distance of the figure, with only the hanging curtain of yellow flowers between them. With one swift move, she reached out a hand and brushed the flowers to one side – and screamed.

The Doctor shot forward, gangly limbs tangling with each other, making his attack seem more like a puppy running for its dinner than anything that might threaten someone.

'CLARA, OUT OF THE WAY!' he shouted, as he struck out at the figure.

He yelped as his knuckles made contact with something solid, the impact reverberating through his body.

'Doctor, it's me!'

'What do you mean it's you?' he said, hopping around in the dirt and clutching his hand to his chest.

'Look, it's me! It's a mirror!'

Still wincing, the Doctor watched as Clara moved the flowers aside and gestured at the wall. It was indeed a mirror – and, as he looked around, he saw that mirrors had appeared everywhere. The walls of the maze were now made of glass instead of stone. There were even some reflective surfaces on the ground.

'It's like the funfair in Brighton,' Clara said. 'A hall of mirrors!'

She was right.

The mirrors varied vastly. They weren't all flat and perfect. Some were warped, and the reflections were contorted, ugly, squat and stretched.

'Clara. This is far more than a normal maze. This is something far *worse* than a normal maze . . .'

Clara moved to the Doctor's side. 'Would now be the time to panic?'

He looked at her. 'Panic is a strong word, Clara. Let's move to "be more concerned" first, shall we?'

*

Short of any better ideas by this time, the Doctor and Clara carried on through the maze, but the mirrors made their progress difficult. They soon became dizzy and disoriented, as they whirled and lurched round corner after corner.

Clara heard her breathing becoming louder and louder, and it echoed in her eardrums until there was a constant hum in her ears. It was unbearable. Lungs almost bursting from the effort, she shouted, 'I can't tell what's real and what isn't!'

'Don't look at the walls!' the Doctor called back. 'Keep your eyes on the ground. It'll stop you from feeling sick.'

It was like being stuck in a terrible nightmare. It began to seem they had been trapped in this awful maze forever, and indeed it soon became evident they had been running around in circles for several hours as, eventually, the gentle light of a new day started to illuminate the pathways and passages ahead of them.

Abruptly, the mirrors disappeared, and the Doctor and Clara stepped into an area that was definitely new: a courtyard brilliantly lit with sunshine, the walls solid and bright white as if freshly painted. Clara could suddenly see and breathe and think clearly again.

'Well, look at this,' the Doctor said, pointing at one wall of the courtyard. Three sturdy doorways, each identical in structure and each with a large exit sign hanging above it, faced them.

'Three doors. Which is the right one?' the Doctor muttered, stroking his chin thoughtfully. This was clearly another puzzle, but as with all the other obstacles they had faced in this maze there didn't seem to be any rhyme or reason to it. It was chaotic, like the maze itself had been left to dream up its own twisted, nonsensical challenges.

Knowing how important it was that Clara believe they were going to get out of here – and that he believe it too – he stated with certainty, 'It's the middle one, of course!'

'Doctor, it can't be as simple as just picking the middle door.'

'Of course it can. It's always the middle one. This maze just wants you to think this puzzle is more complicated than it actually is. Mark my words, when faced with three doors, always go through the middle one. Every time. No doubt.'

Clara sighed. 'We should go through together, just in case anything happens.'

The Doctor nodded. 'Yes. Together.'

He put his hand on the doorknob and turned. It rotated easily, and they both heard the click of a lock opening.

'See,' he said. 'It's *always* the middle door!'

He opened the door as far as it would go, but all that waited for them on the other side was darkness. Hand in hand, the Doctor and Clara stepped through it.

*

After a few seconds in the darkness, the Doctor bumped into something solid in front of him.

'Seems we've got another door here,' he hissed to Clara.

He turned the handle until they heard the familiar click, then opened this new door. They were immediately blinded by sunlight. They'd finally made it out! Clara cheered and hugged the Doctor.

Slowly, her eyes adjusted to the light. Shading her face from the glare, Clara saw the Doctor doing the same thing – and then she realised what had really happened.

They hadn't escaped.

They had walked through the middle door and then come back through the *exact same door*.

They were back in the courtyard again, in front of the three doors, exactly where they'd started.

'We didn't turn round, did we?' Clara asked.

'Maybe we did. It was dark. Let's try again.'

Once more they walked through the middle door, and a few seconds later walked out into the courtyard again.

'I'm not sure it *is* always the middle door, Doctor.' Clara walked towards the door on the left. 'Maybe we should try the others?'

She turned the doorknob and gestured to the Doctor to follow her into the now-familiar darkness, then opened the door that they found beyond . . . and walked through the middle door again, back into the courtyard.

'This is fine,' Clara said, in a deliberately calm, controlled tone. 'It just means that the real exit must be this one.' She walked purposefully to the door to the right of the middle door and opened it.

The Doctor stayed where he was, watching Clara disappear through the right-hand door. Almost immediately she bumped straight into him, as she reappeared through the middle door.

For a moment, their eyes locked.

*Is this it?* Clara wondered. After everything that they had been through, would this be the end?

The Doctor was the one who had brought them here; he thought that this place would be fun, beautiful, even relaxing. But when Clara looked at him now she only felt fear, because for maybe the first time since they'd travelled together he looked lost – as lost as she was.

Then the Doctor turned his head sharply. He'd spied something in his peripheral vision; something he hadn't noticed before. Had it been in the courtyard all this time? It was a narrow passageway between two walls covered in yellow flowers – tiny, but definitely there.

'Clara! Over here!' he said, walking over to the passageway. As he peered down it, he could see another courtyard a short distance away.

'This could be it,' he whispered to himself, turning back to Clara – but Clara was nowhere to be seen.

On the opposite side of the courtyard, he saw that another passageway had appeared. It was the mirror-image of the one he stood next to. Doors, mirrors, passageways, mirror-passageways – the maze was throwing everything it had at them!

'CLARA!' the Doctor yelled, sprinting across the courtyard, desperate to catch her before they lost each other for good. He tore down the passageway, gasping for breath as he reached the mirror-courtyard, and gave another enormous cry, every ounce of his being behind it. 'CLARA OSWALD! ANSWER ME!'

He listened. Nothing but silence. And then he heard it. Far away and quiet, but definitely there.

'Doctor! Where are you?'

'Clara! I'm here! Move towards my voice!'

Clara was in another part of the maze. She had gone through the middle door again and this time found herself in a different courtyard. When she had turned to look for the three doors, however, she had discovered to her horror that they had disappeared. She was sitting on the ground trying to work out her next move when she heard the Doctor calling her name.

'Keep talking!' she called back. 'I'll try to find you!'

She stood up and listened carefully.

'Okay . . . erm, hello! I'm in a maze,' she heard him saying, and despite her fear she smiled. He was rambling. 'It's not the kind of maze that I like. Usually I prefer one in the garden of a nice castle or something. Somewhere you can get an ice cream if it gets too hot. I mean, it's not my fault. Well, it kind of is my fault. But last time I was here I got an amazing pedicure – I didn't think I'd like it, but once you've had your toenails clipped by a tiny air-breathing shark-like creature who uses his actual teeth you'll never go back . . .'

As the Doctor rattled on, Clara worked her way towards him. Finally, she was sure that she was right beside him, but between them stood a wall that was too tall to climb over and too thick to knock down.

'Doctor!' she interrupted him. 'I'm here! Can you hear me?'

On the other side of the wall, the Doctor pressed his hands to the brick, as if by touching them he could get closer to her. 'Clara, I can hear you. Are you okay?'

'I'm fine. I can't see a way of getting through this wall to you, though. Is there a way through it on your side?'

'I'll see.' The Doctor had already started patting the bricks and working his way methodically along the wall, searching for any sign of a potential weak point or gap. 'Sing a song so I can tell where you are.'

'Why do I need to sing? Can't I just talk?'

'No. Sing. Singing is easier to follow than talking. That is a fact.'

There was a moment's silence, then Clara reluctantly started humming a tune.

'Louder than that!' shouted the Doctor. 'Give it some welly!'

Clara started to sing loudly. Amplified by the echoes, her

voice seemed to stretch up to the sky. She stopped to cough and suddenly sneezed. She took out the Doctor's hankie and blew her nose. She sneezed again.

'Keep singing, Clara!' The Doctor sounded further away, so she started singing again, but her nose was blocked.

'Doctor, come back!' she called, coughing. 'You're going the wrong way!'

She was seized by a fit of sneezing. How strange. What could be making her sneeze? She didn't feel like she was coming down with a cold.

She coughed with such force that she had to grab on to the wall to steady herself. As she did so, she brushed against one of the yellow flowers. From it cascaded a waterfall of yellow dust, a shower of tiny pellets that floated in the air around her like a mist.

*It couldn't be as simple as that, could it?*

Clara dropped to the ground, immediately placing the hankie over her nose and mouth. As she took shallow breaths, things slowly began to change in front of her eyes. The walls started to shimmer and became more and more transparent.

That *was* it!

The very flowers that the Doctor had insisted they should stop to smell were trapping them. Clara wasn't sure whether it was a hallucinogenic effect or not – all she knew was that the longer she stayed on the ground breathing through the hankie the more the walls disappeared.

In the distance she could see a figure: it was the Doctor. He was running round and round in a circle. It would have been comical to watch if it wasn't so terrifying. Clara now realised that there were no walls – there had never been any walls – but the Doctor was still seeing them.

'Doctor! I know what's happened!' she called.

'I'm coming for you, Clara!' He looked blindly in the direction of her voice. 'Don't worry! I'm coming for you!'

'Doctor, listen to me. You need to get on the ground and breathe through your hankie!' As Clara finished her sentence, she realised that she had the Doctor's hankie.

'I'm nearly with you!' the Doctor shouted, still running round in a circle.

'Doctor, use your shirt sleeve. Breathe through it. It's the flowers! They're doing something to us!'

'Nonsense!' he scoffed. 'It's a simple puzzle. I'll have it all worked out in a jiffy!'

'STOP!' Clara shouted.

Hearing the tone of her voice, the Doctor skidded to an abrupt halt.

'Do you trust me, Doctor?' she asked slowly and deliberately.

The Doctor turned his head towards the direction of her voice and she saw him smiling. 'Always, Clara.'

'Then get on the ground and breathe through your sleeve.'

'I think a hankie would be more appropriate,' the Doctor said. 'I always carry a spare one for just such an occasion.'

'Doctor, I've got y—' Clara began, but she stopped short and shook her head in amused disbelief as she watched him pull a massive spotted cloth out of the inside pocket of his jacket. He shook it with a flourish, then placed it over his mouth and nose and dropped to the ground.

Within moments, the Doctor saw the walls of the maze shimmer and start to disappear. He could at last see that they were in a small courtyard just beside the alleyway in which they had first entered the maze. All they had been doing for all this time was walking round and round in circles. He set eyes on Clara, and scurried across to her on his hands and knees.

'It seems that there may have been a reason why the people abandoned Cui Palta,' he said. 'What say we do the same?'

Clara didn't need asking twice. Still holding their hankies over their faces, they both got to their feet and ran — back up the stairs, past the temples, until they saw the TARDIS. It was right where they had left it.

Thrusting his hand into his pocket, the Doctor pulled out

the TARDIS key and held it up.

'It must have been here all along,' he said, scrutinising it, as though making extra sure that what he was looking at was indeed really there. 'And the sonic must have been connected with the TARDIS all along too. That pollen did such a thorough job of clouding our senses that we weren't able to see it. Except clever old you worked it out, Clara.'

He pushed the key into the TARDIS's door, then threw the door open. 'After you,' he said, as Clara burst through it. Once they were both inside, she slammed the door shut, taking a deep breath as she sank to the floor.

'Thanks for the relaxing day,' she said, the glimmer of a smile appearing at the corners of her mouth. 'I really needed that.'

The Doctor seemed thoughtful, leaning against the central console with his head bent down. 'All those people, having fun, relaxing . . . driven away by the visions the flowers created, maybe even driven *mad* . . .' He turned to her and fixed her with a serious look. 'Clara, I was wrong to not listen to you sooner. It was the maze, doing funny things to my judgement . . . But I really do trust you. I hope you know that.'

Still catching her breath, she reassured him with a smile in return. 'I do, Doctor. And it's okay. You can owe me: one proper spa break, to be redeemed any time of my choosing.'

The Doctor laughed. 'We'll come back here for a pedicure, shall we?'

'No thanks!' Clara replied emphatically. 'So much for stopping to smell the flowers, eh? I'd find a battle on a planet that's about to self-destruct from fabric-softener overload more relaxing.' She thought of Artie and Angie, and how pleased she was that she'd get to see them again – messy habits and all. 'How about we just go home for a cup of tea?'

'Oh, yes! And, for the trip home, snacks!' The Doctor pulled the remaining popcorn from his pockets, looking rather proud of himself. It had by this time melted together into one big, messy toffee-and-popcorn lump, and bits of grey lint fuzzed the outside edges. Clara grimaced. As the Doctor held it out towards her, a tiny yellow flower detached itself from the sticky mess and floated innocently to the floor of the TARDIS.

The two of them watched it land between their feet, then looked at one another.

'Maybe some biscuits instead . . .' the Doctor conceded.

# BILL AND THE
# THREE JACKETS

·  ·  •  ●  ●  ●  ·  ·

## BY DOROTHY KOOMSON

'I'm telling you, Bill – there are rooms and rooms of jackets in this TARDIS. In fact, I think there's a whole *level* devoted to jackets. Jackets created by some of the most important and noteworthy designers of the modern age! Nardole will help you choose one. You do not need to go out there and *shop*.' The Doctor navigated the console of the TARDIS, an ever-watchful eye concentrating on one multi-coloured control panel while he talked to Bill Potts.

'Yeah, but it's not the same,' Bill replied. Stood on the other side of the main console, she looked at the readings on the screen in front of her but wasn't really paying attention.

The readings were usually interesting, sure, and if the Doctor asked, she would obviously monitor them. But to Bill, the TARDIS felt alive. The console room was its beating heart. Like there was always someone there with her, looking out for its passengers – even when she was by herself.

Bill was tempted to lean down and whisper to the TARDIS how excited she was about her date that evening, but instead she spoke to the Doctor.

'Thing is, Doctor, you can have too much choice. I could go down there, or up there, or out there, or wherever your rooms full of jackets are . . . but too much choice means I might not find anything. If I go into town, I've *got* to decide what I like, by myself, in a normal amount of time. Trust me – it's the best way to pick a perfect outfit for a perfect date.'

'Perfect dates don't exist,' the Doctor snorted. 'I've witnessed many dates on many planets and none of them were perfect. Some have come close, I'll give you that, but my advice would be to expect imperfection. Embrace it!'

'Maybe your standards are just too high,' Bill shrugged.

The Doctor ignored her. 'I don't understand why you need anything new to wear. Did you not meet this "perfect date" when you were dressed in clothes? Was she not interested in you then? Why do you imagine that what you choose to put on your body will change in any way what happens tonight?'

'Oh, come on, I know you're not fashion-phobic. I've seen you wear a hoodie,' Bill grinned. 'What you wear changes how you feel. When I look better, I feel better – know what I mean?'

'But you look *fine*.' The Doctor looked over Bill, with her mass of curly black hair tied up in a red scarf, her features as inquisitive as always, her unique smile lighting up her face. 'In fact, I'd go as far as to say *adequate*.'

Bill sighed as she headed for the door. 'That's the thing about you, Doctor. You understand all this amazing stuff. Time and relative dimension in space! You've been to all these different planets and yet, still, when it comes to emotions, feelings . . . you can be a bit clueless.'

'I don't think that's true.' The Doctor sounded offended by the suggestion that he might not know *everything* about human beings. For a wise, two-thousand-year-old Time Lord who had spent a lot of time on Earth, what Bill was saying was quite a big insult.

'It's *totally* true,' Bill said with a laugh. 'It's not a bad thing. Just the way it is, isn't it? Anyway. Standing here chatting won't get me any closer to finding a new jacket.'

She pushed open the TARDIS's heavy door.

'Bill?' the Doctor called, just before she stepped outside.

'Yes?'

'What you look like tonight really isn't important,' said the Doctor seriously. 'The most important thing is who you are. I may not know everything about emotional stuff, but I do know that. Who you are, the strength of your character . . . that's the most important thing.'

'Yeah. Thanks, Doctor,' Bill replied with a small smile, before she left.

'And you wouldn't be travelling in the TARDIS with me if you didn't have that,' the Doctor added, when the door had shut behind Bill and she had no chance of hearing.

'Well, that looks *awesome* on you,' said the sales assistant, whose name badge read 'Ziggy'.

Earlier, Bill had spotted a shop on a small street on the outskirts of Bristol city centre, mysteriously called *O & Ohhh*. It looked like there were loads of cool clothes inside, but it had been the gold jacket with buckles in the window that had caught her eye and made her decide to come back.

Inside, Bill had discovered a whole rack of colourful jackets, each as unique as the next. Ziggy had insisted that Bill pick three she loved best and only try those on. 'You want to narrow it down straight away. You can have *too much* choice, you know,' Ziggy had said, nodding sagely.

'Exactly,' Bill had replied.

This first jacket was the colour of amethyst, a glorious purple, and when the light hit it, it shone like it had been carved from the precious rock too.

Bill stood in front of the mirror, twisting this way and that, looking at herself in the jacket. Each time she caught a glimpse of herself from a different angle, she liked the look of it even more.

'It could have been made for you!' Ziggy said, beaming.

Bill went to her own denim jacket and took out her mobile phone from the pocket. She returned to the mirror and was about to snap a photo when Ziggy stepped in front of the mirror.

'Oh, I'm sorry,' she said. 'But I'm not allowed to let anyone take photos of the clothes – these are *exclusive* designs, so people come in all the time posing as customers and then they steal the ideas. My boss left strict instructions: no selfies.'

'Oh,' Bill said. 'Okay. No selfies makes it harder to decide, though. I can't work out which jacket looks best against the others.'

'I'm sorry,' Ziggy said, regretfully. Bill looked at her. There was something about her . . . Bill couldn't quite put her finger on it. Ziggy was beautiful, there was no doubt – her dark brown skin was smooth and flawless, her large eyes were a deep, hazel brown and her large lips made her look even more stunning whenever she smiled or, as she was doing now, twisted them in worry.

'I feel really bad!' Ziggy sighed. After a second or two she seemed to make a decision. 'Look, don't tell anyone I did this . . . ' She nipped behind the counter and bobbed down out of sight for a few seconds before reappearing with an old-fashioned instant camera in her hands and a conspiratorial grin on her face. Placing the camera on the counter, Ziggy ran to the door and switched the sign to 'Closed' before she locked it. 'At least this way you haven't *technically* taken any selfies on your phone . . . but we have to be quick!'

She grabbed the camera again and held it up. 'Strike a pose!' she said to Bill with a giggle. Bill smiled, her hands in the purple jacket's pockets. 'Perfect,' Ziggy said. 'Absolutely perfect.'

Ziggy pushed the button at the front of the camera and the image of Bill was captured. There was a whirl and a slow, soft buzz as a white square sheet came out of the front of the camera. Ziggy took the photo and stared at it, like she was willing it to develop faster. 'Quick, try on the next one and we'll get them all photographed before my boss comes back.'

Bill shrugged off the jacket and went to the other she

had chosen. It was a rich emerald green with red roses embroidered all over it. As she reached for it, she felt a bit light-headed. *Must be the excitement of getting ready for the date*, she thought. *That and the secret photoshoot.*

She slipped on the second jacket and, like the other one, it fitted like it was made for her. She stepped back in front of the mirror as Ziggy gasped. 'Wow! That looks perfect on you. Maybe even more so than the other one.' The helpful shop assistant raised the camera again.

Still unsteady, Bill did as she was told as Ziggy took another photo. Again she stared at it, smiling as it developed and placing it carefully on the counter next to the first. 'One more for luck?' Ziggy said with a mischievous smile. Bill was starting to really like her – there was something about Ziggy that made Bill think they would've spent a lot of time getting into trouble together if they'd met at school.

Bill reached for the final jacket – the gold one from the window. The leather was butter-soft under her fingers, and Ziggy gasped when Bill slipped it on. 'I'm really, really glad I'm not the one who has to choose between those three,' she said as she raised the camera again. 'They all look fab on you. Whoever you're going on a date with is very lucky!'

When Ziggy had taken the last photo and laid it beside the other two, Bill took off the jacket and another wave of dizziness almost knocked her over. She had to stand very, *very* still for a moment and squeeze her eyes shut.

'Are you all right?' Ziggy asked.

'Yeah,' Bill replied. 'Just didn't have a proper breakfast, and no lunch. Must just be desperate to get this outfit sorted for tonight!'

'Hmm. I can tell you need a rest,' Ziggy said kindly. 'Why don't you go get a coffee and something to eat, and clear your head? When you come back, the photos will be developed and you can decide which jacket you want.'

Bill wobbled again, then smiled and nodded. 'Yeah, I think you're right.'

Ziggy gently helped Bill to the door. 'You should take better care of yourself! Come back in a bit and we'll choose together. Although, have to say, that gold one is definitely my current fave . . .'

At a nearby café, Bill still didn't feel better. She was sat outside with a coffee that she couldn't drink without feeling even more dizzy, and a sandwich that turned her stomach. She wished she'd just kept the photos Ziggy had taken. She could do with looking at something to take her mind off how sick and weak she felt.

*Well, if I'm gonna sit here, totally useless, I'll close my eyes for a sec* . . . she thought. *Rest them for just one teeny-tiny moment.*

Bill suddenly jerked awake, and sat up. The clock on the face of the building opposite told her that fifty-five minutes had passed since she first sat down. Blinking fast, she tried to get her eyes to focus. *That can't be right*, Bill thought, squinting at the clock. *I've been here five minutes at most.*

'Where'd she go?' The waiter asked her suddenly, his voice with an angry edge to it.

'Who?' Bill asked.

'The girl who was sitting there about half an hour ago.'

'I've been here for nearly an hour,' Bill replied.

'No, the *other* one.'

'What other one?'

The waiter tutted. '*The other girl*. You know, curly hair, light brown skin, big smile. Where'd she go?'

'What was she wearing?'

He frowned. 'A bit like your outfit, really. Red headscarf, denim jacket, black-and-white t-shirt, nice pair of trainers on her, like yours . . . but her outfit suited her *much* better.'

'Oh, well, *thanks*. At least you like my trainers.'
Bill rolled her eyes.

'No, I liked your trainers on *her*. Where'd she go?'

'Okay. Big hair, red headscarf, brown skin, sick trainers

and big smile? Totally cute face?'

'Yes.'

'That's ME.'

'It's *not*,' the waiter replied, exasperated. 'And I need to know where the other girl went because she hasn't paid her bill.'

'What did she order?'

'Coffee, fish finger sandwich with chips, juice.'

'That's what I ordered!'

'Fine, good for you! But it's the other girl who ordered all that and then left without paying the bill that I need to know about!'

'I didn't leave! I'm right here!'

He sighed. 'Look, if you want to play silly idiots, I give up. The manager's going to kill me for her doing a runner . . .'

As confused as he seemed to be, Bill felt bad for the waiter grumbling to himself as he walked away. She took money from her pocket and put it down on the table to pay her bill and got to her feet. *Why do I still feel so odd?* she wondered as she started to walk back towards the shop. She hadn't decided which jacket to buy yet, but it seemed like a good idea to choose any of them and get back to the TARDIS for a lie-down, fast.

Bill turned a corner towards the shop, stopping for a

moment to let a wave of wooziness wash over her. She closed her eyes as she swayed and a barrage of images went through her mind: faces she didn't recognise, her hands in chains, a man in white shouting at her and then waving his hands to tell guards to take her away.

Bill's eyes snapped open. *Whoa!* she thought. *What on earth was that?*

This day was becoming too weird. Never mind the jackets – she had to go back to the Doctor right now and work out what was up. Strange visions were *not* a good sign.

Outside the TARDIS, Bill placed her hand on the door and pushed, but it didn't swing open as usual. She sighed with frustration – the Doctor must have gone somewhere on foot, starting an adventure without her! She reached into her pocket, pulled out her TARDIS key and slotted it into the lock. Nothing. The door still wouldn't budge. Bill took a step back and looked at the blue box. *Why was this day getting weirder and weirder?*

A sudden fear clenched her heart and stomach. The visions she'd had . . . Now the TARDIS wouldn't open, and the strange waiter had thought she was someone else . . . What if someone was messing with her mind?

'Doctor! Nardole!' Bill yelled, hammering on the door of the TARDIS. 'Come on! Let me in.'

Finally, the blue door opened and Bill almost collapsed in relief.

'I have had the weirdest day,' she said, moving to step inside. 'You're the king of weird days, I know, but this one's been weird even by your standards.'

But the Doctor didn't move from the doorway. Instead he just frowned, blocking Bill's way. 'What do you think you're doing? Who are you?' he demanded.

Bill was starting to lose her patience. 'It's me, obviously!' she said. 'Your friend, Bill?'

'Don't be ridiculous. You look nothing like Bill.'

'Not funny, Doctor, not today,' Bill said. 'Move over. I need a rest.'

'Well, you'd better go on home then!' the Doctor replied.

Bill sighed. 'I know it's not really my home, but I love the TARDIS like a really fancy, time-travelling second home. And I think the TARDIS quite likes me too!'

The Doctor looked at her with eyebrows furrowed, as though trying to work out where he'd seen her before. 'How do you know about my TARDIS? Did Bill tell you about it?'

'I *am* Bill. Why would I tell myself something? And you know I wouldn't tell anyone about the TARDIS.'

'For the last time: You. Are. Not. Bill.'

'Yes, I am!'

'Then who's this?' The Doctor stepped aside and pointed to the person standing beside the console of the TARDIS. Bill's mouth slowly dropped open because inside the TARDIS was . . . *Bill.*

Bill stared with her mouth open at the girl standing beside the console. Her curly hair framed her face, and she was wearing the gold jacket Bill had tried on in the shop – and she also wore one of Bill's favourite tops, her jeans and her platform shoes. *That's the exact outfit I was going to wear on my date tonight!* Bill thought. She wondered for a moment if perhaps she had a secret twin she'd never known about – but that wasn't it. This person wasn't her twin. She was an exact replica, an imposter wearing Bill's face and body.

'Doctor, that's not me!' Bill insisted. '*I'm* me. *I'm* Bill.'

'Just stop talking, okay?' the Doctor replied. 'As you can see, Bill is standing right there. Whatever it is you're playing at, we're not interested. And DON'T tell anyone else about my TARDIS!' With that, the Doctor slammed the door.

*Okay*, Bill thought. *Try very, very hard not to panic.* She scrabbled around in her pocket for her phone, then took it out and held it up to her face.

In the black screen, she could see that she was . . .
*not Bill.* She was Bill on the inside, but not on the outside!
Quickly, she unlocked the screen, opened the camera and
took a selfie. The image froze in front of her − her skin was a
darker brown, her eyes were large and pretty but nothing like
her own. Her face had become rounder, and her nose was
small and flatter. Bill stared and stared.

Somehow, her selfie was not of her *self.* Her selfie was of
Ziggy, the oh-so-friendly and helpful sales assistant from the
clothes shop.

'Ziggy stole my face!' Bill exclaimed. She whirled back
around to hammer on the TARDIS door. 'DOCTOR!
NARDOLE! ZIGGY STOLE MY FACE!' She banged and
banged on the police box, but even as she did it, she knew
that the Doctor wasn't going to open it to her. He thought
the imposter was the real Bill! And the fact that the TARDIS
wouldn't let her in meant that even the Doctor's time
machine didn't recognise her.

Feeling fear rising again inside her, Bill wandered away
from the TARDIS in a daze.

*What am I going to do?* she asked herself, slumping down
on to a nearby park bench.

'What you look like doesn't matter,' the Doctor had told

her. *But that's so not true, is it?* The Doctor didn't recognise her. The TARDIS didn't recognise her. Right at that moment, how she looked was the only thing that mattered.

How had Ziggy managed to steal her face and body? And how could she possibly know enough about being Bill to be able to fool not only the Doctor but the TARDIS too? The Doctor wouldn't believe the imposter was Bill simply by looking at her – he would speak to her, listen. Ziggy, the fake Bill, must be able to act *perfectly* to get away with it. She had to be an alien of some kind, didn't she?

Her mind still fuzzy and her stomach churning, Bill realised she was going to need help to convince the Doctor that she was the *real* Bill – but who could help? As far as she knew, Nardole was in the TARDIS with the Doctor. Anyone else Bill could potentially tell this story to would *never* believe her – and they probably wouldn't even speak to her in the first place, because they wouldn't recognise her!

Perhaps she could convince someone of who she was by sharing a secret – a secret only Bill could possibly know. In fact, what she *really* needed was someone to whom she could reveal a secret so trivial, that person would know that Bill would have never bothered to share it with anyone else. *There has to be someone out there like that*, Bill thought, searching her memory. When she'd worked in the university canteen, she'd met loads of people. But none of them had really noticed her. And none of them would help her even if somehow they did believe her.

Her shoulders sagged. It was hopeless. There was no one, except . . . *Of course!* Bill jumped to her feet. She knew who would help her. At least, who she *hoped* would help her . . .

At the university, Bill ran to the canteen. She hoped she'd got there at the right time. She searched frantically amongst the faces – and there she was! A round-faced girl, sitting on her own, reading.

Bill sprinted over to the table and threw herself down in one of the seats. The girl looked up from the book she was reading in surprise. 'Can I help you?' she asked, eyebrows raised.

'Hi, Lou. Look – this is going to sound really odd, and I don't have a lot of time to explain it properly. Well, I do have a lot of time – we've all got a lot of time, because time is relative and everything is happening all at once – but in real, everyday, me-and-you terms, I don't have a lot of time. I'm going to tell you something and I'd really like you to listen. Please?'

Lou was a beautiful girl who Bill used to give extra

portions of chips to every time she served her lunch in the university canteen. There had always been a spark between them. Bill was hoping with all her heart that Lou would still feel that spark, even though Bill now wore a different face.

Lou said nothing, but simply stared, so Bill carried on talking, launching into the best explanation she could give. 'This is going to sound really out there, but it's the truth. The absolute truth.

'Basically, I used to be Bill. I mean, I used to look like Bill. I still am Bill, but I don't look like me any more. Somehow, an alien stole my face and my body, so now no one recognises me.'

Lou's face did not move – not one millimetre.

'Aren't you going to say anything?'

Lou shook her head.

'Why not?'

'Because I think the quickest way to get rid of you, whoever you are, is to listen to what you've got to say, and then politely ask you to leave.'

'Fine. Well, I'm Bill. That's who I am. I used to work here. Behind the counter, on chips.'

'No you didn't,' Lou frowned. 'I remember the girl who used to work on chips. She was lovely, and she looked nothing like you.'

'That's what I'm trying to tell you. Someone stole my face!' Bill paused, because what she said next would be the only way to get Lou to help her. She lowered her voice and leant forwards. 'I used to give you extra chips. You'd give me the nod, a little look – like you knew what I was doing. Extra chips. It was *our thing*.'

Lou's eyes widened. 'How do you know that?' she asked. 'I never told anyone.'

'And neither did I!' Bill replied. 'Well, I told the Doctor, but he doesn't count. I didn't tell anyone else!' Bill thought about it. 'And really, who would I tell? It's not exactly the most interesting thing – I gave a woman extra chips, because I liked her. No one's going to want to hear that, or remember it for more than five minutes.'

Lou folded her arms and sat back, looking over Bill again. After a few long seconds she said: 'What did you say had happened to you?'

Bill breathed a sigh of relief. Lou *might* just be starting to believe her. 'I went into this shop, and there was this really nice assistant – except she *wasn't* nice, because about an hour later, I fell asleep in a coffee shop and woke up looking like this. Like *her*. And then I went to see my friend, the Doctor, and she was there, looking like me. I know that sounds crazy and made up, but that's what happened.'

Lou frowned, and then smiled. 'You're lucky that I read a lot of sci-fi,' she said.

'Yeah?' Bill brightened up.

'Don't get me wrong. You still sound completely crazy. But I've read enough alien stories to know how body-snatching works.' She waved the copy of the book she was reading, which Bill now saw featured a glowing spaceship on the cover.

'So you kind of believe me?'

Lou shrugged. 'Let's just say I haven't got any lectures this afternoon, and I'm interested enough to help you out, if you *really* need it.' A bright smile suddenly lit up her round face. 'I assume the first thing you want is to get your body back?'

'Yeah!' said Bill. 'But it's not just my appearance. She must've taken part of my personality too, otherwise the Doctor would never have been fooled. She took everything about me!'

'Not your memories, though, if you remember giving me extra chips.'

'No.' Bill blinked. 'You're right. Not my memories.'

As she said this, the barrage of images from before – visions of things Bill had not experienced, people she didn't know, being dragged away by guards – galloped through her mind. She swayed for a moment, but recovered quickly. These

things she was seeing – they *must* have something to do with
Ziggy, what she'd done and where she'd come from. Was she
now seeing Ziggy's memories, while Ziggy saw hers?

'Talk me through *exactly* what happened in the shop,'
Lou said.

Shaking slightly, Bill concentrated on her explanation:
about trying on the jackets, Ziggy insisting on taking
photographs, how she started to feel woozy, about falling
asleep, going to the Doctor and finding the other Bill had
taken her place.

'Could it be something to do with Ziggy's camera?' Bill
said, feeling more exhausted than ever once she had finished
her tale. 'That's the only thing I can think of.'

'Hmmm,' Lou said. 'This shop, was it just off the high
street? A sort of cool, boutique-type shop that you never
really noticed – and then you suddenly saw it one day and
decided to go in?'

'Yes! That's exactly what happened. I only noticed it
today, when I needed a jacket for a date tonight.'

Lou frowned. 'It sounds like the same shop I went to last
time I was going on a date and I needed a new outfit. First
time I noticed it too. The woman in there *did* look like you do
now, come to think of it. But she told me she didn't think they
had anything for me. I asked her what she meant and she

said they only had clothes for people "keen to make a good impression on a date".'

'Oh!' said Bill. 'She mentioned my date to me too, actually.'

'I didn't think anything of it at the time, but I wasn't sure —'

'How she knew you were going on a date?' Bill finished. 'I never told her about it.'

'Exactly. Me neither.'

Bill knew that some alien species could read your emotions, even feed off them. *Is that what Ziggy had done?*

'You know,' said Lou, 'a few other people told me that she wasn't interested in them buying things from her shop too. Not just me.'

'So why was I okay, when everyone else wasn't?'

The pair of them fell silent. What had made Ziggy keep Bill and steal her identity, while rejecting Lou?

'Were you nervous about your date?' Bill asked.

'Not really. I was there to buy an outfit for fun, really. I wasn't nervous about the date. I just didn't understand why she wouldn't sell me anything!'

'I was worried about looking perfect. Having the right jacket seemed important at the time.'

'Maybe that's it, then!' Lou grinned. 'I wasn't stressed

about how I looked. Sometimes clothes suit me and
sometimes they don't, but basically, I'm happy as I am.'

Bill looked at Lou. She remembered, embarrassed, that
at one point she'd told the Doctor that she'd 'fatted' Lou.
That she'd stopped her from being good-looking by giving her
extra chips. But Lou didn't see it that way. Lou liked the way
she looked, and it was clear from the way she spoke that she
didn't mind what other people thought of her either.

*She's right*, Bill thought. *That's the difference.* Ziggy couldn't
steal the identity of someone who was happy in their own
skin. Psychic energy, nervous and obvious, must be the thing
that Ziggy could latch on to. Ziggy must have thought she'd
won the lottery having Bill in the shop that day. She was
overflowing with nervousness, with wanting to be perfect, and
so she gave Ziggy the perfect body to steal. Not to mention
giving her the added bonus of getting to travel in time and
space with the Doctor . . .

Bill's heart suddenly dropped. If Ziggy got to travel with
the Doctor, to all those different places and times and worlds,
all those bodies to snatch . . . There was no limit to the havoc
she could cause.

'We have to go,' Bill said, standing up suddenly. 'The
Doctor needs me. The *real* me. And fast.'

Outside, the chill of a breeze moved across Bill's skin as they ran from the canteen, which felt odd.

But *everything* felt odd. This body didn't move in the same way hers had. The feet went out at a different angle – she wasn't properly steady with each step. She was aware of every blink, every swallow, every breath that went in and out. She'd never noticed what it was like to *be* in a body before – how important it was to feel comfortable, to not be aware of every little thing your body did. Now, when she didn't have the luxury of being herself, she appreciated herself so much more. *When I fix this*, she decided silently, *I am never ever going to complain about my brilliant old body again.*

'Where do you want to start looking?' Lou panted, as they ran from the university grounds.

Bill spoke raggedly through hard breaths. 'The shop. There might be clues there – clues about how she's done this. How to stop her.'

As they neared the high street, Bill kept catching glimpses of herself in windows, shuddering as she was reminded what she looked like now. It wasn't that Ziggy looked bad – she was beautiful – just that Bill had never so badly wanted to see her own face, and not someone else's.

The shop was empty, of course – Ziggy must still be off

with the Doctor in the TARDIS. As they looked around for an entry point, Bill gave Lou her theory.

'When I went into the shop, I wasn't *completely* happy with what I looked like. Maybe that's what allowed Ziggy to do this to me,' Bill said as she peered into the darkened shop.

'No one's happy with themselves *all* the time,' Lou said, looking up at a window on the first floor of the building.

'But this was different. When I walked in, I was thinking about being *perfect*,' Bill said. She hadn't admitted this to anyone before, but desperate times called for full honesty. 'And for just a second, I wanted to change who I was – I wanted to be someone else.'

'Welcome to being human,' Lou said sympathetically. 'You didn't do anything wrong, Bill. It's just bad luck that Ziggy ran into you at an anxious moment.' She sighed, looking over the building. 'We might have to smash the window. Unless . . . Hang on – have you tried the door?' She reached for the handle, and the door swung open.

In partial darkness, the shop had an even stranger feel to it. Bill noticed that the three jackets she'd tried on were missing from the rail. She went to the counter and ducked down behind it, searching for the camera. It was there, on a shelf – but the photos were nowhere to be seen. Bill had guessed right, then – somehow the camera and the photos were connected to how Ziggy had stolen her body.

*And now she's taken them with her,* Bill thought. *So the photos must still be important somehow* . . .

'There's something else I should mention,' Lou said. 'The other girls came back from the shop and said they'd felt funny after trying on one or two things, before Ziggy had made them leave.'

'Really?'

Lou nodded. 'That wasn't the weird thing. Thinking about it now, one girl was ill for quite a while afterwards. She said she didn't feel like herself. Like, after that day, she couldn't stack playing cards any more – and that was her party trick. It was like someone had reached into her head and plucked it out. She put it down to a virus. But maybe it was a milder version of what happened to you.'

Bill nodded. 'Spot on, I reckon.'

If the Doctor was here, Bill realised, he'd have a neat theory all worked out by now. He would say: 'Ziggy is from a noble and ancient alien race, Bill! And the jackets are visually cloaked devices that can siphon away a person's energy and emotional qualities! And the camera is either a necessary part of the siphoning process – OR a clever way of keeping people in the jackets long enough to make sure the process completes!'

*Hang on*, Bill thought. *That's a pretty good theory!*

Bill didn't need to wait to speak to the Doctor – she'd come up with this theory on her own! And if she'd learned anything from the Doctor, it was that a theory led straight to a plan.

'How about we play Ziggy at her own game?' Bill said, grabbing Lou by the arm. 'We get the jackets, get the camera and then I take a picture of HER in the jackets to get my body back?'

'Could work!' Lou replied. 'You'll need to be careful, though. It seems like a pretty unstable process. She got your looks and bits of your personality – but you still know you're *you*. You still have your memories. Don't you?'

'Yeah,' Bill replied. 'But I kept getting these flashes of things – things I know I haven't experienced. Ziggy's memories, not mine. Maybe the longer I have this body and this face, the more I'll become Ziggy until there's nothing of me left and I'm just . . . *her*.'

'Okay. It's important that we don't panic . . .' Lou said, looking around the room. 'We just need to find Ziggy, fast. How are we going to track her down?'

Bill took a deep breath. 'I have an idea,' she said, reaching into her pocket and pulling out her mobile phone. 'I just need to make a call.'

'How did you get this number?' the Doctor asked when he answered the TARDIS phone.

'You're going to have to come and meet me to find out,' Bill said. That's when she heard it: her voice, which had remained her own, suddenly broke and sounded exactly like Ziggy's. She was becoming more and more like Ziggy by the moment. Soon, there'd be nothing of Bill left. She glanced at Lou who looked worried too.

'I don't have time for games,' the Doctor replied.

'That's not true, is it, Doctor?' Bill said, grasping for facts that would convince the Doctor of her true identity. 'You always have time for fun stuff. Like playing your electric guitar!'

Bill wanted to tell him more about himself − the real things that only the real Bill would know about the Doctor − but the words wouldn't come. Her mind was a fuzz, a blur, and she found herself unable to explain how much she knew about the Doctor, the things they'd done together, the places they'd been. They'd done *amazing* things. They'd seen *so much*. But at that moment, all Bill could remember was that he travelled in a big blue box and played an electric guitar. Everything else was slipping away. Fuzzy, fuzzy, fuzzy. And more of those other images, the barrages of a life she hadn't lived, came rushing through her head.

'Lots of people play electric guitar.'

'But do they know about the Daleks, and Nardole and
. . . and . . . ?' Panic exploded in Bill's chest – she couldn't
remember *anything*. 'And the girl with the star in her eye,' Bill
blurted out.

The Doctor said nothing on the other end of the phone,
but Bill could tell she'd said the right thing. He was puzzled,
curious even. That was how the Doctor's mind worked, how
*her* mind worked too: neither of them usually took things at
face value. She remembered that about herself at least.

'Aren't you even a little bit curious about how I know all
these things?' Bill said. 'Don't you want to know how I know
that you travel through time and to different planets? In a big
blue box?' She spoke quickly, the words rushing out of her
mouth before they were forgotten, lost into the soup of Ziggy
that was becoming her mind. 'If you meet me, I'll tell you the
answer. The park near the university – you know which one.
As soon as you can get there.'

❋

Lou tried her hardest to steady her nerves, as she hid behind
the tree close to where Bill stood waiting for the Doctor.

She was scared by how quickly Bill seemed to be slipping

away – she was losing that *thing*, the essence that made her who she was. Even though Bill had looked different that morning, Lou had still felt the connection between them. She'd first felt it a long time ago – Lou liked the extra chips, but more than that, she liked to see Bill behind the chip counter. She'd been a comforting sight – a face that was welcoming and kind, friendly and caring, no matter what. And even when Lou had put on weight, and other people had started to give her sideways looks, Bill had still given her extra chips and a smile.

Lou didn't understand how it could be possible, but Bill was clearly in danger. And Lou was going to stick with her, even though she looked nothing like the Bill she used to know.

'It'll be all right,' she whispered loudly to Bill. 'The Doctor will be here soon.'

Bill turned unsteadily towards the tree. 'What will we do when the Doctor gets here?' she asked loudly. And then, after a moment, 'What's wrong with me? Am I ill?'

Lou was alarmed, but forced herself to stay calm. 'We need to get the jackets. Remember? The jackets will turn you back into Bill. You'll be Bill again! Bill who served me extra chips? Remember?'

Bill blinked a couple of times, and the fog cleared. 'Yeah. Yeah, I remember.'

Across the park, Bill saw the Doctor walking towards her. Followed by the fake Bill. The person wearing the body that used to be and was still rightfully hers.

'I can't see the photos,' Bill whispered loudly enough for Lou to hear. 'But she's still wearing one of the jackets. That's going to have to be enough. I'll try to talk to her, and somehow convince the Doctor to help me try it on.'

'Good plan.'

Bill started waving, to make sure the Doctor remembered who he was meeting. He frowned deeper than Bill had ever seen him frown before as he approached her – this person who, to him, looked like a total stranger.

'I don't have much time, so tell me how you know all those things, sharpish, and we can all carry on with our lives,' the Doctor snapped, before Bill had a chance to say hello.

'Liar,' she said instead, gathering her strength and clinging to her memories. 'You know time doesn't run out. You know time isn't set. Everything happens at the same time, and one thing after the other. You know that time is everything and time is nothing. Time and relative dimension in space. Means life. *You* taught me that.'

'I did *not*,' the Doctor replied. 'I mean, it's technically, partially true, but incredibly simplistic.' The Doctor frowned. 'Do I know you?'

*He recognises me*, Bill thought. *Not the body I'm in, but the real me, inside.*

'Come on, Doctor, we haven't got time for this,' the fake Bill said, stepping forward.

'She's not me!' Bill cried. 'She's a fake. Come on, Doctor, deep down you must know that.' Bill stared right at the Doctor. 'This morning – you told me the perfect date doesn't exist!'

'And *I* said that your standards were too high,' Fake Bill cut in.

Bewildered, Bill looked at the creature that had stolen her body and life. For her to know that, she must be becoming more and more like Bill. Stealing her memories. 'Okay, how did I get your phone number on the, the, you know . . . ?' She'd forgotten the word. 'The ship! The box!'

'Bill here explained she lost her phone. She said it might even have been stolen,' the Doctor said, eyebrows raised.

'Let me try your jacket on,' Bill said desperately to Fake Bill. 'I mean, it's fabulous and I'd love one just like it.'

'No!' Fake Bill almost shouted. 'You're *so* weird. I'm not letting you anywhere near me or my clothes.'

Bill looked pleadingly at the Doctor. 'If she's the real Bill, why won't she let me try on her jacket? You know the real Bill – you know I'd be kinder than that, to anyone!'

'Not necessarily to someone who claims you're a liar,' the Doctor said. 'And if you were really Bill, you would know that wearing clothes can be a *very* dangerous business. Psychic energy is transferred on to our clothing – and if certain alien species got hold of your stuff, they could do almost *anything* with that psychic energy.'

'Including stealing your identity?' Bill said, almost in a whisper.

The Doctor's eyes widened. 'Well, yes. If they had access to your psychic energy and a mechanism to capture it, they might create a connection that could continue to siphon off psychic energy, as long as the thief kept a bond with the item, a fixer of some sort . . .'

'So you could, say, steal someone's identity with a jacket and a camera, loaded with, for example, *psychic paper*?' Bill said.

The Doctor looked at Fake Bill, his frown deepening. 'What was the name of the woman with the star in her eye?' he asked.

Fake Bill looked at him blankly, then scoffed. 'Why are you asking me that? You don't actually believe this girl, do you?'

The Doctor turned to Bill and asked the same question. Bill opened her mouth to answer and nothing came out. She couldn't remember. It was a flower. It was a flower and the woman was beautiful. She remembered so much about her, how she felt about her . . . Water – there was water. She was a flower. But she couldn't remember her name. It was there, on the tip of her tongue.

'Heather,' Fake Bill said. 'Her name was Heather.'

Bill's heart sank. 'Doctor, don't you recognise this jacket?' she said, grabbing at the denim jacket she was still wearing, with badges she'd sewn on herself. 'It's the one I always wear. If she's me, then wouldn't she have it?'

'I already told the Doctor – I decided to leave it at the shop because I didn't need it any more.'

'Doctor! Come on! Do you really think I'd do that?'

The Doctor frowned again.

Suddenly, from nowhere, Lou sprang out from behind her tree, running towards them. She barrelled into Fake Bill, causing the both of them to come crashing down on to the ground.

'Quick, Bill!' she shouted. 'Grab the jacket!'

Stunned for a second, Bill stared at the two women wrestling on the ground. Then she came to life and ran to them and began to tug at the jacket. Out of the pocket tumbled the three photos of Bill that Ziggy had taken earlier. She stared at them – they *had* to be psychic paper, the fixers keeping the connection between her and Ziggy going!

Bill snatched the photos up. This was her chance to get her body back – but if she destroyed the photos, would she be hurt too? Possibly, but she could feel herself fading fast, and she couldn't wait any longer. She chose the picture with the first jacket she tried on, the amethyst one, and ripped it a little.

A jolt ripped through Bill's body and a barrage of images, memories, thoughts, feelings came rushing into her brain, her body at the same time. Not the strange ones she'd been getting all day, but her own memories. Her own personality. Bill, Bill, Bill. The psychic connection Fake Bill was using had been damaged by that initial rip and Bill's mind was starting to clear.

'Hurry up!' Lou shouted. 'I don't know how much longer I can hold her.'

Bill ripped the photo in two and her whole body jolted, while a deep, dark amethyst colour lit up her hair, face and body in a glorious display.

*Bill. I am Bill. I really am.* Through blurring vision, Bill could see that Fake Bill was lit up with an amethyst glow too – in fact, there was so much energy coursing through her that Lou was thrown back, letting her go for a moment.

'GIVE THEM TO ME!' Fake Bill roared, pushing Lou

aside. She scrambled to her feet and leapt forward, ready to snatch the photos from Bill's hands.

Bill used every ounce of her remaining strength to rip the second and third photos cleanly in two, tearing apart the images of herself in the jackets, and setting herself free. She dropped the pieces as her whole body lit up with dazzling green light, and then a sun-like burst of gold. Fake Bill glowed in the same colours as Bill, howling with rage as the psychic connection was severed.

When the blinding light finally dimmed, Bill could tell she was back to normal. She had use of her brilliant body again, long limbs and all, and when she moved, everything felt normal. She was Bill again.

'No! No!' Ziggy sobbed, throwing herself to her knees to try to gather the torn pieces of her three photographs.

'I don't think so,' the Doctor said and pointed his sonic screwdriver at the pieces, causing them first to flicker and then the images of Bill to completely disappear.

Bill turned to the Doctor, wondering what he'd done. 'Severed the signal between the jacket and the photographs,' he said, his expression serious. 'No more fixers, and now, no more siphoning device either.'

'What have you done?' Ziggy wailed, pressing the pieces of the now-empty photographs to her heart. 'This was my only chance . . . My *final* chance . . .'

Bill knew she should be furious with Ziggy for what she had done – but Ziggy looked so distressed, so heartbroken, that all Bill felt for her was pity.

To the Doctor and Lou's surprise, Bill got down on her knees beside Ziggy and spoke quietly.

'Why did you do this?'

Ziggy seemed startled by Bill's tone, which was full of kindness and understanding. She looked up, tears soaking her face. 'I just wanted to go home. I didn't want to harm you. Not really. I have been here such a long, long time . . . I just want to go *home*.'

The Doctor stood with his arms folded, glaring down at Ziggy. 'And where is home, exactly?'

'I'm an Ohcho. My planet is Onhwhie.'

'I know it,' the Doctor said. 'The planet of shape-shifters.'

Ziggy wiped her face, but tears still fell from her eyes. 'I was banished here,' she explained. 'Our planet elected a new and dangerous leader. He ruled us with fear, and with pain, and every morning we woke up terrified, our friends and family going missing in the night. Until a number of us decided: no more. We formed groups, we protested, we started to get others to protest too.

'People across the planet began to wake up, taking notice of what we were saying. They started to feel *powerful*. And then one night, I was taken from my house, dragged in chains to see the new leader, and banished. Sent out across the galaxies, landing on Earth by chance. They wanted to crush the resistance, but I hope my friends have stayed strong, that they have carried on our good work.'

She turned to Bill. 'I'm sorry for what I did to you. But I have been so lonely, trapped here for hundreds of Earth years. I discovered a Time Lord had visited this planet and I tracked him down as best I could. I set up my shop in many different places where I sensed an alien presence, and waited for a chance. A chance to meet you, Doctor – to beg you to take me home.'

'If you just wanted to ask him for a lift, why did you steal Bill's face?' Lou said, her eyes narrowed as she stood with her arms folded next to the Doctor. 'How would *that* encourage him to help you?'

Ziggy's shoulders sagged. 'Over time, I built the little psychic technology I had into my camera and my jackets. I would practise on ordinary people who walked into my shop, making sure the psychic link worked, but always ripping up the photographs later. I learned that it worked best on those who were nervous, brimming with negative psychic energy – so that's why I waited until Bill was going on a date to draw her in.

'More importantly, in all that time, I listened for tales of the Doctor. And the more I learned, the more I suspected he would not break the laws of time for just one person. He who had stood by while whole peoples were destroyed, in the name of justice . . . I could not risk him saying no. I knew my best chance was to ask him as his friend. His greatest weakness.'

She looked desperately first at Bill, then at Lou and then, finally, at the Doctor. 'I would have told you the truth, Doctor, and given the photographs and the jacket back so you could restore Bill. I would never have kept her trapped. I know how that feels, all too well. I hope you believe me.' Ziggy began to cry again. 'I am truly sorry.'

There was a moment's silence, and then Bill carefully stretched her arm around Ziggy's shoulder.

'We have to help her, Doctor,' she said, looking up at him, hoping he would understand.

The Doctor looked thoughtfully at Bill.

'She was wronged,' Bill went on. 'They punished her for standing up for the right thing. You were the one talking about character this morning. Did you not believe all that? Ziggy was punished for having character. Don't punish her more.'

The Doctor said nothing, but narrowed his eyes – yet Bill

looked at Lou, and she was smiling.

'I might be new to this whole aliens-time-travelling-
in-space business,' she said, with a grin. 'But really, what's
the point in having the power to travel across the universe
through time and space if you can't help good people?'

'All right, all right.' The Doctor put away his sonic
screwdriver. 'Look. Zaggy, or whatever your name is. Your
planet, Onhwhie – it exists in a completely different era to
Earth. By now, your galaxy won't have existed for thousands
of years.'

'*Doctor*,' Bill hissed. 'Don't tell her awful news just like
that! Show some compassion!'

The Doctor rolled his eyes. 'I just mean we'll have to
travel through space *and* time to get there. If we were to travel
to the planet's coordinates right now – nothing but clear
space. But if we move through time, we'll find it.'

'You'll help me?' Ziggy asked, a smile breaking across
her stricken, tear-streaked face. 'Really?'

'Yes. Now come on, Zoggy, and Bill – back to the
TARDIS *now* – before I change my mind.'

With that, he stomped off across the lawn of the park,
with Ziggy dazedly in tow.

Bill shook her head as she watched him, and then turned
to Lou.

'"Thank you" isn't enough, I know,' Bill said to her, beaming. 'But thank you. You're a life-saver, Lou. Quite literally.'

'It was no bother,' Lou said, her cheeks glowing a faint pink. 'It was fun, actually. Like I said, alien body-snatching, planets with evil leaders, mysterious time-travel machines . . . all right up my street.'

Before she could stop herself, Bill threw her arms around Lou. 'I couldn't have done it without you,' she said with a smile. 'And that tackle to the ground, that was pretty impressive.'

'There's more to me than meets the eye,' Lou replied. 'You and me both.'

'Well, thank you, anyway. And *triple* chips next time.'

'Gotcha.'

'So, Bill – *now* will you make use of my many jacket rooms?' the Doctor asked as he set the coordinates for Ziggy's home planet, and as Ziggy examined the TARDIS's glowing control panels with wonder.

'Absolutely,' Bill replied. She smiled, thinking of Lou. 'Even if I don't find the perfect one, who cares, eh? You were right – it's character that counts. And anyone I go on a date with in the future should believe that too.'

With those words, the Doctor's frown turned to a soft smile, and the TARDIS slowly dematerialised.

**Jacqueline Rayner** has written many books, audio plays and comic strips, many of them set in the world of *Doctor Who*, including the number-one bestseller *The Stone Rose* and two 'Quick Reads' for World Book Day. Before becoming a full-time writer, she worked at BBC Books as an editor on their *Doctor Who* range.

**Jenny T. Colgan** has written twenty-five novels under the name Jenny Colgan and, as Jenny T. Colgan, has published extensively in the *Doctor Who* universe, including the novels *In the Blood* and *Dark Horizons*, and the Big Finish audio drama, *Time Reaver*, starring David Tennant and Catherine Tate.

**Susan Calman** is a comedian, actor, presenter and writer. A regular on *The News Quiz*, Susan has written four series for BBC Radio 4 and her last tour, *The Calman Before The Storm*, sold out nationally. On TV she presents *The Boss*, *Armchair Detectives* and *Top Class*. In 2016 she published her memoir, *Cheer Up Love: Adventures in Depression with the Crab of Hate*, and in 2017, she quickstepped into the nation's hearts as maybe the most joyful contestant ever on the BBC's *Strictly Come Dancing*. An advocate for LGBT and mental health issues, Susan lives in Glasgow with her wife, Lee, and their cats.

**Dorothy Koomson** is the award-winning author of twelve novels. Her third book, *My Best Friend's Girl*, was selected for the Richard and Judy Book Club 2006 Summer Reads and sold more than 500,000 copies. Dorothy's books *The Ice Cream Girls* and *The Rose Petal Beach* were both shortlisted for the British Book Awards, and in 2013 a television adaptation of *The Ice Cream Girls* appeared on ITV1. Since her early days of buying comics and working in a well-known comic store, Dorothy has been a die-hard science fiction fan, so she was delighted to work on this anthology.

**Kelly Wagner** is an illustrator and graphic designer based in Milwaukee, WI, USA. Most of her projects involve branding, product development, illustration, typography and promotional print materials. The foundation of Kelly's work is the belief that all great design should strongly engage, inspire and communicate. It is her main ambition to consistently deliver deeply intentional solutions that are both beneficial and relevant. Her primary medium of choice is Adobe Illustrator.

## Also available:

**Also available:**

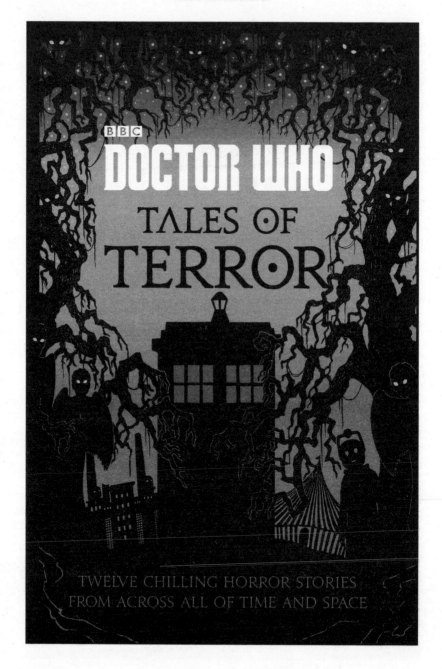